Italy/Australia
Postmodern Architecture
in Translation

Italy/Australia
Postmodern Architecture in Translation

EDITED BY
Silvia Micheli and John Macarthur

EDITORIAL ASSISTANT
Carmen Armstrong

ISBN
978-0-9943966-2-4

PLACE OF PUBLICATION
Melbourne, Victoria

PUBLISHER
Uro Publications

DATE OF PUBLICATION
2018

DESIGN
Jack Loel, Lachlan Richards and Print Ideas

Proudly supported by

Affiliations
Léa-Catherine Szacka, The University of Manchester
Philip Goad, The University of Melbourne
Francesco Vitelli, The University of Melbourne
Silvia Micheli, The University of Queensland
Paul Walker, The University of Melbourne
Karen Burns, The University of Melbourne
Antony Moulis, The University of Queensland
Elizabeth Musgrave, The University of Queensland
Peter Kohane, The University of New South Wales
Gevork Hartoonian, University of Canberra
Ian McDougall, ARM Architecture
Rex Addison, Rex Addison Architect
Mauro Baracco, RMIT University
Conrad Hamann, RMIT University
John Macarthur, The University of Queensland
Enrico Taglietti, Enrico Taglietti Architect

About the editors

Silvia Micheli is a Lecturer at The University of Queensland. Silvia's main research interest focuses on international influences and cross-cultural exchanges in the 20th and 21st century architectural context. Silvia has published extensively on post-war, postmodern and contemporary history of Italian architecture.

John Macarthur FAHA, is Professor of Architecture at the University of Queensland where he teaches history, theory and design. He was the founding Director of the ATCH (Architecture, Theory, Criticism, History) Research Centre. His research on the intellectual history of architecture has focused on the conceptual framework of the relation of architecture and the visual arts from the Picturesque to the present.

Italy/Australia Postmodern Architecture in Translation

Edited by
Silvia Micheli and
John Macarthur

Contents

Thinking Italian in
Postmodern Australia

Silvia Micheli
and John Macarthur

Introduction

6
Thinking Italian in Postmodern Australia
Silvia Micheli and John Macarthur

Essays

12
From Centre to Periphery: Reflections on the Dissemination of Postmodern Architecture
Léa-Catherine Szacka

22
***Colonne e una Torre*: Italian Designs for Melbourne 1978**
Philip Goad and Francesco Vitelli

36
Ciao Australia: *Domus* Looks to the Antipodes
Silvia Micheli

48
***The Architecture of the City*: An American Rossi in Australia**
Paul Walker

62
A Welfare State: *Tendenza* in 1980s Melbourne
Karen Burns

76
Exhibiting Scarpa: Transcriptions of the Narrative Detail in Queensland
Antony Moulis and Elizabeth Musgrave

90
Learning from Kahn and Scarpa: Rigour and Ornament in the Ana Kindergarten
Peter Kohane

104
Romaldo Giurgola: From America with Po-Mo
Gevork Hartoonian

Conversations

164
Culture Mining
Ian McDougall in conversation with John Macarthur and Silvia Micheli

172
Thinking about Gino Valle and a Few Others in My Small Italian Pool
Rex Addison in conversation with Silvia Micheli and John Macarthur

180
Between La Tendenza and Neoliberty: Mauro Baracco Goes to Australia
Mauro Baracco in conversation with John Macarthur and Silvia Micheli

194
Encountering Italian Architectural Culture via USA and Australia
Conrad Hamann in conversation with Silvia Micheli

208
We All Loved Tafuri!
A conversation between Gevork Hartoonian, John Macarthur and Paul Walker

Poem

218
Canberra: The Invisible City
Enrico Taglietti

227
Index

Italy/Australia: Postmodern Architecture in Translation casts light on a particular instance of international influence on Australian architecture and urbanism in the late twentieth century, when the relationship between the two countries was significant to the making of postmodern architecture in Australia. In the 1970s and 1980s, it was typical for architects in Australia and worldwide to consider Italy at the forefront of international trends. In part this was because Australian architecture schools took their model from Britain, and from British investment in renaissance classicism, which had made Italy an essential destination in the grand tours of Australian architects from early in the century, and continued to do so. In part this was also to do with the high prestige that Italian design had gained worldwide: in couture, in furniture and tableware, and in cars and motorcycles. Italy held a high status in Australia at a crucial point of step-change in the process of internationalisation. The Australian fascination for Italian trends became evident with the exhibition "Italy at David Jones", organised in Sydney in 1955. Designed by the Milan-based architect Enrico Taglietti, "Italy at David Jones" was the largest exhibition of foreign merchandise ever seen in Australia to date, and was meant to legitimise Italian culture in Australia and encourage trade between the two countries. The exhibition was part of a wider strategy to identify sophisticated tastes with European imported products and to grow demand for high design.

In architecture, this broad increase of interest in Italian design culture was intensified by the penetration of Italian architectural journals into the Australian market. Since the late nineteenth century, journals had been important in the dissemination of architectural ideas and the phenomenon reached its peak during the postmodern period. In 1980s Italy, underpinned by the values of accumulation and acceleration, architectural magazines turned out to be the perfect vehicle for the circulation of ideas. Intellectually less demanding than books and aesthetically more appealing with their experimental approaches, high-quality photography, colour-saturated images, big titles and slim formats, magazines better suited the necessities of the new dynamic postmodern lifestyle and were within easy reach for the Australian market. Through its renowned architectural journals, including *Casabella, Domus, Modo* and *Abitare,* Milan played a crucial role in the dissemination of Italian postmodern architectural discourse internationally.

Other factors coincided with the tendency to Italophilia in Australian architecture in the late twentieth century. First, and closest to the theme of this book, was the debate on postmodern forms, exhibited at the 1980 Venice Biennale curated by Paolo Portoghesi. Second, the translation into English in 1982 of Aldo Rossi's first book *The Architecture of the City* had an immediate impact on the understanding of architecture related to urbanism. Third, there was the rise of architectural theory and the centrality of the texts of Manfredo Tafuri. The ideas of Italian historians and architects, such as Leonardo Benevolo and Giuseppe Samonà, that architecture was less determined by present-day functional demands and constructional techniques, and rather answered more to the long-term history of urban culture, reached Australia late with the translation of Rossi's seminal publication. It had the effect of freeing architecture from the scientific functionalism of high modernism, and sending it to seek new allegiances with the arts, social sciences, linguistics and history. An account of cities based on their morphology and building typology gave architecture an authority with which to contest the positivistic claims of town planning based in demographics and traffic engineering. Also, the Rossiesque concept of the "autonomy of architecture" offered an alternative approach to the Australian practice-oriented way of understanding design. At the same time, the Italian model of a deep and layered past was clearly an ill-fit with the short history of European settlement in Australia, and raised other questions of the Aboriginal understanding of place, the urban fabric as the record of quite recent contestation, and whole scale importation of appropriate ideas. The misfit of Western European culture in Australia became itself a space of productive and critical thought pursued by Australian architects, just as post-colonial discourse and critical regionalism was rising internationally.

The explosion of European philosophy, linguistics and literary theory, and its promulgation in translation through the American academy, heavily marked architectural discourse in the period. Australian architects, being generally politically progressive and distant from the debates, paid little heed to the differences between the Marxist inheritance of the European mainstream intelligentsia and the rise of structuralism, post-structuralism and postmodern pluralism. Tafuri's texts were then read not so much in terms of their politics and his defence of Marxist historiography against the rising postmodern relativism, and more for a kind of poetics of theory. In Tafuri, and perhaps particularly in Fredric Jameson's version of Tafuri, Australian architects felt that they had a body of theory as important as Derrida was to literature. Italy again provided a locus for a certain idea of the architect as ascetic and removed from everyday debates, while engaged in a longer-term politics of the nature of architecture and its potential for critique.

Based on these premises, the symposium "Italy/Australia: Postmodern in translation" was held in Canberra in November 2015. Chaired by Silvia Micheli in collaboration with Gevork Hartoonian and John Macarthur, the symposium brought together a community of scholars to reflect on the circulation of architectural ideas between Italy and Australia in the post-modern period. Through different perspectives and case studies, national and international experts were invited to explore a phenomenon that had yet to be fully investigated. The information gathered at the symposium has flowed into this edited book, whose focus is to explore the relationships that occurred between Italian and Australian architecture through the analysis of buildings, projects and competition entries, and the dissemination of theories and ideas.

Challenging the idea of a unique understanding of postmodern architecture in the Australian context, the book shows how different responses emerged from the idiosyncratic architectural relation between the two countries. In so doing, the aim of the editors is twofold: on the one hand, the book adds to the ongoing discourse on European influences on Australian architecture. On the other hand, it represents a collective attempt, through a specific topic, to initiate a first critical discussion of postmodern architecture in Australia—whose broad history has yet to be written. The question of translation and appropriation of foreign architectural design methods, forms and theories are underlying themes that pervade the book.

Among the most illuminating discoveries of this joint research is the fact that on many occasions postmodern Italian architectural culture had to pass through America before reaching Australia. The USA, and in particular its East Coast scene, filtered and digested Italian design and theory for its own audience to such an extent that one can talk about an "American Rossi" and a "Jamesonesque Tafuri". Another significant finding is the interest aroused around Italian Neoliberty architecture in 1970s and 1980s Australia, a fascination generated by the strive for "localism" by some Australian architects. While acting as a counterpoint to the hegemony of La Tendenza, Neoliberty provided Australian architects with a strategy for the rehabilitation of historical forms and materials. Carlo Scarpa never set foot in Australia and yet his design was a significant influence, informing the making of postmodern architecture in both Brisbane and Sydney. The success of Scarpa's work in the antipodes, which was drawn through interpretations belonging to UK-based architects and academics, comes across as a surprising discovery. Indeed, his most authoritative Italian scholars are probably not aware of this influence.

The first part of the volume *Italy/Australia: Postmodern Architecture in Translation* includes academic essays that constitute a first attempt to collect and interpret historical materials concerning the impact of Italian architectural culture in postmodern Australia. The book opens with some critical reflections on the relationship between centre and periphery in the postmodern architectural scene at an international level by Léa-Catherine Szacka, who was the key note speaker at the symposium "Italy/Australia". The second part is a set of discussions with architects who witnessed the period under examination and have contributed, in different ways, to the spread of Italian architectural ideas and precedents across the Australian context. In the middle of the volume is a collection of images that visually represent ways Australian architects received and translated Italian ideas and forms within their local environment. The book concludes with a fascinating poem by Enrico Taglietti, which is a tribute to the city of Canberra.

The present volume is an outcome of Dr Silvia Micheli's University of Queensland Postdoctoral Fellowship research, "Recovering the historical roots of post-war regionalism in Australian architecture: The Scandinavian and Italian legacy", conducted at The University of Queensland between 2012 and 2015. The editors wish to acknowledge the ATCH Research Centre (The University of Queensland) for its support in the organisation of the symposium and editing of this book and the University of Canberra for hosting the symposium. In particular, they thank Professor Gevork Hartoonian and Macarena de la Vega for assisting in the coordination of the event. They also want to thank Carmen Armstrong for her valuable assistance in converting the findings of the symposium into a book. A special thank you goes to John Gollings for his generous contribution of photographs.

      This book is dedicated to the Italo-American architect Romaldo Giurgola (1920–2016), co-designer of the Australian Parliament House in Canberra, which opened in 1988. His building has become, over time, one of the most valuable examples of postmodern architecture internationally. Giurgola's decision, as a native-born Italian with a US-based practice, to become an Australian citizen highlights the extraordinary movement between cultures that characterised the relationship between Italy and Australia through postmodernism.

From Centre to Periphery: Reflections on the Dissemination of Postmodern Architecture

Léa-Catherine Szacka

In 1986, nearly a decade after the publication of his seminal book *The Language of Postmodern Architecture,* Charles Jencks, in his foreword to *What is Post-Modernism?*, made the following diagnosis: "The Growth of Post-Modernism has followed a sinuous, even tortuous, path. Twisting to the left and to the right, branching down the middle, it resembles the natural form of a spreading root, or a meandering river that divides, changes course, doubles back on itself and takes off in a new direction".[1] By the mid-1980s, postmodernism had reached most parts of the world, encountering more resistance in some places, while being instrumentalised to the profit of specific political regimes or purely economic enterprises and neoliberal policies in others. What then had happened to postmodernism and, more specifically, to its most tangible manifestations in architecture? Had something been lost in translation when examples of postmodern architecture started appearing around the world, transferring postmodern ideas transnationally while embodying the so-called logic of late capitalism?

Architectural forms and ideas have long been transferred and translated from one geographical context to another. In the 1980s, however, new technologies of transport, communication, and mobility contributed to the reconfiguration of our geographies and sociologies. The commercialisation of the Boeing 747 in the early 1970s, for example, captured the international market and expanded the opportunities for travel of the upper and middle classes, accelerating exchanges and flows of information and leading to a more global architecture culture in which national particularities tended to be diminished to the benefit of a plurality of individual languages—or signatures—repeated everywhere, with no regard to context or local culture.

In architecture, postmodernism was essentially defined by way of negation: it was initiated by a strong reaction against the so-called 'international style', an architecture trend that developed in the United States in the course of the 1930s, only to become dominant in Western architecture during the middle decades of the Twentieth Century—criticised for its lack of ornamentation and decoration, for its rectilinear, undecorated, asymmetrical, and white surfaces, and for its formalism and anti-contextualism. Therefore, the words '"postmodernism' and 'international' somehow call for an internal paradox: if the postmodern had declared war on the 'international style', how could one reconcile these two words and therefore talk of an international postmodernism when referring to a style that favoured local tradition and the vernacular? In other words, is there such a thing as an international postmodernism or is postmodern architecture by nature divided and fragmented in local idioms, condemned to remain mere copies of the originals—or copies of the copies?

One of postmodernism's facets was the propensity to herald the celebration of peripheries, both the peripheries of the world and the peripheries of things themselves. Postmodernism "inhabited the peripheries of practice, often finding its most effective projections through the lenses of gender, race or identity politics," wrote the curators of the Victoria and Albert Museum for the exhibition *Postmodernism: Style and Subversion, 1970-1990*, the first major show to reassess the legacy of postmodernism in 2011.[2] But, despite addressing complexity and denying the idea of centrality to the profit of the glorification of plurality, postmodernism grew out of centres from which it later reached out to the world in different ways and directions. What were these centres and who operated from them? What was, in the short history of postmodernism, the relation between centre and periphery?

Centres: Publications and Exhibitions

Italy, England, and the United States (particularly the East Coast) were hotbeds for postmodernism. Contacts between these leading countries flourished in the 1960s and 1970s as many American architects were fascinated by Italy, particularly Robert Venturi after his fellowship at the American Academy in Rome in the mid-1950s and also Michael Graves, Robert Stern, Peter Eisenman, and many more. The 1972 exhibition organised at MoMA, *Italy: The New Domestic Landscape*,[3] the 1973 XV Milan Triennale,[4] and the 1976 *Europa-America: Centro storico-suburbio* exhibition at the Venice Biennale of Architecture reflected the scope of Italian post-modernism while leading to a greater internationalisation of the profession.[5] This was especially evident with the changing direction of the *Congrès International d'Architecture Moderne* (CIAM) meetings, as ideas were no longer merely travelling one way—from Europe to America—but were moving in the opposite direction, the new world increasingly influencing the old.

The terms 'postmodernism' and 'postmodern' had been used since the late Nineteenth Century, yet they became common in the 1970s.[6] It was in England, around 1975, that the word emerged in association with architecture when writer and critic Charles Jencks used it in his essay "The Rise of Post-Modern Architecture" to denote an era marking the point at which the modern period came to be regarded as a part of the historical past—like classical antiquity or the medieval period.[7] The same year, Greek-Cypriot editor Andreas Papadakis, founder, proprietor, and editor-in-chief of Academy Editions,[8] one of the most important publishing houses of the moment, acquired the financially troubled *Architectural Design* (*AD*) and, with editors Haig Beck and Martin Spring, transformed it into the leading architectural magazine of the time.[9] After he had heard Jencks talking about postmodernism in Melbourne in 1974, Beck introduced Jencks to Papadakis. From the meeting of Jencks and Papadakis, two like-minded men, would result a long and fruitful professional relationship. Jencks was travelling the world, bringing back images of work by foreign architects, sometimes completely unknown to the Anglo-American audience. According to Jencks, Papadakis would "publish everybody as he was very fast, much faster than anybody else in the world".[10] The dynamic marriage between the two men proved to be extremely successful in ensuring the initial circulation of the idea of postmodern architecture as both Jencks and Papadakis "played an operative role in promoting the movement," wrote Elie Haddad in *The Journal of Architecture*.[11] Most importantly, the collaboration between Jencks and Academy Editions would result in the first publication, in 1977, of *The Language of Post-Modern Architecture*, a major vehicle for the dissemination of Jencks's ideas and of a plethora of architectural images from all over the globe.

The Language of Post-Modern Architecture was one of the first easily accessible, cheap, glossy, full-colour books on architecture. Resembling something between a magazine and a book—the original edition was only 104 pages—it quickly became a huge publishing success. Appearing some two decades before the popularisation of the internet as a search engine and source of images, the book stood on the drafting table of many students and architects in search of more diversified examples of architectures from around the world. It was issued by Academy Editions (in collaboration with Rizzoli for the American edition) in seven revised editions, "in each case readjusting the defining parameters of the new movement" (1977, 1978, 1981, 1984, 1987, 1988, and 1991) and an eighth, *The New Paradigms of Architecture*, in 2002,[12] translated into 11 languages, and pirated in others.[13] *The Language of Post-modern Architecture* was promoted through Papadakis's journal *Architectural Design* and sold more than 160,000 copies.[14] Its release was also accompanied by an exhibition and symposium at Peter Cook's Art Net Gallery.[15]

In 1980, three years after the initial publication of *The Language of Post-Modern Architecture*, the first International Architecture Exhibition of the Venice Biennale, *The Presence of the Past*, marked an important meeting point for postmodernism. It saw the coming together not only of a group of like-minded international architects (the twenty main exhibitors and the fifty-five younger exhibitors on display on the mezzanine) but also of an artificially created group of critics who were to define the scope of the exhibition and the extent of the participants. The exhibition, unlike any other Biennale, travelled abroad, first to Paris and later to San Francisco. There, it not only spread the message of postmodernism, it transformed its content due to changes in context, timing, and venue. In Paris, the exhibition, which incidentally changed title from the direct translation *La Présence du Passé* to *La Présence de l'Histoire*, was strongly associated with historicism and was caught up in a larger polemic between French architects defending a continuing modernity and those interested in postmodernism. When the exhibition arrived in San Francisco two years later, it was very much associated with a local real estate initiative. It was brought to the West Coast by Joseph Weiner, a real estate developer, and his wife, PR agent Virginia Westover. Weiner and Westover had fallen in love with the exhibition in Venice and organised an American version, with the intention of giving credence to a new postmodern architecture. In favour of a more commercial aspect of the movement, the San Francisco exhibition saw the addition of many local architects (the San Francisco façades) and of an Italian Marketplace.

The catalogue of *The Presence of the Past*, published in several editions (two in Italian in 1980, two in English in 1980 and one in 1981, and one in French in 1981) was also an important source for the dissemination and later translation of postmodern architecture. It contains images of work by more than seventy architects and essays by Paolo Portoghesi, Charles Jencks, Christian Norberg-Schulz, and Vincent Scully.

Peripheries: Norway and Poland

In order to touch upon the transnationality of postmodernism, many peripheral contexts could be explored—contexts that, in opposition to centres such as Italy, the UK, or the US, came across postmodernism rather late and through an operation of 'translation'. How did postmodern ideas travel in these countries and what was the result in terms of debate and built forms? How were they integrated into a new culture and what were the outcomes? How was the complex and the contradictory plurality of postmodern architecture absorbed and digested by colonies, former colonies, or countries experiencing a rapid economic growth or an abrupt change of political regime? Scandinavia and Eastern Europe appear as two interesting case studies of postmodern translation in the 1980s and 1990s. More specifically, here we consider Norway, the homeland of postmodern theorist Christian Norberg-Schulz, and Poland, a country in which the shift from communism to capitalism happened rapidly and with important consequences for the image of the nation.

In Norway, post-war architecture followed more or less the same trajectory as that of the rest of the Western world. But while in the 1970s Europe plunged into postmodernist speculations, Norwegian architects held back. Very little was happening in Norway in terms of experimentation and the return to communication in architecture or in relation to the need for a greater sense of history. "Functionalism appealed to the practical minds of Norwegian people," wrote Ingerid Helsing Almaas, an architect and editor-in-chief of the journal *Arkitektur N*.[16] Almaas continued: "The only part of European Post-Modernism that reached Norway was the attempts headed by architects like Krier and Moore to reformulate the vocabulary of form and detail found in classical architecture".[17] For Almaas, the fact that only some postmodernist ideas reached the country may be explained by the scarcity of messengers. Indeed, only two architectural theoreticians really contributed to the development of postmodern architecture in Norway at the time: historian and theorist Christian Norberg-Schulz, a long-time friend of Paolo Portoghesi and an internationally renowned figure at the time, and Thomas Thiis-Evensen (both teaching at the Oslo School of Architecture and Design). Norberg-Schulz and Thiis-Evensen "concentrated their writings on presenting architecture as a language – Norberg-Schulz through an approach rooted in his understanding of Heidegger's phenomenology, which he described in *Genius Loci – Towards a Phenomenology of Architecture* (1980), and Thiis-Evensen in a kind of architectonic dictionary, *Archetypes in Architecture* (1987)".[18] And while most Norwegian architects continued a largely modernist practice, only isolated figures such as Jan & Jon (an office formed by Norwegian architects Jan Digerud and Jon Lundberg,[19] incidentally the sole architects representing Norway at the 1980 Venice Biennale of Architecture)[20] and Arne Henriksen produced in the 1990s buildings that we could classify as postmodern.[21] However, their production remained modest and, wrote Almaas, "it became clear that Norway would not see anything approaching the frenzied experimentation that was opening so many doors elsewhere in Europe".[22]

The few examples of postmodern building in Norway include Jon Lundberg's home at Holmen in Oslo, a building that expresses postmodernism's playful attitude toward room positions and space; the Villa Normann built in Jessheim by Jan & Jon (1979) and largely inspired by Robert Venturi's Vanna Venturi House (1962–64); the Sheraton Oslo Fjord Hotel in Sandvika (partly designed by Jan Digerud in 1985), in which the interior appears with all of postmodernism's use of classical elements; Rådhusgata 23B, completed in 1986 by Jan Digerud, the vertical extension of an office building in the centre of Oslo, which paraphrases the older façade in neo-baroque (1917) from the hand of architect Henrik Bull using strong colours and Venturian broken gables at the top; and the Holmia station near Oslo by Arne Heriksen (1982) that borrows some elements from Aldo Rossi's architectural language.

But, despite the very timid concretisation of postmodern architecture in Norway, the debate between the modern and postmodern reached the country and was repurposed in the local press. In Norway, post-war architecture and architectural thinking were characterised by a strong aversion to history due to a still vivid modernist ideology. However, at the Oslo School of Architecture and Design, a group of intellectuals, including Thomas Thiis-Evensen, Erik Collett, Einar Dahle, and Robert Esdaile, were gravitating around Norberg-Schulz, using the magazine *Arkitektnytt* as an important venue for the debate on postmodernism. For example, at the end of the 1970s, two letters published in the magazine reported on Collett and Dahle's travel to the US and the changes they observed in American architecture. Collett wrote:

> With Chicago and Mies van der Rohe the United States marked itself strongly with the International Style. They are now equally marking themselves against it. The monotone, so-called perfect buildings that ignore their surroundings, are now giving space to softer solutions with an adaptability that more strongly creates a sense of place. The buildings are more irrational, poetic and extroverted.[23]

In Norway, as in many other countries, postmodernism provoked a heated debate in the press. The reaction was very strong and may perhaps be explained by the fact that Norway has traditionally shown a political preference for social democracy and more sober architectural expression.

Poland seems particularly interesting as a case study of the translation of postmodernism from the USA and Italy to another, very different socio-political context. Perhaps the last bastion of European postmodernism, Polish architecture of the last thirty years remains relatively under-studied or at least under-disseminated within an Anglo-Saxon context. However, Polish postmodernism has been recently explored by Lukasz Stanek in the exhibition and catalogue *Postmodernism is Almost all Right* as well as by Alicja Gzowska and Lidia Klein, editors of the two-volume publication *Postmodernizm Polski – Architektura i Urbanistyka*.[24] In their introduction to this publication, Klein reminds us that, in Poland, postmodernism was a late-born child that only burgeoned after the downfall of Communism in 1989 and the following democratic transition leading to Poland's entry into the European Union in 2004. After the fall of the wall—which, in a way, confirmed Jean-François Lyotard's diagnosis of the end of the meta narratives—optimism was ever greater in Eastern European countries. Yet, as Klein argues, postmodernism in Poland remained mostly disappointing, due to the incongruence of the theoretical frame in which Polish postmodernism flourished. For Klein, this failure boils down to one fundamental question: can we speak of postmodernism in the context of a just-nascent market economy? In other words, how could architects translate what Fredric Jameson had qualified as the "cultural logic of late capitalism" into a context in which capitalism was still in its infancy?

In Poland, the term postmodernism (as applied to architecture) appears for the first time in 1979, in the pages of the monthly magazine *Arkitektura* under the byline of Anna Wronska. The discovery of architecture as an artistic discipline brought a wave of enthusiasm that liberated architects from the series of rules imposed on Polish architects in the 1970s because of the uniformisation due to the standardisation of most building design.

Things started to change in the early 1980s. As explained by historian Piotr Marciniak, with an unprecedented economic crisis and the establishment of the *Solidarnosz* (Solidarity) movement in 1980, Poland witnessed a greater openness of public life and a greater freedom of expression that led to the critique of modern architecture.[25] Following this, in June 1981, Jencks visited Warsaw for the 14th International Union of Architects (UIA) Congress on "Architecture – Man – Environment".[26] This important event was the first occasion to situate Poland's achievements, attitudes, and expectations within the larger international milieu.[27] According to Marciniak, the congress also coincided with "the emergence of regional and new historicist architectural trends and references" and an intensified intellectual debate.[28] In 1987, the publication in Polish of *The Language of Post-Modern Architecture* "stirred major ferment in Polish architecture schools and introduced the concept to a larger public".[29]

One of Polish postmodernism's most famous icons is the Solpol department store, built in 1993 in Wrocław, the largest city in Western Poland. The bright pastel colour and strange geometric forms of Solpol embody Poland's violent optimism in the early 1990s, when the *tristesse* of decades of communism was replaced overnight with capitalism's promise of opportunity. With time, Solpol became Poland's symbol of transformation from the state-run economy of the 1980s to the capitalism of the 1990s and one of the county's best examples of postmodern architecture.

Norway and Poland provide instructive examples of different translations of postmodern architecture. If, in Norway, postmodern architecture only had a few timid manifestations, in Poland, the translation from centre to periphery was instrumentalised by a new capitalist explosion that needed a new language conveying a sense of wealth but also extravagance, colourfulness, and eccentricity. Therefore, in the latter case, the translation sometimes exceeded the original, the context creating an amplification of the postmodern message.

From Centre to Periphery: The Italy/Australia Case

Many other contexts could have been explored in this essay in order to understand the flow of ideas between centres and peripheries. Elsewhere in this volume, the relationship between Italy and Australia is thoroughly analysed to illuminate how the idea of postmodern architecture might have been brought to and translated into the Australian context of the 1980s and 1990s. One of the most poignant examples of the cross-cultural exchange between Italy and Australia in the postmodern period remains, however, Parliament House in Canberra, built in the 1980s by Italian architect Romaldo Giurgola. How did Giurgola transport postmodern forms and materials, as well as the notion of axiality and monumentality, to the Australian context? Working on his project for almost a decade, Giurgola, strongly influenced by Louis Kahn and part of the so-called Philadelphia School, built a Parliament house dominated by a sense of place and a strong symmetry; a building, which, highly contextual, follows the landscape to become both monumental and anti-monumental at once. By the time

Parliament House was completed, Giurgola had made Canberra his permanent home. And while, as reported by Jencks, postmodernism was taking different directions and meanders in the peripheries, the US was already moving away from postmodernism, the 1988 MoMA *Deconstructivist Architecture* exhibition marking a turning point and a conscious reorientation of the architectural discourse.

[1] Charles Jencks, *What is Post-Modernism?*, London: Academy Editions; New York: St. Martin's Press, 1986, 2.

[2] Glenn Adamson and Jane Pavitt, eds., *Postmodernism: Style and Subversion, 1970–1990*, London: V&A Publishing, 2011, 13.

[3] New York's Museum of Modern Art (MoMA) hosted a ground-breaking 1972 exhibition *Italy: The New Domestic Landscape*, which emphasised the dynamic context of radical Italian design and architecture in the 1970s. An innovative exhibition, it was the first presentation of experimental domestic 'environments' and attendant films by the most vibrant Italian architects and designers of the period. See Felicity Scott, *Architecture or Techno-Utopia: Politics After Modernism*, Cambridge, Massachusetts: MIT Press, 2007.

[4] The 1973 Milan Triennale is mostly remembered for its architecture section, *Architettura-Città*, curated by Aldo Rossi and featuring the work of many protagonists of the architectural movement called *Tendenza*. It also focused on the legacy of rational architecture and the importance of the relationship between architecture and the city. See Ezio Bonfanti, Rosario Bonicalzi, Aldo Rossi, Massimo Scolari, and Daniele Vitale, *Architettura Razionale*, Milan: Franco Angeli editore, 1973.

[5] For more on this exhibition, see Léa-Catherine Szacka, "Debate on Display at the 1976 Venice Biennale" in *Place and Displacement: Exhibiting Architecture*, eds. Thordis Arrhenius, Mari Lending, Wallis Miller, and Jérémie Michael McGowan, Zurich: Lars Muller Publisher, 2014, 97–112.

[6] Hatje Cantz Verlag, "Art Dictionary, Postmodernism", accessed 13 November 2016, http://www.hatjecantz.de/postmodernism-5051-1.html.

[7] Charles Jencks, "The Rise of Post-Modern Architecture", *Architectural Association Quarterly*, 7, 4, October/December 1975, 3–14.

[8] Andreas Papadakis opened the Academy Bookshop in Holland Street, Kensington, in 1964 and Academy Editions in 1967.

[9] Steve Parnell, "AD Magazine and Post-Modern Architecture" in *Proceedings of the 2nd International Conference of the European Architectural History Network*, eds. Hilde Heynen and Janina Gosseye, Koninklijke Vlaamse Academie Van Belgie Voor Wetenschappen en Kunsten, 2012, 401.

[10] Charles Jencks, interview with the author and Eva Branscome, 16 February 2009, London, cited in Eva Branscome, "The Project Postmodernism and its Midwives" in "Hans Hollein and Postmodernism: Art and Architecture in Austria, 1958–1985," PhD thesis, UCL, The Bartlett School of Architecture, 2014, 104.

[11] Elie Haddad, "Charles Jencks and the Historiography of Post-Modernism," *The Journal of Architecture*, 14, 4 (2009): 493.

[12] Haddad, "Charles Jencks and the Historiography of Post-Modernism", 496.

[13] Charles Jencks, *The Story of Post-Modernism: Five Decades of the Ironic, Iconic and Critical in Architecture*, Chichester, UK: John Wiley & Sons, 2011, 46. In *The Story of Post-Modernism*, Jencks writes that *The Language of Postmodern Architecture* had been translated into German: *Die Sprache der postmodernen Architektur – Entstehung und Entwicklung einer alternativen Tradition*, Stuttgart: Deutsche Verlags-Anstalt, 1978; French: *Le langage de l'architecture post-moderne*, Paris: Denoël, 1979; Czech: *Jazyk post-moderní architektury*, Samizdat: self-published version, 1979; Spanish: *El Lenguaje de la Arquitectura postmoderna*, Barcelona:

Léa-Catherine Szacka

Gustavo Gili, 1981; Russian: *Jazyk architektury postmodernizma*, Strojizdat, 1985; Serbian: *Jezik postmoderne arhitekture*, Beograd: Vuk Karadžić, 1985); Chinese: 後現代建築語言, Chu ban, 1986; Polish: *Architektura postmodernistyczna*, Arkady, 1987; Japanese: ポストモダン建築の言語; Hungarian, *A posztmodern építészet nyelve*; and Italian, only in parts.

14
Parnell, "AD Magazine and Post-Modern Architecture", 401.

15
Ibid.

16
Ingerid Helsing Almaas, "Norwegian Architecture?" in *Arkitektur N*, published 10 May 2010, http://www.architecturenorway.no/questions/identity/almaas-norwegian-arch/.

17
Almaas, "Norwegian Architecture?".

18
Ibid.

19
Jan Digerud was trained at Washington State University and Yale University from 1963 to 1965. In 1969, he established, together with Jon Lundberg, the office Jan & Jon in Oslo. Before returning to Norway, Digerud had worked for Skildmore, Owing and Merrill (SOM) between 1963 and 1965. He also worked for Platou arkitekter from 1966 to 1969 and 1983 to 1995. During his stay in the US, Digerud had been strongly influenced by Louis Kahn and Robert Venturi (with whom he had studied when at Yale University).

20
Thomas Thiis-Evensen, in his monograph on the work of Jan & Jon, claims that Digerud and Lundberg introduced Postmodernism not only to Norway but also to the whole of Scandinavia. See Thomas Thiis-Evensen, *The Postmodernists Jan & Jon*, Oslo: Universitetsforlaget, 1984.

21
Arne Henriksen graduated from the Norwegian Technical University in Trondheim (NTH) in 1971. Henriksen worked for Norwegian Railways (NSB) from 1975 to 1989 before establishing his own office, Arne Henriksen Arkitekter AS, in 1989. From 1989 to 1993, he was a professor at the Oslo School of Architecture and Design, mainly teaching drawing.

22
Almaas, "Norwegian Architecture?".

23
Translated by the authors: "Med Chicago og Mies van der Rohe som utgangspunkt makerte USA seg sterkt i den internasjonale stilen og markerer seg nå tilsvarende sterkt vekk fra den. Den monotone, såkalt perfekte bygg som ignorerer sine omgivelser i kraft av sin gastalt, skal vike plass for mykere løsninger med tilpasningsevner som mer skaper et sted. Byggene er også ofte irrasjonelle, poetiske og ekstroverte." Erik Collett, "Amerikatur og arkitektur", *Arkitektnytt* 1 (1980), 4–5.

24
Lukasz Stanek, *Postmodernism is Almost all Right: Polish Architecture After Socialist Globalization*, Waraw: Museum of Modern Art Warsaw, 2012. Lidia Klein and Alicja Gzowska, "P1 Postmodernizm Polski Architektura i Urbanistyka," *Antologia Tekstow Pod Redakcja Lidia Klein*, Warsaw: 40000 Malarzy, 2013.

25
See Piotr Marciniak, "The Search for a New Concept of Space and the City. Postmodernism in Poland: Theory and Practice in the 1980s" in *Proceedings of the 2nd International Conference of the European Architectural History Network*, eds. Hilde Heynen and Janina Gosseye, Brussels: Koninklijke Vlaamse Academie Van Belgie Voor Wetenschappen en Kunsten, 2012, 390–395.

26
This occurred on 15–21 June 1981.

27
Piotr Marciniak, "The Search for a New Concept of Space and the City", in *Proceedings* of the 2nd *International Conference of the European Architectural History Network,* eds. Hilde Heynen and Janina Gosseye, Koninklijke Vlaamse Academie Van Belgie Voor Wetenschappen en Kunsten, 2012, 390

28
Ibid.

29
Ibid.

Colonne e una Torre: Italian Designs for Melbourne 1978

Philip Goad and
Francesco Vitelli

On 4 December 1978, the conservative Liberal State Government of Victoria, Australia, launched an international ideas competition for a landmark for its capital city, Melbourne. The project site was nominally the vast Flinders Street rail yards, which lay between the southern boundary of the city's 1837 colonial grid plan and the Yarra River. From across the world, 2300 architects, firms and private individuals registered to enter the competition, and more than 1900 entries were received.[1] It was at a time when neoliberal politics was on the rise and architectural theory globally was taking a more openly self-reflective and postmodern turn, and the competition entries offer an internationally significant insight into what a sizeable cross-section of the architecture profession at the end of the 1970s believed might be suitable answers to questions of monumentality, representation, and urban rehabilitation. Largely forgotten today, the competition entries are now archived in the Public Records Office of Victoria (PROV).

The Search for an Idea
The Melbourne Landmark Ideas Competition had all of the elements that would come to mark the rise of the visually 'iconic' projects of the 1990s and early twenty-first century, when architects as image-makers partook and became complicit in a process in which speculative development funded a mix of large-scale public and private infrastructure in the name of urban renewal and revenue raising for the state. Even the report produced at the end of the assessment process suggested the provision of a combination of elements that might include a 'landmark symbol' (denoted diagrammatically as a slender, pencil-like tower) as just one component of the larger site, the remainder of which could be devoted to functions such as a 'residential village', a 'civic approach', 'pleasure gardens', an 'Australiana centre', 'casino/exhibitions/conventions', and a serpentine connecting 'transport system', all the while retaining the train lines beneath.

Victorian Premier Rupert Hamer announced the competition outcome on 18 December 1979.[2] Forty-eight Australian and overseas entries shared the $100,000 prize money. The conclusion of the eight-member panel of assessors was that there was no individual project of outstanding merit.[3] The local reception was scathing, even from one of the competition assessors.

Professor Patrick McCaughey stated publicly that the competition had attracted "an appalling standard of entries" and that they "give banality a new dimension and demonstrate a megalomania that makes the pyramids look like pimples".[4] Certainly, the number of entries that featured giant kangaroos, boomerangs, and even a replica of the Welcome Stranger gold nugget appear to confirm McCaughey's strident opinion.[5]

However, the competition, advertised widely in the international architectural press, elicited a number of entries from well-known local and international architectural practices, as well as celebrated Australian artists such as Norma Redpath and Stanislaus Ostoja-Kotkowski.[6] Significant international entrants included the architect Cedric Price (UK), with his prophetic, multi-level series of hydroponic urban farms; Coop Himmelb(l)au (Austria), whose entry featured an adjustable 'rock' that opened and closed for concerts; Alison and Peter Smithson (UK), who submitted 'Magic Mountains'; and expatriate Melbourne architects Peter Wilson and Jenny Lowe, whose entry, titled 'Melbourne Banqueting Wall and Ballroom', was drawn in a style that echoed the lyrical constructions of Italian architect, painter and designer Massimo Scolari. Other significant entrants included Warren Chalk (ex-Archigram, UK), Peter Salter (UK), Will Alsop (UK), Eva Jiřičná (UK), Harry Weese (USA), and Jack Diamond (Canada). Few of these entries were ever published, though Austrian architect Raimund Abraham's 'World Science Centre', with its building impaled by a plane, featured on the cover of the American journal *Artforum* in March 1981, and American architect Steven Holl's 'Bridges of Melbourne' entry was famously included in Holl's *Pamphlet Architecture 7: Bridge of Houses* (1981) and *Anchoring: Selected Projects 1975–1988* (1989).[7]

    A select number of competition entries went on public display for one week at Collins Place at 35 Collins Street from 6 January 1980.[8] Most of the winning Australian entries were safe, even genteel, in their deference to either heritage or romantic concepts of the public garden. The city as a speculative entity to be challenged, or as a sovereign claim on land that might be questioned, was neatly sidestepped. Bates, Smart & McCutcheon, for example, proposed the world's largest indoor garden enclosed by a giant transparent roof. Denton Corker Marshall's bucolic, Krieresque scheme tried to satisfy all the competition requirements and would find part realisation twenty years later on another riverbank, in Brisbane, with the South Bank Grand Arbour (1997–2000).

The Italian Contribution

While criticism could be levelled at the naive, oft absurd, but mainly insipid Australian entries and even the cultured gentility of the winning local schemes, the Italian entries in the competition (mostly from Milan) showed—unselfconsciously—many shades of grey. There was, like the Australian entries, a diversity of approach but with no guarded fear of the monumental (such as Filippo Tartaglia and sculptor M. Carlo's entry #3124), no fear of radically recasting the concept of city (such as Giorgio Lo Cascio's megastructural 'The Hub'), nor any fear of the wildly organic (such as entry #1991 by forgotten Milanese architect Mario Galvagni). Studio Nizzoli (entry #1993) labelled its scheme 'Melbourne's Post Modern Skyscraper', depicting an enormously tall Ionic column that not only answered the competition's simple brief but also prefigured its amputation and realisation a year later as the Domus Editorial Headquarters in Rozzano, Milan (1980).

All of these Italian entries reinforced Manfredo Tafuri's assessment of Italian architecture at the end of the 1970s as "leading to a crisis of models and to the ineffectiveness of passwords".[9]

Amongst the general dross were two unpremiated Italian entries that deserve special note: one was a series of pillars, the other a tower. Both entries spoke to European conceptions of the New World: one about the limits of the civilised world, the other about an 'unknown city', a ghostly echo of Melbourne's mark on the land as a classical project of colonisation. The two projects, one by Florentine architect Adolfo Natalini, the other a combined entry by Milan-based Aldo Rossi and Gianni Braghieri with collaborator Stefano Getzel, demand documentation and theoretical location within the context of Melbourne's architecture culture, then poised on the edge of postmodern discourse, and a local political culture in which the call for 'landmarks' was a none too subtle preparation for what Melbourne had always forged its future upon: the spectacle of capital.

Colonne: 'The Pillars of Melbourne'

Adolfo Natalini's entry (#3143), registered under the name of Superstudio, comprised a single sheet that included a block of typewritten text, a series of ten small images taped roughly onto the sheet (some hand-drawn, others collaged), photographs, two postcard-sized images of the site (one aerial view, the other a distant view) from the competition brief, and a large-scale partially hand-drawn view of the upper level of Natalini's 'Pillars of Melbourne'.[10]

In stark contrast to the humour and irony of "magic boomerangs" and boxing kangaroos holding dollar signs aloft, Natalini, unusually it might seem for someone who had never been to Melbourne, sought inspiration from Indigenous Australian culture. As Alison Clarke has observed, Italian radical architects, including Superstudio and Natalini in particular, were at the time deeply interested in pre-industrial craft-based genres, where "anthropologically inspired ideas around material culture, ritual meaning, and emphasis on users and co-design underpinned their newly forged design philosophies".[11] Natalini, for example, made reference in his competition text to the "Arandas, called the Achilpas", who:

> carry with them in their periodical wanderings, the sacred pole known as kauwa-auwa, the symbol of the centre of the world, and that pole is planted facing the direction of their journey. The pole connects the cosmic planes (sky and earth), and by representing the centre of the world, puts an end to the anguishing search for land.[12]

For Natalini, this practice reminded him of the Pillars of Hercules, which marked the limits of the ancient world, the gateway into the unknown.

According to Roman sources, legend has it that Hercules had to cross the mountain that was known as Atlas, and, instead of climbing it, he smashed his way through it and, in doing so, connected the Atlantic Ocean to the Mediterranean Sea, forming the Strait of Gibraltar. The two mountains formed by the split, one Gibraltar, the other Jebel Musa in Morocco, have since become known as the Pillars of Hercules. For Charles V of Spain, these pillars became part of his country's coat of arms. They represented not the gateway to the Mediterranean but the entrance to the rest of the world: they were a symbol of Europe's colonial project.

Natalini then made the connection with trees, columns, towers, and skyscrapers:

> Since myths are not to be disregarded, I thought that pillars could once again become a landmark—for Melbourne. The Pillars of Hercules marked the end of the ancient world. The Pillars of Melbourne will mark the beginning of the new.[13]

Natalini arranged a series of pillars—200-metre-high steel cylinders, each with a diameter of ten metres—in the pattern of the Southern Cross and nearby stars. Each pillar was to represent one of the six continents of origin of Melbourne's inhabitants: it was a monument to migration. According to Natalini:

> During the day, they project long shadows, like sundials, and with the help of sun and wind produce sounds. At night, they are illuminated and can be seen from the sea.[14]

Natalini's project is metaphysical, elegant poetry. The series of hand-drawings of trees and images are borrowed from Dante's *Inferno* (1308–20). It is different—formally—from the surrealist, anti-classical projects of Superstudio such as *Monumento Continuo* of 1969, which Manfredo Tafuri argued "turned the project into dream material transcribed with an irony 'that made nobody laugh'".[15] Both Natalini schemes were rhetorical but dressed in the avant-garde pictorial media of their day. As a collective, Superstudio had abandoned working together in 1978, but their work had already lost its potency by the mid-1970s, only to be replaced after 1979 by Natalini's patrician retreat into the Florentine traditions of drawing and genteel form.[16]

Una Torre: 'The Tower of Memories'

The message behind Aldo Rossi, Gianni Braghieri, and Stefano Getzel's entry (#1251) was rhetoric of a different kind. The Rossi team submitted five sheets: three black and white dyeline prints (one showing indicative plans and an elevation, another elevation with roof plan, and an isometric view) and two semi-perspectival views drawn over a hard-line elevation and then coloured with a sepia wash and solid block colours in oil pastel and watercolour. There was neither text nor a title.[17]

The project was for a skyscraper: 380 metres high, ninety-five storeys, taller than the Eiffel Tower, and, tellingly, just twenty metres short of Tatlin's Monument to the Third International. In Rossi's words, his proposal directly addressed the concept of a 'landmark':

> This tower built over the railway, in an unknown city, with no function or use except perhaps that of being a symbol, was to have been the symbol par excellence; the tower to end all other vertical constructions envisaged, vaguely drawn, and seldom if ever built.[18]

Octagonal in plan, the skyscraper was a stepped tower with a lift core at its panoptic centre, the entire structure sitting on a square base that straddled the railways beneath.

Facing west, the tower was shown in fact to be hollow. The line work of the three black and white drawings, presumably delineated by Braghieri, exude professional competence. They exhibit a commercial quality that recalls the sheer mirror glass forms then in vogue in Australia and the United States, especially Cesar Pelli's blue glass Pacific Design Center, Los Angeles (1975), which had been lionised during the running of the Landmark Competition by Arthur Drexler's MoMA exhibition, *Transformations in Modern Architecture* (1979).[19] As if to counter these sleek homages to commerce, Rossi's tower had no explicit function and was to be clad in red glass. It was an homage instead to the collective urban monumentality of one of his favourite buildings, Karl Ehn's red stuccoed Karl Marx Hof housing, Vienna (1927–30). It is as if Rossi, like Adolf Loos before him, asks questions of the skyscraper: Can it be a monument? Can a tower hold, even convey, collective memory?

The two-coloured drawings appear to have been intended to read as a pair. Both are versions of Rossi's 'analogous city'—collections of his typological researches but depicted in dream-like settings. One is green, almost pastoral, and depicts not just the Melbourne tower but also the Student Housing at Chieti (1976), the Gallaratese housing in Milan (1973), the Hotel on the Grand Canal in Cannaregio West in Venice (1979), and his most recent project, il Teatro del Mondo, Venice (1979). The other is darker. There are few trees, the background is dominated by towers—a career-long preoccupation—and many of the same buildings appear. Il Teatro del Mondo and the Gallaratese housing appear again, but now there is also the Villa at Borgo Ticino (1973), the School at Fagnano Olona (1973–76), and his competition entry for the Civic centre tower at Pesaro (1979), as well as, significantly, in the foreground, the Cemetery of San Cataldo at Modena (1971–78). In the Melbourne competition drawing, the stepped skyscraper tower takes the place of the projected crematorium chimney at Modena. The skyscraper becomes the factory chimney of the speculative city behind; a haunting echo of the memory conjured at Modena, where the chimney stood—unsettlingly— in front of the segregated Jewish cemetery behind.

The telescoping forms of Rossi's 'Tower of Memories' also echoes Tafuri's critical encapsulation in 1973, in reference to Cass Gilbert's Woolworth Building, of the skyscraper being "an element of mediation, a structure that does not wholly identify with the reasons for its own existence, an entity that remains aloof from the city".[20] Sitting alone— alienated—above Melbourne's rail yards, Rossi's tower performs the same rhetorical role as Loos's 1922 project for the *Chicago Tribune*, which Tafuri described as having the following intention:

> In 1922, in full view of the Chicago Loop, he [Loos] wished deliberately to 'reflect on values'; in an obsessive search for non-ephemeral forms, he wished to compromise the very symbol of order—and in its most authentically classical version—by using it in an everyday manner. The estrangement of the column became an allegory of urban estrangement.[21]

Rossi's hollow tower has the same aim, to challenge the nature of the very city it accompanied. While the two projects by Natalini and Rossi reveal much about contemporary architecture in Italy and stand as powerful reflections of both architects' career trajectories at the time, Melbourne architects in 1979 were blissfully unaware of these two entries. It was not until the March 1982 edition of *Domus* was published that both entries were seen publicly together for the first time. This was where Rossi and Braghieri's project was first labelled as 'The Tower of Memories'.[22] March 1982 was also the month that Micha Bandini's article, 'Fashion and consumption: notes on Aldo Rossi', appeared in the Melbourne-based journal *Transition*.[23] A decade later, Rossi's competition entry had bequeathed a visual legacy to Melbourne's central city skyline with the completion of 222 Exhibition Street (1989) and 101 Collins Street (1991) by Denton Corker Marshall Architects and 120 Collins Street (1991) by Hassell Studio and Daryl Jackson. In contrast to Rossi's didactic hollow tower, however, each of these buildings was a high-rise commercial office tower with a square-planned floor plate maximised for real estate yield, expertly dressed in monumental guise, and, if nothing else, at least reclaiming the spirit and morphological consistency of Melbourne's 1920s street architecture.

An Architecture Culture in Transition

In 1977 to 1979, at the time of the Landmark Ideas Competition, Melbourne's architecture culture was on the cusp of change. By the end of the 1960s,

Melbourne as a city had embraced the post-war American vision of modernity and succumbed to consumption. Whole city blocks had been razed for speculative office buildings as Melbourne's inner heart was effectively "de-housed" and zoned as a mono-functional city.[24] Only Melbourne's colonial grid stood firm as development proposal after development proposal challenged its near unassailable form.

At the same time as the ousting of the Federal Labor Government due to financial scandal in 1975, unrest had begun to brew amongst the younger members of the architecture profession. Between 1975 and 1980, a series of significant events occurred within Melbourne's architecture culture: the rise of conservation and heritage, which saw the formation of the Collins Street Defence Movement in 1976;[25] the ill-fated attempts in 1978 to form an alternative chapter of the Royal Australian Institute of Architects and the infamous meeting at the Last Laugh Restaurant in May 1978; the rise of a local architectural discourse that included Charles Jencks's visit to Melbourne in 1974; Norman Day's turbulent term as editor of *Architect* from May 1976 before his sacking in late 1977; the launching of the Half-Time Club in January 1979;[26] and also the founding of *Transition* magazine by Ian McDougall and Richard Munday in July 1979. At the same time, local architectural aesthetics was shifting and finding its social project not in the central city but in the suburbs[27]—specifically the fine-grained needlework of the inner suburbs, where the Victorian Ministry of Housing had from 1980 begun to make postmodern incursions in the form of infill terrace housing.[28] All of a sudden, the promising urban reappraisals of Daryl Jackson and Evan Walker's City Edge Housing in South Melbourne (1972–77) and Earle Shaw's Carlton Housing Co-operative scheme (1970) were forgotten—even by their own authors and became architectural anomalies by the 1980s. These were signal events in a turbulent five years, which were to set a different course for Melbourne's architecture culture in the 1980s.

Despite appearances to the contrary, there was no theoretical or polemical vacuum. The city's architectural historians, most notably George Tibbits and Miles Lewis at the University of Melbourne, did not merely theorise on its form and project. They were deeply involved with others in urban activism and obsessed with heritage and conservation as a response to a city under siege. This was not an abdication of the urban project but a rallying call to save the historic city. At the same time, these historians led crusades to document the inner suburbs, almost as if a bulwark against unchecked speculation. This was not a rejection of modernism per se, but a defence against the worst aspects of capital, speculation, and laissez-faire government. Meanwhile, other local theoreticians such as Peter Downton, Daryl Le Grew, David Watson, and Kim Dovey were deeply enmeshed in people/environment and human relations in architecture, a parallel campaign to shift design perceptions rather than shape urban politics.

Colonne e una Torre: Italian Designs for Melbourne 1978

If the city was a battleground, architects such as Peter Corrigan and an emerging generation of graduates and students turned to the suburbs for sustenance, critique, and physical results. Rossi's lesson, for the most part, was the recognition that in the suburbs there existed a genuine social politic that had, for decades, been ignored.[29]

When the final competition report was released in December 1979, it was introduced by a letter to Premier Rupert Hamer from the Chairman of the Landmark Committee, businessman and developer Ronald Walker. Part of his letter gave a clue to what, in retrospect, might have been the whole venture's ultimate aim:

> The conclusion of the Panel is that there is no single brilliant idea, but that a combination of a number of excellent ideas are worthy of recognition.

The ideas selected take into account the multi-cultural background of Melbourne, our national pride and great interest in all sporting activities, the uniqueness of our national flora, fauna, marine and bird life and our great tendency to gamble.[30]

The Melbourne Landmark Ideas Competition pre-empted the 1980s development of Southbank further down and on the other side of Melbourne's Yarra River.[31] But perhaps more critically, it planted the political and economic seed of what would eventually be realised in the 1990s as Crown Casino (1992–99), the massive complex west of Southbank, devoted to gambling, retail, and hospitality and steered in large part by Ronald Walker and businessman Lloyd Williams, whose development company Hudson Conway not only developed the casino but was also its first operator. In retrospect, the Melbourne Landmark Ideas Competition might be regarded as a cynical foretaste of urban renewal as a wealth begetting exercise.

1979: *Anno di delirio*

In 1976, Aldo Rossi and others at ETH Zurich produced his now-famous collage, *La Città Analoga* (*The Analogous City*). The spectacular artwork included the artfully disordered meshing of Rossi's own works and drawings, as well as those of Michelangelo, Borromini, and Schinkel, amongst others. As David Dunster observed, Rossi explained his understanding of 'analogous' by quoting Jung's letter to Freud in 1910:

> Analogical or fantasy thinking is emotionally toned, pictorial and wordless, not discourse, but an inner-directed rumination on materials belonging to the past.[32]

For Rossi, this dream-like or delirious state meant "a different sense of history, conceived of not simply as fact, but rather as a series of things, of affective objects to be used by the memory or in a design".[33] What could then be described as the delirium of Rossi's 'analogous city' (1976) was quite different from the seriousness of his early works and especially his commitment to the social, revolutionary, and research aims of the modern project. His later projects lack this earlier compulsive introspection. In 1979, Rossi gets caught up in his own internal reverie. The Melbourne competition project and Il Teatro del Mondo in Venice, both designed in the same year, can thus be seen in the same light: as a turning point in his career. It is as if Aldo Rossi's composites of multiple buildings of his own authorship, which comprise his multiple 'analogous city' images of the late 1970s and early 1980s, constitute a personal delirium. They are also an eerie acknowledgment of Erastus Salisbury Field's famous and ultimately prophetic painting *Historical Monument of the American Republic* (ca. 1875) with its collection of telescoping towers, which appeared in Alison Sky and Michelle Stone's *Unbuilt America* (1976) and was published at exactly the time Rossi was writing and teaching in New York.[34]

It's tempting at this point to ask whether others might have been caught up in Rossi's delirium of an 'analogous city' and then see what trajectory might have played out. Melbourne architects did not know of Rossi's entry in 1979. But many architects, especially the city's younger generation of recent graduates and students, were well aware of his work, as well as the design work of other contemporary Italian architects as a sometime counter or parallel to the strong Melbourne interest in the work of American postmodern architects such as Robert Venturi and Charles Moore. For example, in 1979, Melbourne's National Gallery of Victoria would host the Ettore Sottsass exhibition, an event that would be influential to the young firm Biltmoderne, the directors of which, Dale Jones-Evans, Roger Wood, and Randall Marsh, later split, the latter two forming Wood Marsh.[35] However, it was Aldo Rossi's work and writings—understood as a body of critical ideas rather than an architectural language to emulate—that had deeper local influence, channelled largely through the English and US architectural press and through exposure to a new generation via Melbourne's schools of architecture. In 1977, issue 45 of the popular large format *Global Architecture* series featured Yukio Futagawa's haunting photographs of Rossi's Gallaratese housing in Milan,[36] which in turn was visited by numbers of Melbourne architecture students and graduates in the early 1980s.[37] Rossi's floating Teatro del Mondo, Venice (1979), was well known in Melbourne (notably by architects Peter Corrigan, Alex Selenitsch, and Greg Missingham), as were the three *Oppositions* books that featured Rossi's writings, namely, *The Architecture of the City* (1981), *A Scientific Autobiography* (1981), and his introduction to *Spoken into the Void: Collected Essays 1897–1900* (1982), the special *Oppositions* book of the collected essays of Adolf Loos, a figure of intense interest in Melbourne at the time, given Ian McDougall's professed admiration for the Viennese architectural theorist's problematisation of the monument.[38] *The Architecture of the City* was on reading lists at Monash University from 1981 and the University of Melbourne by 1983. Together with Manfredo Tafuri's *Architecture and Utopia* (1976) and *Theories and History of Architecture* (1980, English translation)—understood largely through their presentation through *Oppositions*—Rossi's buildings and writings were promoted by *Transition* from 1981 and by Kim Halik at Melbourne's Half-Time Club from 1985.[39]

Interest in contemporary Italian architecture was not new in Melbourne, however. Journals such as *Domus* and *Casabella* were well known, as was the furniture of designers such as Achille Castiglioni and Mario Bellini.

The difference between post-war interests in Italian architecture—such as Roy Grounds' admiration for the museum work of BBPR in Milan and Ezio de Felice in Naples and its translation into the National Gallery of Victoria (1959–68)[40] or Giancarlo De Carlo's 1971 talk in Melbourne as part of Robin Boyd's Melbourne Architectural Papers[41] or Peter Elliott's interests in Carlo Scarpa in the 1970s and a general awareness of Scarpa's work experienced again through Futagawa's photographs in *GA*[42]—and the early 1980s interest in Italian architects and theorists was the focus on theory.

Yet, in the competition entries submitted by local architects in 1979, there was no evidence of a turn to European, specifically contemporary Italian, urban theory. Instead, there were different, more localised concerns. Especially popular were schemes that suggested alternative energy production. Of these, one is noteworthy for its expression of a different but no less polemical 'delirium' to that explored by Aldo Rossi. Entry #3968 by Kevin Greenhatch, Ian McDougall, George Hatzisavas, and Betty Greenhatch, entitled 'The Science Playground', comprised a giant solar collecting 'tree' that supported the four worlds of nature, humanity, science, and reality. It was a virtual fun park of diagrammatically disparate elements, almost as if the idea of landmark was to be Luna Park, the vision of Australia at play by the beach, a theme that would be further played out by McDougall's later firm, ARM Architecture, in its competition entry for Federation Square (1997) and its built scheme for the National Museum of Australia (NMA) in Canberra (2000). However, ARM Architecture's subsequent renewal and refurbishment of the Shrine of Remembrance (2001–14) in Melbourne does accord with Rossi's respect for the monument. At the other end of the Swanston Street axis, the same firm's use of the image of William Barak, the last traditional elder of the Wurundjeri-willam clan, on a speculative residential tower means that memory collides with capital, an uneasy and disturbing reminder of Melbourne's perennial obsession with its own dubious presence.[43]

An Unfinished Project

The riverside setting for Melbourne's Landmark Ideas Competition in 1979 has long been a site of urban projection. In the 1880s, for example, architect William Salway proposed an imperial gateway to the city with symmetrical civic institutions and a new bridge. In May 1925, in conjunction with James Smith's competition-winning project to roof the Flinders Street rail yards, the journal *Building* commented:

> Mr Smith traced history back to the time of the old aboriginal ford on the site of the present Princes Bridge over the Yarra, and showed that that has been a dominant factor and that the whole arterial system of Melbourne, its suburban tram system and its greatest business activities are today on that spot.[44]

Melbourne's urban development has been told in competition and has been steeped in speculation ever since its founding. The monument of its grid is a monument to colonial sovereignty and its claim over the land. Today, Melbourne architects, one might argue, have emerged from what Tafuri would describe as the "negative prologue" of the mid-1970s.[45] The complexity of the city is understood; so is its history, its memory, and its ability to haunt. Melbourne is a city that prides itself on its architecture and urbanism as a sophisticated marker of European settlement and future design thinking. But this is also part of its ongoing anxiety; how does it reconcile that past and anxious present earned through the dark spectacle of capital with a landscape known and settled by others? Perhaps, then, it is appropriate to return to Aldo Rossi's 1979 competition entry. His 'Tower of Memories'—which continues to act like a spectral conscience. Its brooding shadows suggest there is a history and a project still to be uncovered.

1
The Public Records Office of Victoria (PROV) holds 1973 competition entries. See Landmark Competition Drawings, Series No. VPRS 2869, Consignment numbers P0002 and P0003, PROV, Shiel Street, North Melbourne.

2
"48 attempts to make Melbourne memorable," *The Canberra Times*, 19 December 1979, 9.

3
The panel of eight assessors included Fine Arts Professor Patrick McCaughey, architect Barry Patten, and Director of the Victorian Ministry of the Arts, Dr Eric Westbrook.

4
"Professor says landmark-contest entries 'banal'", *The Canberra Times*, 18 December 1979, 3.

5
The so-called Welcome Stranger is the biggest alluvial gold nugget ever found. The 97 kg nugget was discovered at Moliagul, Victoria, in February 1869 by prospectors John Deason and Richard Oates.

6
The well-known Australian architecture practices and architects who submitted entries included Baird Cuthbert Mitchell; Bates, Smart & McCutcheon;

Kevin Borland; Graham De Gruchy; Denton Corker Marshall; Holgar & Holgar; Stuart McIntosh; Peter Myers; Geoff Nairn; Joyce Nankivell Associates; Anthony Styant-Browne; McGlashan & Everist; Gerry Rippon; Paul Ritter; Romberg & Boyd; Peter Staughton; and Yvonne von Hartel.

7
Steven Holl, *Pamphlet Architecture 7: Bridge of Houses*, New York: Pamphlet Architecture, 1981, and Steven Holl, *Anchoring: Selected Projects, 1975–1988*, New York: Princeton Architectural Press, 1989.

8
Geoff Walsh, "Landmark ideas go on display," *The Age*, 7 January 1980, 3; "Landmark entries," *The Canberra Times*, 7 January 1980, 3.

9
Manfredo Tafuri, *History of Italian Architecture, 1944–1985*, Cambridge, Massachusetts: MIT Press, 1989, 146. Originally published as *Storia dell'architettura italiana, 1944–1985*, Torino: Giulio Einaudi editore spa, 1982, 1986.

10
However, when the project was published in 1982, the authorship was cited as solely Adolfo Natalini. See "Le Colonne di Melbourne – Melbourne Pillars", *Domus*, 626 (March 1982), 30

11
Alison J. Clarke, "The Indigenous and the Autochthon", in *Global Tools, 1973–1975*, eds. Valerio Borgonuovo and Silvia Franceschini, Istanbul: SALT/Garanti Kultur AS, 2015, 126. See also Alison J. Clarke, "The Anthropological Object in Design: From Superstudio to Victor Papanek", in *Design Anthropology: Object Culture in the 21st Century*, ed. Alison J. Clarke, Vienna and New York: Springer, 2010, 74–87.

12
Quotation from Adolfo Natalini and Superstudio, Florence, Italy, "The Pillars of Melbourne," Landmark competition drawing, VPRS 2869, P0002, Unit 1269, PROV.

13
Ibid.

14
Ibid.

15
Tafuri, *History of Italian Architecture, 1944–1985*, 99.

16
See Vittorio Savi, *Adolfo Natalini: architetture raccontate*, Milano: Electa, 1989.

17
The project's descriptor as Entry 1251 in the Public Records Office of Victoria collection is "Stepped Tower". See VPRS 2869, P0002, Unit 511 (Entry 1251), PROV.

18
Aldo Rossi, "The Tower of Memories," *Domus*, 626 (March 1982), 28.

19
Arthur Drexler, *Transformations in Modern Architecture*, New York: Museum of Modern Art, 1979. The book was based on an exhibition held at the Museum of Modern Art, New York, 23 February to 24 April 1979.

20
Manfredo Tafuri, "The Disenchanted Mountain: The Skyscraper and the City", in Giorgio Ciucci et al, *The American City: from the Civil War to the New Deal*, Cambridge, Massachusetts: MIT Press, 1979, 389. This book was first published in Italian as *La città Americana della Guerra civile al New Deal*, Rome: Laterza, 1973.

21
Tafuri, "The Disenchanted Mountain," 402.

22
See "La Torre dei Ricordi – The Tower of Memories" and "Le Colonne di Melbourne – Melbourne Pillars," *Domus*, 626 (March 1982), 28–30.

23
Micha Bandini, "Fashion and Consumption: Notes on Aldo Rossi," *Transition*, 9 (March 1982), 6–14.

24
For an account of the modern project and the Australian city, see Philip Goad, "Absence and presence: Modernism and the Australian city", in *Fabulation, Papers from the Twenty-Ninth Conference of The Society of Architectural Historians, Australia and New Zealand*, eds. Stuart King, Anuradha Chatterjee, and Stephen Loo, Launceston: SAHANZ, 2012, 10.

25
The most public of these was the conservation and the battles over Melbourne's rich nineteenth century building stock, which was being and had been rapidly depleted during the 1960s building boom. One of the Federal Labor Government's chief contributions to the built environment was the formation of the National Estate from May 1973 and the Australian Heritage Commission in mid-1975. At a local level, the Collins Street Defence Movement was formed in September 1976 by members of the architecture profession, under the direction of Evan Walker and Professor Charles Robertson. Other forms of activism took place in Melbourne's inner suburbs. See Graeme Davison, Renate Howe, and David Nichols, *Trendyville: the battle for Australia's inner cities*, Clayton, Victoria: Monash University Publishing, 2014.

26
The Half-Time Club, a Melbourne-based meeting/club/discussion circle of graduate architects and students,

'principally young (under 30) architects', first met on January 16, 1979. Minutes and subjects of its meetings (1979–88) can be found in *Backlogue: Journal of the Half-Time Club*, 3, 1999.

27
The Melbourne turn to the suburbs theoretically and formally is best recounted in Conrad Hamann, *Cities of Hope: Australian architecture and design by Edmond and Corrigan, 1962–1992*, Melbourne: Oxford University Press, 1993.

28
John Devenish, "Victorian Ministry of Housing: style replaces stigma," *International Architect*, 4 (1984), 20–7. See also Karen Burns and Paul Walker, "Publicly Postmodern: Media, Image and the New Social Housing Institution in 1980s Melbourne", in *Proceedings of the Society of Architectural Historians, Australia and New Zealand: 32, Architecture, Institutions and Change*, eds. Paul Hogben and Judith O'Callaghan, Sydney: SAHANZ, 2015, 68–81.

29
A key article that recognised this was Richard Munday, "Passion in the Suburbs," *Architecture Australia*, 66:1 (February–March 1977), 52–61.

30
Ronald Walker, "letter to The Honourable R.J. Hamer, Premier of Victoria," dated 11 December 1979, in *Landmark Competition Report*, Melbourne: Landmark Committee, Department of the Premier, Government of Victoria, December 1979.

31
A detailed account of the development of Melbourne's Southbank and the Melbourne Docklands from 1983 to 2004 can be found in Kim Dovey, *Fluid City: Transforming Melbourne's Waterfront*, Sydney: University of New South Wales Press, 2005.

32
David Dunster, caption to *La Città Analoga*, 1976 in *Aldo Rossi: Architecture, Projects and Drawings*, London: Institute of Contemporary Arts, 1983, 48–49.

33
Aldo Rossi, quoted in *Aldo Rossi: Architecture, Projects and Drawings*, 49.

34
Alison Sky and Michelle Stone, *Unbuilt America: forgotten architecture in the United States, from Thomas Jefferson to the space age*, New York: McGraw-Hill, 1976.

35
See, for example, Ettore Sottsass jr., *from the end product to the product's end*, Sydney: Australian Gallery Directors' Council, 1979, the catalogue of an exhibition held at the National Gallery of Victoria, Melbourne, 20 February to 11 March 1979; Ballarat Fine Art Gallery, Ballarat, 18 March to 8 April 1979; and S.H. Ervin Museum and Art Gallery, Sydney, 19 April to 13 May 1979.

36
Yukio Futagawa, ed., *Global Architecture 45: Housing complex at the Gallaratese quarter, Milan, Italy, 1969–74*, Tokyo: ADA Edita, 1977.

37
For example, this author (Philip Goad) and Deborah Fisher, then both architecture students, made a special visit in 1982 to photograph the Aldo Rossi and Carlo Aymonino–designed housing blocks at the Gallaratese quarter in Milan on the recommendation of older architecture students at the University of Melbourne.

38
Evidenced in physical terms by Ian McDougall's design of his own home, 'Haus am Grosvenorstrasse', in Grosvenor Street, Prahran, Victoria, 1984. See Doug Evans, ed., *Aardvark II*, Melbourne: Department of Architecture, RMIT, 1992, 71.

39
For example, "Minutes, Half-Time Club, 13 May 1985," *Backlogue*, 3 (1999), 69–71.

40
Philip Goad, "An Oriental Palazzo: Roy Grounds and the National Gallery of Victoria," *Backlogue* 3 (1999), 72–105.

41
For a transcript, see Giancarlo De Carlo, *An architecture of participation*, South Melbourne: Royal Australian Institute of Architects, 1972.

42
GA 50 (1979) and *GA 51* (1979) both featured the work of Carlo Scarpa, extensively photographed by Yukio Futagawa.

43
For a detailed critique of the Barak tower project, see Sandra Kaji-O'Grady, "Swanston Square," *Architecture Australia*, 5 (September 2015), 28–34.

44
Building, 12 May 1925, 142–143.

45
Tafuri, *History of Italian Architecture*, 146.

Ciao Australia: *Domus* Looks to the Antipodes

Silvia Micheli

Distance, in its deeper sense of remoteness, is a condition of the Australian mentality that always affected the nation's intellectuals across the nineteenth and twentieth centuries. The opportunity for Australian architects to explore a historical reference to architecture's past and gain exposure to contemporary movements was impaired[1] by what the Australian historian Geoffrey Blainey called the "tyranny of distance".[2] Although it is recognised that this state of physical and cultural isolation has provided local architects with exceptional opportunities and enviable conditions of intellectual freedom, there is also a constant need for new ideas, cultural exchange, and dialogue.[3] If it is true that, since the 1970s, international air connections have made Australia 'closer' to the main centre of cultural production, they were an expensive way to visit foreign sites of interest to the profession. In these circumstances, the Australian architectural community would have risked remaining disconnected from the international intellectual circuits if not for the architectural publications that provided a fairly immediate and cheap source of information. Since the late nineteenth century, books and architectural journals have offered to Australians a cerebral link to foreign architecture, playing a crucial role in the dissemination and exchange of architectural ideas across different continents.

As there was a strong motivation to see Modernism as a European phenomenon, libraries in Australian universities and architects' offices had a wide range of European magazines from Germany, Scandinavia, France, and Italy, which became popular after World War II and throughout the postmodern period, including *L'Architecture d'Aujourd'hui*, *Casabella*, *Domus* and *Arkkitehti*, just to mention a few. The presence of this published material in university libraries offered students the opportunity to have access to different critical and visual content, allowing for a broader understanding of architectural production internationally beyond that presented by the English and American professional press.[4]

In the second part of the twentieth century, the Italian magazine *Domus* became a point of reference for post-war and postmodern Australian architects and industrial designers. Harry Seidler observed: "*Domus* has been a superb visual medium over the years. It is exciting visually, provocative in its imagery and stimulating always".[5] James Birrell travelled to Milan as part of a planned study tour of Europe and the United States during his Sisalkraft Travelling Scholarship in 1961. It was on that occasion that he had the chance to visit the office of the architectural journal *Domus* and meet the then-editor Gio Ponti. Although there were language difficulties, the two reportedly "got on like a house on fire".[6] Rex Addison, who worked under Birrell at the University of Queensland, shared the same fascination for *Domus*. Addison was convinced of the necessity to overcome the cultural cringe that oppressed architectural circles in Brisbane, recovering Queensland vernacular architecture and facilitating its development.

He came across Gino Valle's house in Udine, published in an issue of *Domus* in 1967, prior to his trip to Italy in 1971.[7] For Addison, like many other Australian architects, *Domus* was a source of discovery, inspiration, and planning prior to their field trips, for which the Italian magazine operated like a "mental guide".[8] *Domus* was "the bible", according to Marc Newson, who discovered it as a design student at the Sydney College of the Arts at the beginning of the 1980s, while working part-time in a newsagency. "I used to borrow [*Domus* issues], and they were my windows into the world of design",[9] said Newson, confirming that *Domus* assisted Australian architects to cope with the tyranny of distance and remain up-to-date with the main architectural and design trends internationally in more recent decades.

Domus in the International Context

Domus was founded by the Milan-based architect Ponti in 1928. He was joined in 1929 by the publisher Gianni Mazzocchi with Editoriale Domus, which was created specifically to publish the magazine. From its outset, *Domus* played a unique role in Italian and international architectural culture, manifesting a broad sensibility for architecture, art, and applied arts and industrial design. In contrast to other coeval architectural journals published in Italy, *Domus* avoided any ideological stance or political approach. Instead, it adopted an inclusive attitude, with a strong interest in setting new stylistic trends and embracing exotic design experiences. With a short break between 1940 and 1947, Ponti maintained his role as chief editor of *Domus* until 1979, spanning different architectural phases from Modernism to the beginnings of postmodernism.[10] His long editorship, exceptional for an architectural journal, was made possible by his sense of inclusivity in terms of different design agendas and his acceptance of divergent ideological positions and social needs, but it was also thanks to the international network he built up over time. In any case, Ponti prioritised the improvement of a collective taste across the nation on art, architecture, and furniture, updating the Italian middle class's social and cultural behaviour and offering an alternative direction for the international audience. This mission, which informed the journal from the outset, kept going throughout all stages of its development until the postmodern phase.

The articles published in *Domus* were mainly descriptive and enriched by large colour photographs, primarily documenting the domestic environment. This is one of the reasons why *Domus* became so popular amongst Australian architects, commonly focused on new forms of living for a fast-growing suburban population. Another appealing factor for the Australian audience was the great sensibility with which *Domus* understood and presented the relationship between centre and periphery. Ponti's journal paid considerable attention to new ways of producing art, architecture and design in different parts of the world, thus unveiling and celebrating the culture at the fringes. This interest in cultural diversity enhanced *Domus*'s internationalism, with a significant reach in remote regions. *Domus*'s consistency in the translation of its texts into English favoured its accessibility to a foreign audience, and the extensive use of drawings and pictures facilitated intercultural communication. These strategies secured *Domus* a position of supremacy in the competitive world of architectural magazines.

Domus was the Italian architectural magazine that engaged most with Australia, with architecture from the antipodes featured fairly regularly in the journal.[11] Although undeniable cultural differences occurred between the two countries, issues like the domestic environment, the role of industrial design in the making of indoor spaces, and the sensibility for reinventing the vernacular were aspects common to both in local debates. Also, Australian late Modernism and its adaptation to a remote region offered original examples to the spreading international style.

The presence of Australian architecture in Ponti's *Domus* was undoubtedly facilitated by personal connections. For instance, in the mid-1950s the Milan-based architect Enrico Taglietti was offered the opportunity to design an exhibition about Italian design in Sydney for the Australian department store David Jones. Taglietti was an energetic architect embedded in Milanese architectural circles, who studied at the Milan Polytechnic between 1948 and 1954 under distinguished teachers, including Ponti, Carlo De Carli, Marco Zanuso, Franco Albini, Ernesto Nathan Rogers, and Pier Luigi Nervi. Through them, Taglietti was involved in the Milan Triennale's activities, and, in 1954, he was made responsible for the foreign section of its tenth exhibition. In the 1950s and 1960s, the Milan Triennale was an international stage for exhibiting new ideas and a lively cultural environment for industrial designers, architects, and artists, fostering the integration of industry and arts in a city that was perceived as Europe's capital of design. Charles Lloyd Jones was abreast of the international relevance of the Milan Triennale when he attempted to involve Ponti in the set-up of an exhibition on Italian contemporary design to be held at David Jones stores in Sydney in 1955. The attempt to reach Ponti failed and Taglietti was recommended instead.[12] The exhibition was naturally documented in *Domus* with the title "An Italian exhibition in Australia".[13] After the Sydney exhibition, Taglietti moved to Australia and contributed to the bridging of architectural ideas between Italy and the antipodes, with his Australian projects regularly featured in *Domus*.[14]

Ponti would eventually visit Australia more than a decade later in 1967, when he was invited as a speaker at the Australasian Architecture Student Association (AASA) Convention in Brisbane (20–27 May).[15] His presence at the conference helped deepen Brisbane architects' interest in contemporary Italian architecture: a few years later, his colleague Marco Zanuso, one of the most prominent architects and industrial designers in Milan, was invited by the Industrial Design Council of Australia to deliver the Dunhill Industrial Design lecture at the Lennon's Hotel on 8 March 1971.[16] The Australian voyage certainly improved Ponti's understanding of the local architecture and consolidated his interest in Harry Seidler's architectural work. Ponti presented Seidler as "the architect whom I love",[17] publishing his buildings in *Domus* regularly from the early 1950s on.[18] With Ponti withdrawing from the *Domus* editorship in 1979, the interest in Seidler's architecture and more generally in Australian late Modernism diminished. Nevertheless, the presence of Australian architecture in the journal was confirmed by ongoing coverage of the postmodern period.

Postmodern *Domus* and its Reach

Domus's engagement with Australian culture changed its nature when the Milan-based architect and industrial designer Alessandro Mendini became its new editor in 1979, adopting a new program for the Milanese architectural journal. Mendini edited *Domus* in the crucial period between 1979 and 1985, when the discussion around postmodern architecture reached its peak. Given the international reputation and reach of the journal, *Domus* had a special role in his agenda, as it operated as an international showcase for a new way of conceiving architectural and industrial design. From 1980, *Domus* stood out as an active laboratory and influential magazine for the diffusion of postmodern ideas at a national and international level. Its distinctive approach to the production and presentation of postmodern ideas was supported by the understanding of design as non-specialised and anti-industrial. Compared to other coeval journals, *Domus* was more militant about the definition of a postmodern language in that it was animated by architects and designers who practised postmodernism instead of theorising it. Described by the journalist Barbara Radice as "a catalyst of situations and supplier of doubts and energies, a sophisticated intellectual", Mendini was able to turn *Domus* into one of the most interesting crossroads for postmodern culture, bringing about a shift in the design culture in Italy—and internationally.[19] Mendini introduced the idea of the Postmodern not as a trend but as a method of work to be applied to every design and architectural project. This method featured the use of history as a "store" from which to pull out design inspirations "in a sensitive and not scientific way".[20] The path he followed was labyrinthine, portraying an individual and romantic approach. Mendini's strategic use of *Domus* as both laboratory and megaphone contributed to the shaping of a new postmodern lifestyle, reorienting the Italian and international architectural discourse towards hedonistic, transgressive, narcissistic, excessive, and formalist values of design and architecture and opening it up to new formal possibilities and alignments.

In its promotion of postmodern architecture, *Domus* avoided the celebration of its style, instead exalting its formal strategies: the accumulation of signs, the eclectic assembly of forms, and the crossing of different disciplinary boundaries and communication techniques. Mendini articulated a discourse based on understanding design culture as a combination of fragments, parts, and details from different sources and world regions—American and European, in particular. Yet architecture and industrial design were not the main focus of the journal. With articles dedicated to extramural topics such as objects, fashion, food, scenography, photography, music, and art, *Domus*'s editorial team attempted to critically present architecture embedded in the popular culture of its time. This approach was evident from the innovative covers that Mendini carefully organised to convey the new concept of the journal.

In one of the early issues, Mendini dedicated more than thirty pages to the presentation of the first Venice Biennale of Architecture (1980), being personally involved with the exhibition *L'oggetto banale* [The banal object], with the intention to showcase the banal object "for a good taste of the bad taste [for an] aesthetic neutralisation of the everyday object".[21] In his editorial addressed to the commercial architect Morris Lapidus, Mendini explained the meaning of the Venice Biennale:

> It is the transition from the prohibitionist rhetoric of the Modern Movement, towards a period of free, spontaneous behaviour, where figurative past, present and future will be considered natural ingredients for obtaining images of high fantasy. It is a passage from the sad, dull design of rationalism towards arbitrary and festive design, towards their vital reinstatement among the applied and decorative arts.[22]

Looking at the Antipodes

It is in this context of the rise of postmodernism and the breaking down of distinctions between high design and everyday culture that *Domus* special issue 663 dedicated to Australia should be framed. Despite the consistent interest in foreign architecture, industrial design, and art, *Domus* rarely dedicated monographic issues to regional architecture. And yet special attention was paid to Californian architecture in issue no. 604 in 1980; in 1981, issue no. 622 edited by Marco Dezzi Bardeschi was dedicated to Austria; and, in 1984, Daniele Vitale edited issue no. 655 on Portugal. The motivation of such peculiar and occasional choices came from the degree of experimentation provided by the architectural examples of such 'insular' countries.

In 1985, it was Australia's turn with the issue 663 entitled *Ciao Australia. Coast to coast: The last wave*. In the contents page, it is specified that *Domus*'s research for the issue was supported by the Design Arts Board, the Craft Board, and the Visual Arts Board of the Australia Council, the federal government's arts funding and advisory body.[23] The promotion of Australian culture in articles and special issues of international journals was a consolidated strategy in the activities of both the Literature Board and the Visual Arts Board.[24]

In 1979, the Visual Arts Board subsidised the travelling exhibition *Ettore Sottsass jr: From the end product to the product's end*, shown at the National Gallery of Victoria, the Fine Art Gallery of Ballarat, and the S.H. Ervin Museum and Art Gallery in Sydney.[25] The exhibition, which was initially conceived for the International Design Centre in Berlin, moved to the Venice Biennale, the Pompidou Centre in Paris, then to Barcelona and Jerusalem, and eventually arrived in Australia, where its catalogue was translated into English for the first time.[26] The exhibition had the task of introducing the work of the Italian designer and disseminating his postmodern aesthetic. Almost simultaneously, Sottsass developed the design concept of Mendini's new *Domus*.

Australian institutional support for the circulation and exchange of postmodern cultural ideas between Australia and other continents coincided with a high point in Australia's engagement with and celebration of its own national identity through pop culture. Music and movies contributed to export the image of a new continent and its experimentation in pop culture: "Stayin' Alive" was released by the Bee Gees in 1977 and Men at Work's "Down Under" in 1981. "The One Thing" by the rock group INXS gained global success in 1982. Amongst the most famous movies sit Peter Weir's mysterious *The Last Wave* (1977)—from which the *Domus* subtitle comes— the apocalyptic cult film *Mad Max* (1979) by George Miller, and the broad comedy *Crocodile Dundee* (1986).

Australia: A new Frontier for Pop Culture
The interview of Mendini with Seidler that opens the issue *Ciao Australia. Coast to coast: The last wave* can be understood as a homage to the Australian master and his friendship with Ponti, as well as a quick valediction to Australian Modernism. In point of fact, the *Domus* editorial board was intrigued by the 'Australian case' for its new postmodern architectural outcomes. Australian experimental approaches could offer new insights into and interpretation of those themes that *Domus* was investigating, adding to *Domus*'s cultural project. Most importantly, it was the impossibility of reducing the Australian case to one 'style' or 'movement' or 'school' that fascinated the Italians. The distance between Australian cities, and their cultural and climatic diversity, generated eclectic responses to national problems. Fulvio Irace noted a new direction in Australian architecture:

> Stuck in the international fame of a few isolated masters, Australian architecture seems very much to have reached a fork in the road between the insistence on a conditioned loyalty to the canons of modern, and the controlled freedom of a less obsequious, individually freer experimentation.[27]

Australia offered a fresh and original interpretation of postmodern architecture, both in the public and private realms, showing the coexistence of different design methods.

On the one hand, a group of projects published in the issue 663, *Ciao Australia,* indicated the tendency to follow European postmodern design. The Market Three Campus for the New South Wales Institute of Technology (1984–85) by Philip Cox and Partners involved the refurbishment of the Fruit and Flower Markets building in Haymarket, Sydney. Here, there was a strong interest in retaining some historical fragments such as the brick campanile and façades as a medium with the street. The emphasis on the fragments and the use of geometry in the composition of the plan refers to the architecture of Aldo Rossi and James Stirling. In the wake of Rossi's theory and world of references is Ian McDougall's House (1983), built in the chic outskirts of South Yarra, Melbourne. Conceived as an homage to Adolf Loos, the volume of the house is the result of the abstract combination of a cube and an arrow.

On the other hand, two houses in Sydney reveal sympathy for a more openly American aesthetic, with the House in Rose Bay (1982–83) by Andrew Metcalf Architects showing admiration for Richard Meier's pure modernist forms and the pompous entrance a la Graves of Espie Dods Architect's Ashton House (1984). Informed by a Venturiesque interest in popular architectural language are Public Housing (1983), designed by Norman Day Architects in Northcote, and the Kay Street Infill Houses (1984) by Maggie Edmond and Peter Corrigan, built in Melbourne and respectively commissioned by the Melbourne City Council and the Victorian Ministry of Housing. The housing in Northcote is a set of five houses that represent the celebration of the ordinary through the use of typical building elements and their formal exaggeration. Through the ostentation of the brick façade, the stereotypical use of the gable roof, the change in the form of the windows, and the use of exuberant colours, the architect intended to experiment with the recovery and reinvention of suburban residential forms and materials. In referring to the project for the Kay Street Infill Houses, the architects talk about an exercise of myth making. Here, Corrigan's attention to the emphasis in architectural language was partly due to his working experience for such notable American postmodern architects as Phillip Johnson, Paul Rudolph, Cesar Pelli, and Kevin Roche in New Haven and New York. A completely different response to residential design came from the state of Queensland, represented through three timber houses designed by the local firm Noel Robinson, the design of which seems suspended between the tradition of timber technology and the innovation of internal spaces.

The New Parliament House (1980–88) in Canberra, designed by Mitchell/Giurgola & Thorp Architects, represented one of the highest points of experimentation in postmodern Australian public architecture. The Australian New Parliament House project is the culmination of Giurgola's many years of architectural research and is an original response to the postmodern design of monuments. Nestled into the hilltop, the architectural organism is positioned symmetrically on the city's land axis and is organised according to a geometrical scheme, fitting deftly in the development plan for Canberra designed by Walter Burley Griffin in 1911. Two concave walls open the building to the surrounding landscape, thus emphasising the 'spirit of the place'. The result is an anti-monumental building, designed according to an understated and unassertive approach. Its accessibility, connection to the context, and human scale express Australian democratic principles to be transferred, through architecture, to future generations. Only when one reaches the rooftop does the dimension become monumental—from here it is possible to contemplate the view as far as the eye can see—yet it is not the monumentality of architecture but rather the vastness of the Australian landscape. The building also operates like a podium for the giant flagpole, meant to be the umbilicus of the nation, the metallic structure of which refers to the formal solution proposed by Griffin for the culmination of Capital Hill.[28]

Other public projects were presented in *Ciao Australia*, including sports facilities and infrastructures such as an airport and a prison. The architectural language adopted for these buildings is less formal and seems to promote, through different design solutions, a harmonious connection with the environment. However, despite the typological variety deployed in *Ciao Australia*, it was the theme of the Australian house that played a central role in a moment in which *Domus* was focusing its attention more and more on the domestic environment: "The house still constitutes the best and most convincing Australian architectural performance; an exemplary paradigm in which it is forced to speak the aseptic language of international Esperanto, dialectal inflections and regional accents", as observed in the opening article by Fulvio Irace.[29]

The article "Learning from suburbia" by Peter Corrigan draws attention to the vitality of the suburban domestic environment and the concept of the house as a background for human life, a topic that *Domus* had always been keen on. Also, the attention paid to the everyday life in the article is in step with the "praise of the banal" celebrated by Mendini. But, while Mendini took up the task of subverting the rules by introducing the "praise of the banal", in Australia 'the ordinary' already retained a favourable position in the imagination of architects and clients. Thus the Australian suburb, the natural ground for the ordinary and a source of inspiration for Robin Boyd's renowned books *Australia's Home: Its Origins, Builders and Occupiers* (1952) and *The Australian Ugliness* (1960), was seen by the Italians as a spontaneous laboratory of formal eclecticism.

In *Ciao Australia*, architecture was framed in the broad design spectrum, complemented with sections dedicated to regional design, art, and fashion. Although it was recognised that Australia had never had a real fashion industry, new postmodern phenomena such as 'street fashion', video clips as a vehicle for spreading new fashions, and a fascination for the 'Japanese style' had contributed to the revision and enrichment of the nation's fashion design production. Regional and international motives combined together in experimental ways offered a non-homogeneous range of solutions based on the contrasts of bright colours and imported materials, shapes, and patterns. The selection of models presented in *Domus* featured clothes designed by Kathy McKinnon, Kate Durham, Reva, Martyn Thompson, Peter Morrissey, and Leona Edmiston, celebrating the exoticisation of Australia seen at the crossroads of Western and Asian cultures.

Looking holistically at *Domus*'s monographic issue 663 *Ciao Australia*, one can appreciate how postmodern design culture had found an original translation in Australia, despite the tyranny of the distance, or actually thanks to it. Considering the high urban concentration of the Australian population in the capital cities and their quite strong differences due to location, climate conditions, and regional connections and influences, Australia did not come across as a nation with 'one' postmodern approach but rather as a nation with a rich plurality of responses to common questions. The lack of a recognisable and consistent stylistic approach must have stood out as one of the most attractive sides of Australia, for which postmodernism meant the building of a new phase of its urban environment and future society, despite all the idiosyncrasies and contradictions that it could generate. In this particular circumstance, Australia's preoccupation with finding new architectural expressions for the nation's building was more urgent than breaking with the disciplinary rules of Modernism, which was a much larger concern for the Italians.

1
Robin Gibson, "The A.S. Hook Address," *Architecture Australia* 78, 8 (1989): 68–70.

2
Geoffrey Blainey, *The tyranny of distance: How distance shaped Australia's history*, Melbourne: Sun Books, 1966.

3
Philip Goad, "Isolation and introspection: Fortune and Folly of Australian architects", *Casabella* 550 (1988): 50–54.

4
Domus has been purchased by the University of Melbourne since the mid-1940s and by the University of Queensland and the University of Sydney since the 1950s.

5
Alessandro Mendini, "Colloquio con Harry Seidler," *Domus* 663 (1985), 1.

6
Interview with James Birrell by John Macarthur and Andrew Wilson, 13 July 2012, accessed 5 September 2016, https://goo.gl/1TEy56. James Birrell, *A Life in Architecture: Beyond the Ugliness*, Brisbane: University of Queensland Press, 2013, 78.

7
"Una casa a Udine," *Domus* 446 (1967), 1-9. In Addison's personal library there are issues of *Domus* published between 1967 and 1970 that document his interest for the Italian and international architectural culture of that time.

8
Rex Addision, in discussion with the author, Brisbane, 3 March 2014.

9
Alice Rowsthorn, "Made in Italy," *W* (September 2010), accessed 4 May 2017, https://goo.gl/tsgvKb.

10
During these few years, Ponti founded and edited the magazine *Stile. Domus* was then edited by Ernesto Nathan Rogers, who is more commonly renowned for editing another influential Italian architectural journal, *Casabella-continuità*, in the 1950s and 1960s.

11
For instance, Australian architecture was little represented in the other influential Italian architectural journal, *Casabella*. While, in 1961, the Australian architect Robin Boyd was invited to contribute to an international forum organised by *Casabella* to reflect on the "deviations from the main stream of the modern movement", this remained a rare case in which Australian architecture would appear in *Casabella*; see *Casabella* 261 (May 1961), monographic issue "Quindici anni di architettura italiana" [Fifteen years of Italian architecture].

12
Silvia Micheli, "Building European taste in broader communities: The role of the David Jones stores in the promotion of design and architecture in Australia" in *Investigating and Writing Architectural History: Subjects, Methodologies and Frontiers*, ed. Michela Rosso, 3rd EAHN International Meeting, 19–21 June 2014, Turin: EAHN, 2014, 824–832.

13
Enrico Taglietti, "An Italian exhibition in Australia," *Domus* 311 (1955), 50.

14
For instance, see "In Australia: Una casa fra gli eucaliptus", *Domus* 413 (1964), 31–33.

15
See Ponti's conference talk transcription in "Gio Ponti", *Architecture Student Magazine* 5 (1967).

16
"Eminent Italian designer will lecture here", *Centreline* 82 (1971), 3.

17
Gio Ponti, "Seidlers' house in Sydney," *Domus* 465 (1968), 17.

18
The articles included a "House near Sydney," *Domus* 267 (1952), 10–11; "House for weekend," *Domus* 288 (1953), 16; "House in Sydney," *Domus* 413 (1964), 34–37; "Seidlers' house in Sydney," *Domus* 465 (1968), 17–24; "Pavillion for exhibition in Sydney," *Domus* 508 (1972), 20–21; "Government offices in Canberra," *Domus* 574 (1977), 6–10; and "Australian embassy in Paris," *Domus* 588 (1978), 20–27.

19
Barbara Radice, ed., *Elogio del banale*, Turin: Lo studio forma; Milan: Alchymia, 1980.

20
Alessandro Mendini, in discussion with the author, January 2016.

21
Radice, ed., *Elogio del banale*, 10.

22
See Alessandro Mendini, "Dear Morris Lapidus", *Domus* 610 (1980), 1.

23
"Contents," *Domus* 663 (1985).

24
"Sponsored visits by writers and editors from international art journals had resulted in articles on Australian art in *Domus* and *Flash Art* (Italy); *Art Monthly* and *Studio International* (UK); *Art Press* (France); and *Art Forum* and *Art in America* (US)", Paul Walker and Karen Burns, "Architecture and the Australia Council in the 1980s" in *Proceedings of the Society of Architectural Historians Australia and New Zealand*, Vol. 32, eds. Paul Hogben and Judith O'Callaghan, Sydney: SAHANZ, 2015, 688–700.

25
Ibid.

26
Ettore Sottsass jr: From the end product to the product's end, exhibition catalogue, Ballarat: Ballarat Fine Art Gallery, 1979.

27
Fulvio Irace, "Old trends new directions," *Domus* 663 (1985), 2–3.

28
Silvia Micheli, "Vale Romaldo Giurgola AO, 1920–2016," *Architecture Australia* 105, 6 (November/December 2016), 107–109.

29
Irace, "Old trends new directions", 2–3.

The Architecture of the City:
An American Rossi in Australia

Paul Walker

Fig. 12—14

Aldo Rossi's *L'Architettura della Città* [*The Architecture of the City*] was first published in Italian in 1966, the same year that Robert Venturi's book *Complexity and Contradiction in Architecture* appeared. This is a conjunction that has been widely noted, for example, by Mary McLeod, Joan Ockman, Diane Ghirardo, K. Michael Hays, and Harry Francis Mallgrave and David Goodman.[1] The predominant view of these authors is that the simultaneous appearance of the two publications is a hinge in the development of post-war architectural culture. Like Venturi's book, *The Architecture of the City* seems to have had a long germination in the thought of a young architect: in his *A Scientific Autobiography* (1981), Rossi suggests that he had formulated the arguments of *The Architecture of the City* by 1960.[2] Those arguments are cogently described by Joan Ockman—with Diane Ghirardo one of the translators of *The Architecture of the City* for its English language edition of 1982—as follows:

> [In] the assertion of the city as the fundamental artefact of human culture and the repository of collective memory [...] Rossi evoked the role of the singular place – the *locus*, whether a natural element or a man-made monument – within the formal repertory and historical transformation of the urban fabric. He stressed the complexity of the city's evolution, condemning "naïve functionalism" while insisting on the value of typological study as a rational basis for design.[3]

In *A Scientific Autobiography*, the design approach of the mature Rossi had shifted somewhat, ironically, given that book's title, to a stance based not on the science of urbanism that *The Architecture of the City* projected but on something more personal and particular, on the one hand, and, on the other, caught up with projecting the diffuse but profound power of collective memory.

Such as it can be identified, the influence of *The Architecture of the City* in Australia comes through its English language edition, published in 1982 by MIT Press on behalf of the New York–based Institute of Architecture Urban Studies (IAUS), as part of that organisation's Oppositions Books series.[4] There is no evidence that Rossi was widely known or discussed in Australia before the Institute of Architecture and Urban Studies (IAUS), the think-tank established by Peter Eisenman in 1967, introduced his work to the American scene. This is not to preclude the possibility that Rossi's work was known by some in Australia before this, given the presence here of architects with Italian family connections and also given the regard with which the Italian architectural journal *Casabella* was held; Rossi contributed to *Casabella-continuità* from 1955 and served as an editor for that journal between 1961 and 1964. Rossi's winning entry for the competition of the San Cataldo Cemetery in Modena of 1971 and his Gallaretese housing project in

Milan of 1970 were widely published in the international architectural press.[5] However, these seem to have had no immediate impact in Australia; Rossi entered the consciousness of Australia's broader architectural community only after he started engaging with American institutions, in particular the IAUS.

Advocating Rossi in the United States of America

The promotion by the IAUS of Rossi's work was part of a wider agenda that it pursued during the 1970s and 1980s of introducing European architectural culture to American audiences. Other significant European figures hosted by the IAUS included the Italian historian and theorist Manfredo Tafuri, whose American reception was tightly bound with Rossi's, and Rem Koolhaas, who, with George Baird and Michael Graves, was a keynote speaker at the Royal Australian Institute of Architects 1980 conference "The Pleasures of Architecture".[6] Tafuri was one of several Italian figures teaching at this time at the Istituto Universitario di Architettura di Venezia (IUAV) in Venice who were to be associated with the IAUS and in particular with its journal *Oppositions: A Journal for Ideas and Criticism in Architecture*, which was established in 1973. These included Massimo Cacciari, Giorgio Ciucci, Francesco Dal Co, and Giorgio Grassi. Among many other theorists and architects from continental Europe who contributed to IAUS activities or to *Oppositions* were Ignasi de Solà-Morales, Rafael Moneo, and Léon Krier.[7] These figures do not represent a single position on architecture, the city, or architectural history. However, whether primarily practitioners or scholars, historians or theorists, they had in common an approach to architecture as an intellectual enterprise, a problematic rather than a profession. Though such an attitude had been introduced to US schools of architecture through the arrival of figures such as Colin Rowe, Kenneth Frampton, and Alan Colquhoun—reinforced in the 1970s by the Argentinian contingent of Emilio Ambasz, Rodolfo Machado, Jorge Silvetti, Diana Agrest, and Mario Gandelsonas—it was still remote from the American mainstream.

While Rossi was, then, certainly not the only European whose international profile developed through IAUS connections, in his case these connections had consequences that were both profound and immediate.[8] In the four years between 1979 and 1982, Eisenman and the IAUS facilitated the appearance of three Rossi books that had wide impact in the English-speaking world and enhanced his international reputation; a catalogue of his drawings (1979), *A Scientific Autobiography* (1981), and *The Architecture of the City* (1982).[9]

The IAUS's Oppositions Books series, which included *A Scientific Autobiography* and *The Architecture of the City*, Rossi's two major theoretical works, also published an English translation of Adolf Loos's *Spoken into the Void: Collected Essays 1897–1900* with an introduction by

Rossi, a translation of *Style and Epoch* by Moisei Ginzburg, and a collection of essays by the English architect and Princeton professor Alan Colquhoun. The English translation of Manfredo Tafuri's *The Sphere and the Labyrinth* was also intended to be published in the Oppositions Books series, though this was published by MIT Press alone after the IAUS had ceased operations. Other books projected for the Oppositions Books imprint had similar fates or did not happen at all.[10]

As mentioned above, the introduction of the work of Rossi to American audiences is closely tied to that of Tafuri.[11] Tafuri's first book translated into English, *Architecture and Utopia: Design and Capitalist Development* (1976; Italian edition 1973), features a Rossi drawing on its cover. In the next translation of a Tafuri book into English, *Theories and History of Architecture* (1979; Italian edition 1968), the only architects discussed more than Rossi are Kahn and Le Corbusier. Finally, Tafuri's book on post-war Italian architecture, *History of Italian Architecture, 1944–85* (1989; Italian edition 1986), devoted one of its brief chapters on the immediately contemporary to Rossi and, with painful circularity, discusses the drawing by Rossi dedicated to Tafuri that features on the cover of 1976's *Architecture and Utopia*, an image titled by Rossi "L'architecture assassinnée" [Murdered architecture]. It needs to be noted, however, that, while they undoubtedly had high regard for each other and shared a disdain for the reductivism of much architectural thinking, the connections between Rossi and Tafuri that were emphasised through the virtually simultaneous reception they enjoyed in the United States belied their distinct intellectual trajectories and interests. In particular, during the 1960s, significant differences existed between them on architecture's role vis-à-vis urban planning; these have been examined in detail by Pier Vittorio Aureli.[12]

The IAUS's channelling of European architectural thinking (both contemporary and historical) into the American East Coast intellectual scene is reflected not only in the books it published but also in its journal, *Oppositions*. The journal's founding editors were Eisenman, Frampton, and Gandelsonas. Anthony Vidler joined them from issue 6 and Kurt Forster from issue 12; the last issue (26, Spring 1984) was edited by Vidler, Gandelsonas, and Agrest.[13] In *Oppositions*, Rossi and Tafuri again go together and figure largely. The first of five Tafuri essays that appear in *Oppositions* between 1974 and 1979 was "*L'Architecture dans le boudoir*: The language of criticism and the criticism of language", a discussion of the work of James Stirling, the New York Five (including Eisenman), and Rossi as exemplifying a retreat from architecture's engagement with the "domain of the real" to a "degree zero of all architectural ideology", that is, to various modes of architectural ideal or abstraction (above all, the history, composition, and memory of *form*).[14] Indeed, that Eisenman and Rossi share some intellectual ground is central to their interaction across the 1970s.[15] Much of *Oppositions* 5 (Summer 1976) was devoted to Rossi—he is discussed in Mario Gandelsonas's editorial "Neo-Functionalism", is the subject of an article by Rafael Moneo focused on the Modena cemetery design, and is the author of another, "The Blue of the Sky" and to an essay by Tafuri on the New York Five.[16] Anthony Vidler's well-known piece "The Third Typology", written as the editorial for *Oppositions* 7 (Winter 1976), riffs on Rossi's ideas on urban types from *The Architecture of the City*; the article by Dal Co in *Oppositions* 13 (Summer 1978), "Criticism and Design", is substantially a discussion of Rossi's approach to his work, referring to the Modena cemetery (again), the Gallaratese housing, student housing at Chieti, and the Palazzo della Regione at Trieste; and Rossi's Teatro del Mondo is critiqued by Daniel Liebeskind in *Oppositions* 21 (Summer 1980). And by no means is this an exhaustive list of references to Rossi in *Oppositions*. The last issue of the journal, number 26 (Spring 1984), contains a section devoted to Rossi's recent drawings, including further work at the Modena cemetery but mostly studies for large Italian urban projects that were to remain unbuilt.[17] In the book of key essays from *Oppositions*, published as the *Oppositions Reader* in 1998, among architects, only Le Corbusier and Venturi receive more entries in the index than Rossi, and Tafuri is the preeminent historian/theorist.[18]

The American entanglement of Rossi and Tafuri is taken further in the 1979 IAUS Rossi catalogue, *Aldo Rossi in America*. Eisenman's essay in that volume, "The house of the dead as the city of survival", starts with a discussion of the Rossi drawing "L'Architecture assassinée". As already mentioned, this is the Rossi drawing that features on the cover of Tafuri's *Architecture and Utopia*. But Eisenman suggests that it is not the death of architecture but rather its abandonment that is the subject of Rossi's drawings: the abandonment, we must presume, of architecture's prospect of being socially transformative. He suggests that Rossi's work reflects the impossibility both of traditional pre-modern modes of habitation and of the modernity sought by Enlightenment reason. Both these are foreclosed in the aftermath of the mass deaths of the Holocaust and atomic bombings.[19] Rather than based in reason, Rossi's work of the 1970s finds its *modus operandi* in "analogous thinking". Eisenman illustrates this aspect of Rossi's work by the transformation of three types of dwellings in three of Rossi's key Italian works: that of the pedimented hut, the putative basic dwelling house, in the Monument to the Resistance in Segrate (1965–67); the apartment building in the San Cataldo Cemetery in Modena (1971–78); and the Baptistery in the Fagnano Olona Elementary School (1972–76).[20] Such transpositions depart from the urban discipline proposed in *The Architecture of the City*, though Rossi introduces the idea of analogous thinking in his preface to that work's second edition, which is included in the English translation of 1982. It is through the operations of such analogous thinking that Rossi enfolds into his architectural drawings objects that are not usually part of architecture's repertory and buildings from beyond the geographical and cultural bounds of the urban sources of Rossi's native northern Italy. The former include coffee pots most notably, while the latter include the twin towers of New York's World Trade Center. The subsequent fate of the towers now gives the Rossi drawings that depict them an added poignancy. Rossi's inclusion of American skyscrapers in his drawings of this period also echoes Tafuri's interest in the skyscraper and the American city, explored in his contributions to *The American City: From the Civil War to the New Deal*, a book he co-authored with IUAV colleagues Giorgio Ciucci, Francesco Dal Co, and Mario Manieri Elia.[21]

Transition's Take on Rossi

The University of Melbourne Library accessioned its copy of the *Aldo Rossi in America* catalogue in July 1981, the year before *The Architecture of the City* was available in English and probably also before *A Scientific Autobiography* had reached Australia. If Rossi, as the evidence suggests, is first read in Australia through Eisenman and the IAUS, he is in a sense read in reverse, with an awareness of the more personalised and poetic position he assumed in the 1970s in his drawings and then in *A Scientific Autobiography* subsuming and subverting the impulse to system in *The Architecture of the City*.

If, during the late 1970s and the early 1980s, American architecture (or rather those American architects, architectural scholars, and architectural junkies at home in New York think tanks and Ivy League schools) looked to Europe for intellectual leads, in Australia at the same time, even the most thoughtful architects appear to have been looking to the United States.

This can be seen in the early issues of the Melbourne architectural journal *Transition*, established by Ian McDougall and Richard Munday in 1979. *Transition*'s ambitious program to establish an arena for critical reflection and discourse in Australia's architectural culture—set out in its first editorial—was particularly influenced by American formulations of and debates about postmodern architecture. While in retrospect it is possible to discern in Melbourne architecture in particular a line of architectural inquiry that starts from Robert Venturi and continues to develop to this day in the work of leading practices such as those of Edmond and Corrigan, Ashton Raggatt McDougall, and Lyons Architecture, the American orientation of Australian architecture in 1980 was much wider than this.

Writing on Australian architecture in the 1980s under the title "Pleasures of Architecture" (taken from the Royal Australian Institute of Architecture conference that brought Baird, Graves, and Koolhaas to Australia), Australian architectural historian Jennifer Taylor demonstrated how general the American influences were on charismatic new design work at this time.[22] This is not to say that the Australian reading of the US was always accurate. Paul Hogben has pointed out Michael Graves' comment on "The Pleasures of Architecture": "In the US, you rarely get a conference that involves architecture. Conferences like this usually talk about pipes or money or getting clients. Calling it "The Pleasures of Architecture" would have meant they were going to talk about making dough".[23]

Transition clearly demonstrated an affinity with the emergent critical architectural culture of the United States across its early issues. The first issue of *Transition* indicated that the journal's title was taken from that of Chapter 11 of John Maxwell Freeland's *Architecture in Australia: A History* (1968), which is much concerned with the influence of American domestic architecture in Australia in the 1920s and the impact of Walter Burley Griffin's arrival.[24] Nevertheless, it is important to recall that there was a buoyant *local* cultural scene in Melbourne at the time of *Transition*'s establishment, apparent in the founding of other 'small magazines', notably the theoretically oriented art journal *Art + Text*, which started in 1981. *Art + Text* introduced into the Australian art scene discussion of post-structuralist figures such as Jean Baudrillard, Jean-François Lyotard, and Gilles Deleuze and Félix Guattari. It seems reasonable to surmise that, like *Art + Text*, *Transition* in its first phase also had an ambition to engage with the theory turn that was occurring in architecture as well as in the visual arts, but this was filtered through the American orientation that was simultaneously a general aspect of Australian architecture. Thus, while the title of *Transition* ostensibly has a source in a local text, albeit one concerned with historical connections between Australian and American architecture, the echo in *Transition* of the IAUS title *Oppositions* is hard to disregard.[25]

Transition's early American cast is apparent in several ways. *Transition* number 1, for example, includes an article by Philip Drew on Mannerism drawing heavily on Venturi, a design by Sydney architect and teacher Swetik Korzeniewski that *Transition*'s editors suggested demonstrated the influence of Louis Kahn, a lengthy article by Jeff Turnbull on Charles Moore, and a review of a book on the California arts and crafts architects Charles and Henry Greene. The second issue focuses much more on Australia: Jennifer Taylor on the Sydney School, Graham de Gruchy on Brisbane, and nine Melbourne entries to the competition for New Parliament House. But in the article "An exhibition by four Melbourne architects", one of the reviewers, Philip Drew, declares Australian architecture's New York state of mind:

> Melbourne architecture has changed since the Tavistock Place exhibition of Boyd, Burns, Clerehan, MacGlashan, and Waybrowski, in 1964 – indeed much of the conventional wisdom of the sixties has now been overturned. This is illustrated by the "Four Melbourne Architects" exhibition. No doubt it had the New York "Five Architects" in mind, and seeks to establish a similar purchase for the Melbourne four as did the New York event.[26]

An actual alumnus of the New York Five, Graves, is interviewed in the fourth issue of *Transition* (October 1980) on the occasion of his visit to Australia for "Pleasures of Architecture"; the images of his work that accompany the interview indicate that in 1980 "grey" was prevailing over "white"—the riven visage of American architecture of 1973 was at least temporarily pasted over by a postmodern consensus from which there was momentarily little dissent. The other two international keynotes from the "Pleasures of Architecture", Rem Koolhaas and George Baird, were also interviewed. The *Transition* interview with Koolhaas continually returns to the pivot of *Delirious New York*, a book that Koolhaas wrote while a fellow at the IAUS and which is also reviewed in the same issue of the journal. All of the books reviewed in *Transition* during its first three years had American origins.

It is not until volume 2 no 3/4 of *Transition* (September/December 1981) that there is any substantial, direct engagement with contemporary European architectural culture: a tortured interview with Manfredo Tafuri. By this time, English translations of four books by Tafuri had been published and could have been available to Australian readers: *Architecture and Utopia* (1976), *Theories and History of Architecture* (1979), and the co-authored titles *The American City* and *Modern Architecture* (both 1979).[27] Interviews with notable international architects and critics were a significant part of *Transition*'s early editorial strategy. As with the book reviews, the interviews were skewed to the US.[28] *Transition*'s Tafuri interview was conducted by the Melbourne architect Su Dance, who was undertaking an architectural conservation course in Rome.[29] The questions for the first part of the interview were prepared in advance in Melbourne (probably by Paul Munday, one of *Transition*'s editors), answered by Tafuri in Italian and then translated; the second part was conducted in English as a conversation between Tafuri and Dance. The encounter is a tussle between interviewers and interviewee over the relevance of his work to contemporary architecture. Tafuri denies any significance in such a question; *Transition* keeps pressing the issue. The different register of questions and answers is not surprising given Tafuri's disdain for 'operative criticism', but the discussion in the interview is nevertheless engaging. Questioned on the proclamations of the "death of architecture" attributed to him, Tafuri responds first by connecting such an idea to Walter Benjamin's conception of the disappearance of "aura": "'The fall of the aura' is not something that just happened from one moment to the next. Benjamin says that when the 'aura' falls, it leaves an area of shadow, patches of shade. Architecture is going across one of those patches".[30] He then goes on to comment: "Certainly architecture is no longer a cosmological synthesis of knowledge and the sciences".[31] This is to say that it is no longer serious business; rather, architecture has become mere divertimento, the playful manipulation of form.

The Architecture of the City: An American Rossi in Australia

Transition's interview with Tafuri is the venue for the first reference to Rossi in the journal; the connection of Rossi to Tafuri in the American reception of both is repeated in their introduction to Australian audiences. The initial reference to Rossi comes when *Transition* asks Tafuri if Rossi exemplifies the alienation he comments is entailed in divertimento. Tafuri is somewhat evasive:

> Aldo Rossi is only an architect. I don't see in him anything more than can be seen in other architects. He's just a good architect. He isn't a prophet, as many critics, many young architects and architecture students are making of him. He's only someone who's singing his own collective memory and who therefore should be seen in this way.[32]

These comments are accompanied by the first Aldo Rossi images that can be found in Australian publication; a plan of the Fagnano Olona Elementary School of 1972 and a drawing of the San Cataldo Cemetery in Modena of 1971.

The next issue of *Transition* leads with a considered introduction for Australian readers to Aldo Rossi's work to date. The author of this piece was Micha Bandini, an Italian architect then teaching at the University of Sydney; her introduction to *Transition* may have been through the Sydney-based architect Ken Kennedy, who occasionally wrote for the journal, including a piece on Tafuri carried on the pages immediately before the interview with him.[33] Under the title "Fashion and consumption: Notes on Aldo Rossi", Bandini commented that Rossi's career started in the context of the Italian intellectual left of the mid-1950s. She argues that Rossi had remained consistent in his lines of architectural inquiry across different phases of his career, culminating by the 1970s in the formulation of architectural typology and "the analogous city" as central to his thinking.[34] However, while Bandini finds merit and the potential for a critical architecture in Rossi's typological concerns, she is suspicious of the vagueness of Rossi's idea of the analogous city: "His written accounts of the concept seem to suffer from a hollow circularity".[35] This is exacerbated by the vapid, acritical reception that Rossi enjoys in the international scene by the late 1970s and the evaporation of the Italian cultural left out of which Rossi's position had developed. Bandini sees Rossi—and Tafuri along with him—as somewhat lost. She concludes:

> No longer gramscian and intellectually committed (between structure and superstructure in their social responsibility) they both look instead towards the negative tradition of philosophy (Nietzsche, Benjamin and Foucault). In them they find the authority and legitimacy for their position, one which having witnessed the impossibility of a framework of belief redeems everything into a "fragment" for a "discourse".

> Outside Italy, where socio-political conditions are perceived in a less extreme fashion and where the tradition of the committed intellectual has often been less influential, only the tip of this condition is perceived and only its more immediate concepts are consumed as quick passwords. [...] Tafuri then becomes in popularising articles the Marxist prophet of the death of architecture and Rossi just one more producer of images. [...] Within the context of the world in which they exist the logic of their game digested them too.[36]

From Bandini's account, one could propose that there are at least two Rossis. There is the figure who has negotiated his way through the Italian Neo-avant-garde of the 1950s and through a number of changes in institutional setting and theoretical and practical pre-occupation but has always remained committed to conceptions of urban locus and architectural type, drawn from the city and transformed in being reinserted back into the urban setting.[37] And there is the celebrity Rossi, who makes hotels in Japan and coffee services for Alessi. It is presumably this celebrity Rossi who gets invited to speak at the Royal Australian Institute of Architects 1984 conference, an invitation confidently announced in *Architecture Australia* but which, in the end, Rossi doesn't accept.[38] These two Rossis are neither simply the same nor simply different. It would not be entirely fair to characterise the two Rossis implied by Bandini as the Italian one and the one reinvented for American consumption by the IAUS. The transformations in Rossi from theoretically reflective public intellectual to producer of images in Bandini's analysis reflected changes in the Italian scene itself, changes that curtailed architecture's potential and its political ambitions. Moreover, it seems likely that one of the attractions to American audiences (at least of the kind that attended events at the IAUS and read its publications) of Rossi (and of the Tafuri with whom he was perennially linked) was exactly the vague Marxist aura he trailed with him. While the Europeans (and Europeanised Argentinians) the IAUS cultivated and accommodated generally brought with them an intellectualism absent from the American architecture profession, in Rossi's case one senses a sort of delighted naughtiness in Eisenman's introduction of him to those who attended IAUS events and the exposure of students from conservative 'liberal arts' colleges to Rossi as Rossi contributed to the IAUS's educational programs.[39]

Nevertheless, the Rossi honed through the American editions of his books is different to the Italian original. This difference is declared most cogently by Eisenman in the *Transition* interview with him that appears in volume 4, no 3/4 (April/July 1984). Eisenman says, "There is no question I was very influenced by having to read *The Architecture of the City* and having to edit, rewrite it practically. I spent three years on the translation of that book, it's practically mine, because if you took the literal translation from Italian it makes no sense."⁴⁰ Having erased the translation work of Ghirardo and Ockman, Eisenman then aligns his projects of "artificial excavation" with *The Architecture of the City*, rather implying that his own design work has more allegiance to that book's rigour than do Rossi's contemporaneous designs insofar as Rossi's images lend themselves to emulation by students in a way that his (Eisenman's) do not. References to *The Architecture of the City* in English-speaking countries were often misused to promote a bland postmodern 'contextualism'. This was certainly an aspect of Australian architecture in the early 1980s, particularly for urban infill housing. Ghirardo's concerns about the misapprehension to which Rossi was subject, however, focus rather on Eisenman's insistence in the introduction to the English translation of *The Architecture of the City* that Rossi sees the city as "the house of the dead".⁴¹ This is underwritten by the very title of Eisenman's essay in the IAUS catalogue for its Rossi exhibitions, "The house of the dead as the city of survival", and that essay's theme of 'abandonment'. Ghirardo maintains that Rossi entertained no such nihilism and that Eisenman had refashioned Rossi's ideas "as a projection of his own".⁴² This refashioning served to valorise Eisenman's 'archaeological' approach of the early 1980s.

By 1984, the IAUS was nearly finished.⁴³ The interest of the RAIA (Royal Australian Institute of Architecture) in bringing Rossi to Australia coincided with a sense of scepticism starting to appear in *Transition*'s own editorials. In the *Transition* with Micha Bandini's tough account of Rossi (and of Tafuri), the editorial suggested that a contemporary Australian architecture might find its most significant resources in myth rather than in history. As its argument was made, referring both to Tafuri's *Theories and History of Architecture* and to Dal Co's article "Criticism and design" in *Oppositions* 13 (1978), this editorial also specifically rejected Tafuri's prioritising of history over myth.⁴⁴ The editorial in the *Transition* with the Eisenman interview observed that the dearth of critical and reflective opportunities for architecture in Australia that motivated the establishment of *Transition* had, in the intervening years, apparently been addressed. But, implying that architecture's philosophical prognostications had become too remote from design's daily grind, the editors note that "the antagonism to discourse over the drawing board may be a myth – for, in fact, it is an absurdity to believe that formal, intellectual or metaphysical questions are absent from the mind of the designer".⁴⁵

1
Mary McLeod, "Review of *The Architecture of the City*," *Design Book Review* 3 (Winter 1984), 52; Joan Ockman, "Venice and New York," *Casabella* 619–620 (January/February 1995), 57; Diane Ghirardo, *Architecture After Modernism*. London and New York: Thames & Hudson, 1996, 13, 20–21; K. Michael Hays, "Introduction" in *Architecture Theory Since 1968*, ed. Hays, New York: Columbia Books of Architecture, 1998, xiv, note 1; Harry Francis Mallgrave and David Goodman, *An Introduction to Architectural Theory 1968 to the Present*, Chichester: Wiley-Blackwell, 2011, 18. Mario Gandelsonas's editorial in *Oppositions* 5 (Summer 1976), under the title "Neo-Functionalism", suggests that the "present architectural scene" could be characterised in the antagonism between the "neo-rationalist" ideology of Rossi and the "neo-realist" ideology of Venturi. See also Pier Vittorio Aureli, "The Difficult Whole," *Log* 9, 2007: 39.

2
Aldo Rossi, *A Scientific Autobiography*, trans. Lawrence Venuti, Cambridge, Massachusetts: MIT Press, 1981, 15.

3
Joan Ockman and Edward Eigen, *Architecture Culture 1943–1968: A Documentary Anthology*, New York: Columbia Books of Architecture and Rizzoli, 1993, 392.

4
Aldo Rossi, *The Architecture of the City*, trans. Diane Ghirardo and Joan Ockman, Cambridge, Massachusetts: MIT Press, 1982. The title page of the book states that it was revised for the American edition by Aldo Rossi and Peter Eisenman and that it was published by the MIT Press for The Graham Foundation for Advanced Studies in the Fine Arts, Chicago, and the Institute for Architecture and Urban Studies, New York.

5
Diane Ghirardo, "Aldo Rossi in the United States: A Meditation on Artifacts over Time" in *La città nuova: Proceedings of the 1999 ACSA International Conference, 29 May-2 June 1999, Rome*, eds. Katrina Deines and Kay Bea Jones, Washington, DC: Association of Collegiate Schools of Architecture, 1999, 3. As well as several articles that appeared in publications associated with the IAUS and which are discussed later in this chapter, the major articles in English on Rossi that appeared in the international architectural press before 1980 include Vittorio Savi, "Aldo Rossi," *Lotus International* 11 (1976), 42–56; and Savi, "Conception and Reality of Aldo Rossi," *Architecture + Urbanism* 65 (May 1976), 55–120. Several shorter articles on Rossi's design projects were also published between 1976 and 1979. Savi's major Italian survey of Rossi's work, *L'architettura di Aldo Rossi*, Milan: Franco Angeli, 1976, is reviewed by Joseph Rykwert in the *Journal of the Society of Architectural Historians* 38, 3 (October 1979), 304.

6
See Paul Hogben, "The Aftermath of 'Pleasures': Untold Stories of Post-Modern Architecture in Australia" in *Progress: Proceedings of the 20th Annual Conference of the Society of Architectural Historians, Australia & New Zealand*, eds. Maryam Gusheh and Naomi Stead, Sydney: SAHANZ, 2003, 146–151.

7
Joan Ockman, "Resurrecting the Avant-Garde: the history and program of *Oppositions*" in *Architecture production*, ed. Beatriz Colomina, New York: Princeton Architectural Press, ca. 1988, 192.

8
Ockman, "Resurrecting the Avant-Garde," 189.

9
Aldo Rossi in America: 1976 to 1979, New York: Institute for Architecture and Urban Studies, 1979.

10
A full list of the books planned for the Oppositions series can be found in Suzanne Frank, *The Institute of Architecture and Urban Studies: An Insider's Memoir*, Bloomington: AuthorHouse, 2011, 116.

11
Tafuri was invited to the IAUS by Agrest. See Frank, *The Institute of Architecture and Urban Studies*, 46.

12
Aureli, "The Difficult Whole," 51–55; Pier Vittorio Aureli, *The Project of Autonomy: Politics and Architecture within and against Capitalism*, New York: Buell Center, Columbia University and Princeton Architectural Press, 2008, 59–63.

13
Ockman, "Resurrecting the Avant-Garde," 183–185, 193–197.

14
Manfredo Tafuri, "*L'Architecture dans le Boudoir*: The language of criticism and the criticism of language," *Oppositions* 3 (May 1974), 37–62. The other Tafuri essays in *Oppositions* are "American Graffiti: Five x Five = Twenty-five," *Oppositions* 5 (Summer 1976), 35–74; "Giuseppe Terragni: Subject and 'Mask'", *Oppositions* 11 (Winter 1977), 1–25; "The Dialectics of the Avant-Garde", *Oppositions* 11 (Winter 1977), 73-80; and "Historical Project", *Oppositions* 17 (Summer 1979), 55-75. The French edition of Tafuri's *Theories and History of Architecture* is reviewed by Yve-Alain Bois in "On Manfredo Tafuri's *Theories et histoire de l'architecture*", *Oppositions* 11 (Winter 1977), 118-132; and Manfredo Tafuri and Dal Co's *Architettura Contemporanea*, Milan: Electa, 1976 is reviewed by Massimo Cacciari in "Eupalinos or Architecture," *Oppositions* 21 (Summer 1980), 106–116. On the key role of Tafuri in *Oppositions*, see K. Michael Hays, "The Oppositions of Autonomy and History" in *Oppositions Reader: Selected Readings from a Journal for Ideas and Criticism in Architecture, 1973–1984*, ed. Hays, New York: Princeton Architectural Press, 1998, ix. See also Frank, *The Institute of Architecture and Urban Studies*, 113. Tafuri also contributed an essay to the IAUS exhibition catalogue of Massimo Scolari drawings, *Massimo Scolari, Architecture Between Memory and Hope*, New York: IAUS, 1980.

15
A complete account of their interactions, and those of Tafuri and his American interlocutors, is found in Ockman, "Venice and New York".

16
Rafael Moneo, "Aldo Rossi: The Idea of Architecture and the Modena Cemetery," *Oppositions* 5 (Summer 1976), 1–34; Aldo Rossi, "The Blue of the Sky," *Oppositions* 5 (Summer 1976),31-34; Tafuri, "American Graffiti: Five x Five = Twenty-Five". See also Ockman, "Venice and New York".

17
Aldo Rossi, "Recent Works," *Oppositions* 26 (Spring 1984): 65–96; Ockman, "Resurrecting the Avant-Garde," 199.

18
K. Michael Hays, ed., *Oppositions Reader: Selected Readings from a Journal for Ideas and Criticism in Architecture, 1973–1984*, New York: Princeton Architectural Press, 1998.

19
Peter Eisenman, "The House of the Dead as the City of Survival" in *Aldo Rossi in America: 1976 to 1979*, New York: Institute for Architecture and Urban Studies, 1979, 5.

20
Ibid., 13–15.

21
Giorgio Ciucci, Francesco Dal Co, Mario Manieri Elia, and Manfredo Tafuri, *The American City: From the Civil War to the New Deal*, trans. Barbara Luigia La Penta, Cambridge, Massachusetts: MIT Press, 1979; Italian edition, 1973.

22
Jennifer Taylor, "The Pleasures of Architecture" in *Australian Architecture Since 1960*, 2nd edition, Canberra: RAIA, 1990. See also Hogben "The Aftermath of 'Pleasures': Untold Stories of Post-Modern Architecture in Australia," 148.

23
Hogben "The Aftermath of 'Pleasures': Untold Stories of Post-Modern Architecture in Australia," 148; Hogben in turn refers to the interview with Graves in *Transition*; "Michael Graves", *Transition* 1: 4 (October 1980), 6. The interviewers for *Transition* were Cathy Peake, Grant Marani, Ian McDougall, and Richard Munday. Marani and Munday were later to make careers as architects in the US (my thanks to Philip Goad for this information).

24
John Maxwell Freeland, *Architecture in Australia: A History*, Melbourne: Cheshire, 1968.

25
As *Transition* has a kind of analogous relationship to *Oppositions*, so does *Art + Text* to the art and theory journal *October*, founded in 1976, which was also initially produced under the auspices of the IAUS. On *October*, see the interview with Joan Copjec in Frank, *The Institute of Architecture and Urban Studies*, 227.

26
"Four Melbourne Architects: An Exhibition," *Transition* 1: 2 (November 1979), 11.

27
Architecture and Utopia: Design and Capitalist Development, trans. Barbara Luigia La Penta, Cambridge, Massachusetts: MIT Press, 1976; Italian edition, 1973; *Theories and History of Architecture*, trans. Giorgio Verrecchia, New York: Harper & Row, 1979; Italian edition, 1968; Tafuri, Ciucci, Dal Co, and Manieri Elia, *The American City: From the Civil War to the New Deal*, trans. Barbara Luigia La Penta, Cambridge, Massachusetts: MIT Press, 1979; Italian edition 1973; Tafuri, Ciucci and Dal Co, *Modern Architecture*, trans. Robert Erich Wolf, New York: H. N. Abrams, 1979; Italian edition, 1976.

28
Apart from Baird, Graves, Koolhaas, and Tafuri, early *Transition* interview subjects (up to 3, 3–4, April/July 1984) were the Americans William Turnbull, Charles Moore, Stuart Cohen, Frank Gehry, Steven Izenour, Stanley Tigerman, Peter Eisenman, and Daniel Libeskind. Kenneth Frampton is also arguably American. Other interviewees were Melvin Charney (Canada); Louis Hellman, Richard Burton, Piers Gough, and Peter Cook (UK); Kazuo Shinohara (Japan); Hans Hollein (Austria); and Haig Beck (Australia/UK). There are no other Australian interviewees and no Italians other than Tafuri. Leon van Schaik surveys *Transition*'s first ten years in "Ten Years of *Transition* in Review," *Transition* 29 (Winter 1989), 29–32.

29
Karen Burns, "Dance, Su" in *The Encyclopedia of Australian Architecture*, eds. Philip Goad and Julie Willis, Melbourne: Cambridge University Press, 2012, 191.

30
"Interview: Manfredo Tafuri", *Transition* 2, 3–4 (September/December 1981): 8.

31
Ibid.

32
Ibid.

33
Ken Kennedy, "Manfredo Tafuri: Criticism and the Australian myth," *Transition* 2, 3–4 (September/December 1981), 5–6.

34
Micha Bandini, "Fashion and Consumption: Notes on Aldo Rossi," *Transition* 3: 1 (March 1982): 11

35
Ibid., 11.

36
Ibid., 13.

37
Aureli has outlined in detail the trajectory of Rossi's intellectual development up to the 1966 publication of *L'architettura della città* in "The Difficult Whole".

38
The announcement is in *Architecture Australia* 73, 2 (March 1984), 32–33.

39
See Frank, *The Institute of Architecture and Urban Studies*, 135–137.

40
"Interview: Peter Eisenman," *Transition* 3, 3–4 (April/July 1984), 39. On the production of the American edition of *The Architecture of the City*, see Frank, *The Institute of Architecture and Urban Studies*, 116–118.

41
Peter Eisenman, "Introduction" in *The Architecture of the City*, trans. Diane Ghirardo and Joan Ockman, Cambridge, Massachusetts: MIT Press, 1982, 10.

42
Ghirardo, "Aldo Rossi in the United States", 5.

43
Frank, *The Institute of Architecture and Urban Studies*, 60–65.

44
Ian McDougall and Richard Munday, "Editorial," *Transition* 3, 1 (March 1982), 5.

45
Ian McDougall, Conrad Hamann, Greg Missingham, Peter Corrigan, "Editorial," *Transition* 3, 3–4 (April/July 1984), 4.

A Welfare State: *Tendenza* in 1980s Melbourne

Karen Burns

In 1983, the American art historian and theorist Hal Foster introduced a collection of essays on postmodern culture by addressing the thorny problem of postmodernism's definition. Running through various interpretations of the term such as a "break with the aesthetic field of Modernism", Foster organised the category around key conceptual oppositions.[1] After cataloguing a list of positions amongst his essayists, Foster observed that the various postmodern dissenters were united by a common belief that "the project of modernity is now deeply problematic".[2] This essay begins by focusing on one aspect of postmodern architecture's 'oppositional discourse', its antagonistic relationship to welfare state Modernism, before examining the renewal of the welfare state project in mid-1980s Melbourne by younger practitioners working with resources derived from the Italian *Tendenza*. The most widely known *Tendenza* architects, Carlo Aymonino, Aldo Rossi, and Giorgio Grassi, circulated in the English-speaking world under the umbrella term 'Neo-Rationalists'. More colloquially, they were known as the 'Neo-Rats'.[3]

Welfare state building programs and the projects of civil servant architects are a key but under-examined topic in postmodernism. In 1970s transatlantic discourse, from John Turner's *Freedom to Build* (1972), Charles Jencks's *The Language of Post-Modern Architecture* (1977), Malcolm MacEwan's *Crisis in Architecture* (1974), and Colin Rowe and Fred Koetter's *Collage City* (1978), to pivotal issues of architectural journals and the *trouble in Utopia* episode of Robert Hughes documentary series *Shock of the New* (1981), the post-war "architecture of bureaucracy" was conflated with Modernism generally and, in Britain, with brutalism in particular.[4] The architecture of government agencies was described, critiqued, and widely rejected. Critics frequently organised ideas of the architectural project after Modernism through a negative relationship to key welfare state buildings.

For polemical reasons, these postmodern texts did not address experiments in late welfare state architecture begun in the 1960s, nor did subsequent editions catalogue significant changes in government architectural agencies and projects.[5] In mid-1980s Melbourne, changing patronage conditions enabled small, private architectural practices dominated by young architects to become key designers of projects for, or within, the reformed Public Works Department of Victoria. Thus, within ten years of the postmodern 'crisis' of bureaucratic architecture, designers were forced to face the task of 're-thinking' state agency and state architecture. A range of designs from these salaried government architects and private agents were collected into the pages of a small Australian architectural magazine, *Transition*, and accompanied by descriptions. These pages form the core text of this essay.

It is interesting to investigate how a local turn to the buildings, ideas, and sources of the Italian *Tendenza* provided a crucible for distilling a new approach to government building projects and the problem of the 'institution', as well as contesting prevailing modes of 'vernacular' postmodernism.

Tafuri had argued that the *Tendenza* was a set of methods conflated into a school, the defining characteristic of which was an attempt "to construct architecture with its own elements and *of those elements only*".[6] Writing in *Oppositions* in 1976, Rafael Moneo declared that the Tendenza "supported a common ideology": all were committed to understanding the "specific aspects of architecture".[7] The *Tendenza*'s influence on local Victorian projects is hazy and imprecise. With no intention to offer a forensic reception of key theoretical Italian texts, which are rather thin on the ground, I suggest that *Tendenza* drawing practices, design techniques, and shared sources sedimented a set of *Tendenza* approaches in local work. These projects harboured heterogeneous traces. Local architects worked concurrently with recent Italian projects, the more distant 1920s and 1930s avant-gardes, and the bureaucratic reformist present.[8] These mixed references and time periods confound ideals of straightforward translation and influence. Translation is an inadequate mode of speech to describe the practices of hybridised postmodernity.[9]

Examining this local 'translation' of the *Tendenza* contributes three things to debates on postmodernism. This case study places government agencies and their arts of government—how they manage civics, citizens and communities—into the landscape of postmodernism. The analysis brings another strand of postmodern architecture into view, expanding Australian postmodernism beyond the vernacular and neoclassical approaches promoted by the Australia Council in the first half of the 1980s.[10] Thirdly, this case study exposes the complex transnationality of postmodernism.

Local Context

Victoria's welfare state building agencies went through a period of dramatic public crisis and renewal from 1970 to 1985. These changes form the background to the mid-1980s *Tendenza*-inflected architectural experiments. Through the 1960s and 1970s, North American, British, and Australian citizen activists and experts contested the policies and development plans of government housing, education, and planning agencies.[11] Aided by local corruption scandals and politics, public debates and protests eventually forced change upon these agencies. Some dwindled or were deliberately starved of government funds. The ascension to power of conservative governments pursuing neo-liberal agendas in North America and Britain has helped cement a historical narrative of postmodernism as the agent of privatisation in a declining public sphere.[12] In the attacks on government agencies that preceded these changes, the problem of State building projects was often dramatically encapsulated for architectural audiences through a focus on a signature building. In North America, Britain, and Australia, critics located the 'failures' of Modernism and industrialised, bureaucratic building systems in a local piece of architectural Modernism.

In North America and Britain, two public housing tower complexes signified a modernist 'crisis': the demolition of three blocks of the Pruitt-Igoe public housing towers in St Louis in April 1972 and a gas explosion in May 1968 at East London's Ronan Point tower. In Australia, various battles over government development plans in Woolloomooloo, Sydney, and Brookes Crescent, North Fitzroy achieved extensive media coverage. Within the local profession, however, another modernist high-rise villain emerged centre stage to dramatize discontent.

In 1975, the Royal Institute of Victorian Architects awarded its most prestigious prize to the sleek, black BHP Corporate Tower (1969–72) in Melbourne, designed by Yuncken Freeman and Irwin Johnson and Partners.[13] At the award ceremony, the announcement of the prize to a building for a mining giant was greeted with "boos and hisses".[14] The building had been under the microscope for a number of months. In the previous October, international critic Charles Jencks had visited the city to deliver a lecture, and, in the course of his visit, had made pointed comments on the building to the press. He reprised these remarks in an Australian interview for *Architecture Australia*, but these comments were not printed until the February 1975 edition. Placing the BHP building within the context of the energy crisis and polarised debate around the relations between architects and users, he declared that "it's movingly awful, or if you are willing to subscribe to the values of technocracy and capitalism – it's a beautiful thing".[15] In the interview, Jencks catalogued and criticised "the public system" of "the local or government authority working in a welfare capitalist system with restricted money".[16] The Jencks interview included pictures of Pruitt-Igoe's detonation. A caption beneath the images noted that the estate was "the most inflexible space thought of, and created by elitism".[17] His remarks echoed the recent words of Royal Institute of British Architects' Director of Public Affairs, Malcolm MacEwan, in condemning both private and public corporations and the profession's elitism.[18] Indeed, Jencks commended the first two chapters of Malcolm MacEwan's book *Crisis in Architecture* (1974) to readers of the interview.[19]

The 1974 *Crisis* report investigated the status of the profession in Britain, but MacEwan situated his critique within the context of the current economic and environmental crisis, opening with: "In a few months, the vast balloon of expectations built on false assumptions about the world's resources was pricked".[20] In Melbourne, BHP embodied the resource crisis, capitalism, and the corporate client. Moreover, following Jencks's visit, the most significant local interrogations of the problems symbolised by the building carried strong echoes of MacEwan's arguments. These dealt in part with the problem of the institution, a topic that defined building projects, patronage groups, social relations, and the architect's role.

In late 1975 and early 1976, local architectural dissent used the BHP award as a lens for examining architectural values and professional responsibilities. Architect Peter Corrigan wrote a polemic on the award decision and the building for the literary magazine *Meanjin Quarterly*.[21] He urged architects to understand that they had the capacity "to change the nature of our institutions" and argued in humanist terms for the values of the "imagination" and the "spirit".[22] BHP was also the target of another architectural essay in *Meanjin,* Deborah White's "Women and Architecture: A personal observation", which appeared five months before Corrigan's essay.[23] White's article is the first feminist publication on architecture in Australia, and, in passing, she used BHP as a trope for rejecting the social role embraced by many architects. She dismissed the building as an "extravagant Neo-Classical monument to Capital" and added: "An indefensible amount of our personal resources are being expended on extravagantly commercial and institutional prestige buildings of irrational design".[24] For White the "community in general, and not individuals and institutions or even 'Architecture' in particular [...] is the proper object of architectural concern".[25] Corrigan and White's essays had placed the problem of the "institution" at the centre of debate but differed on the terms by which these organisational structures would be changed.

In North America and Britain, a signature project from the State's building agencies was mobilised to visibly embody the crisis of Modernism. This was not the case in Melbourne; a corporate mining company tower assumed the villain's role in local debates. However, this crisis stimulated discussions of a broad range of 'institutional' buildings beyond the commercial world. Discussion of the fate of the public 'institution' was revived in 1980s architectural circles when the Victorian profession's fortunes (its sources of work) were linked to State agencies.

By 1979, the corruption scandals engulfing the Victorian Housing Commission highlighted problems of reform in the State's architectural programs. After two public inquiries, including a Royal Commission in 1979, the Victorian government declared in a 1980 Green Paper that the agency would not be dismantled. In a series of reforms culminating in the appointment of Sydney architect John Devenish as Group Manager of the Rehabilitation and Redevelopment of the new Ministry of Housing, the agency was reinvented. In October 1985, *The Age* newspaper would declare that "Revolutionaries invade the public works", highlighting the recruitment of John Devenish to reform the Public Works Department of Victoria (PWD) as the new General Manager (Design and Construction) and of architect Peter Crone as his Assistant General Manager.[26] The following year, Melbourne's little architectural magazine *Transition* published a nine-page spread on the new-look PWD. The Department had already issued two publications, but the *Transition* folio placed the reform of building procurement, client relations, and architectural design firmly in the context of contemporary architectural debates. And here the influences of the *Tendenza* asserted themselves.

Asserting Presence

"Most large public buildings suffer from a poetically inspired fear of expression", wrote Ivan Rijavec in 1986.[27] Only a few select designs from the new-look Public Works portfolio were presented in *Transition*. In an issue devoted to the activities of a local architectural association founded in 1979, 'The Half-Time Club', the magazine focused on the Public Work buildings of its members and their shared approaches. The seven projects comprised two police stations, an extension to a health training facility at an institutional psychiatric care home for children, a school building, a coronial services centre and a jail. The folio bundled together a range of sites in which schooling, health, and justice were administered to citizens. Each building offered a rich site for studies of bio-politics, the term coined by Michel Foucault to describe the procedures and technologies employed by the State to regulate, govern, produce, and inscribe the bodies and conduct of subjects.[28] For Foucault, bio-politics lay at the heart of the new liberal arts of government developed in the late eighteenth century. The "management of populations"—their health, security, education and welfare—was part of this purview.[29]

All seven projects are accompanied by texts that in various ways address the managerial or administrative role housed in these buildings. The descriptions explain compositional choices, aligning key elements as expressions of the liberal ideals and governing functions of each organisation. All projects rely on typological approaches, which can range from a quite general sense of a 'public' building type to analysis of specific building morphologies. A desire to assert the public or institutional type through architectural means evokes Rafael Moneo's reading of the Rossian type as an analytic tool: "a structure" in which things are "revealed and made knowledgeable".[30] Moneo emphasised morphology, and the Half-Time projects also assert the role of particular elements in expressing key managerial principles or liberal ideals.[31]

Three distinct approaches to the governmental can be discerned. The first asserts the 'institutional' nature of the building and is evident in Shane Murray's McKinnon High School Music Complex, Melbourne. The second approach expresses the civic and public nature of the building and is evident in Ivan Rijavec's Victorian Coronial Services Centre (designed and documented at Bates, Smart and McCutcheon) and his Whittlesea College of TAFE. The third approach expresses the contradictory values and demands of governance placed on the services housed by the building, often expressing these in a dualistic fashion.

The third approach was most pervasive. Mardi Butcher's Kew Children's Cottages School of Nursing Extension acknowledges the existing 1965 building as a design for a time when (psychiatric) nursing was seen as apolitical. Butcher's design works with the idea of repair and energy as well as permanence and stability. The two police stations negotiate dual roles. Andrew Hutson's Gisborne 24 Hour Police Station acknowledges 'regulation' and 'virtue' and slices a curved form through a low rectangular block to capture this binary. Bill Goodwin's Campbellfield 24 Hour Police Station expresses the civic nature of the building, using gable elements derived from local industrial vernacular and classical pediments. The northern façade deploys enlarged modified versions of these elements to express the building's policing functions. The Watch House is defined by a brooding gable with a cut-out slot (a reference perhaps to panoptic symbols). Opaque panels of regular, off-form concrete produce a blank wall to signify the regular cell blocks housed within. Francesco Timpano and Alex Selenitsch's scheme for the Regional Prison in Castlemaine expresses its penal function in cell block plan form with a dominating watch tower/panopticon imagery at the nodal point joining individual wings, but many of the stylistic elements and overall site planning drew on suburban precedents of house and street to explore notions of individual and communal identity.

The role of government buildings and their relation to their users was addressed in the *Transition* pages through an examination of institutions and type. These Half-Time projects recover the institutional role of the buildings. Shane Murray's text openly addresses the recent history of antagonism towards institutions. He cautions against the "romance" of "de-institutionalisation".[32] Originally a 1960s-movement dedicated to removing patients from total psychiatric institutions into community-based care, Murray's use of the phrase de-institutionalisation allows the idea to enter architecture.[33] The phrase and ensuing discussion suggest engagements with the rejection and reform positions articulated by local architects ten years previously.

Murray exposes the "romance that architecture can somehow manipulate institutions".[34] This is quite a different position to the social change agenda promoted by Corrigan for institutional reform or White's rejection of institutions and corporations in favour of a community basis for architecture. Murray's remarks frame his explanation of the design logic driving his secondary school project. He argues against the use of domestic imagery and plan organisation in schools and asserts that:

> institutions are constituted by fundamental and enduring relationships between history, convention and authority, not by the buildings they inhabit. Protagonists of "de-institutionalisation" merely sentence us to a built environment composed of endless permutations of a bland domestic vernacular.[35]

His proposition is "that architecture should evidence their [institution's] various roles".[36] This position does not adhere to either Corrigan's call for the reinvention of institutions nor White's outright rejection of them in favour of community organisations. Continuity and analysis are embraced. The Italian architect Giorgio Grassi had argued in favour of historical and urban continuity, apparent in repeatable morphologies, and against the deliberate novelty and the de-familiarising experimentation of the avant-gardes.[37] Grassi's interest, however, extends beyond historical sources to assert the material presence of architecture, a technique that appears very strongly in the Melbourne welfare state *Tendenza*. As Grassi noted, "It [architecture] judges, searches for the truth and the necessity of the object; it recognizes what is stable within it" and it calls "attention to the specific conditions of architecture".[38] Murray and Rijavec assert the role of architecture in providing material presence to institutional buildings. Murray declares that his building "unashamedly announces its scale and non-domestic role".[39] Not one of the seven architects featured in the *Transition* portfolio uses the word 'monumental', but each project makes monumental gestures, even in the tiniest of buildings.

The discussion in *Transition* is driven by a concern for the 'expression' of the institution in its visible, tangible elements, and spaces. Institutional identity is articulated through continuities with historical building typologies or civic and 'institutional' typologies in the case of the TAFE College and the Music Complex. Through strategies of self-conscious presentation, buildings are forced into a condition of self-acknowledgement of their roles. These techniques align with a broader mid-1980s interest in architecture's social role as a conduit and constructor of relations of power. In 1985 New York–based critic and historian Mary McLeod parsed the Venetian School's understanding of architecture "as an instrument of an existing power structure".[40] 'Unmasking' these relations of power is a different critical project to that offered by the Victorian works. The local designs converge around a common technique of showing institutional presence. These clearly defined, austere forms are often amalgamations of component parts, with separate elements presenting spatial and symbolic expressions of the competing managerial and liberal desires of government services. This focus on binaries, tensions, and differences reveals the various forces at work in the art of governing. Even as the buildings assert the physical presence of institutions, their component parts suggest the irreconcilable aims of managerial liberalism. Nurture and reform coexist with regulation and discipline.

Reviving the Avant-garde
Beyond the designs and declared intellectual positions, the Neo-Rats' influence exerts itself in the austerity of their black and white line drawings. The illustrations emphasise plan and elevation views and are rarely peopled.

The buildings are presented in white space rather than contextualised within landscapes. The viewer is directed to study the forms themselves and their compositional aspects. Images draw attention to the familiar neo-rationalist preferences for austere architectural forms dominated by façade views of plain walls with the sparse ornamentation of fenestration, doorways, and the occasional stairwell and lobby. Andrew Hutson's Gisborne 24 Hour Police Station directly references neo-rationalist precedents. The formal lobby and entrance façade is uncannily close to Grassi's Chieti student housing of 1980, which Grassi had aligned in turn with vernacular classicism, Karl Friedrich Schinkel, and Heinrich Tessenow. Mostly the buildings drew on the avant-garde source material that had fascinated the other Neo-Rat, Aldo Rossi: the work of the classicising modernists Adolf Loos, Auguste Perret, Peter Behrens, and Hannes Meyer, all described and analysed in Rossi's reviews for the Italian architectural journal *Casabella-continuità*.

    The Melbourne designs reflected the Rossian modernist and neo-rationalist antecedents but also expanded to include other references from the 1920s and 1930s German, Austrian, and Dutch avant-gardes. Mardi Butcher's extension and Murray's Music Complex appear to reference Oud, with Murray's building being particularly indebted to Oud's cubic compositional method for the 1927 Weissenhof Housing Estate. Butcher's skillion roofs mix in bits of Aalto or Scharoun's expressionistic planning (influential on the earlier Melbourne generation of Edmond and Corrigan and Greg Burgess). Expressionistic influences often appear in the Melbourne Neo-Rationalists' plan forms.

    The reworking of this source material reflects a broader interest in the Dutch and Germanic avant-gardes that propagated in the circles aligned with Ian McDougall and Richard Munday's *Transition* journal and the Melbourne Half-Time Club. These interests were declared at the beginning of the 1980s in Ian McDougall's own house in South Yarra (1981–83), with its Loosian motifs on the front façade, and his 1981 Kensington Community Health Centre (1981-85), which reimagines the austere, white masonry façades of *mitteleuropa* Modernism in local Aussie timber. The Health Centre is composed from three blocks: a central flat-rooved form with flanking blocks of planar Modernism topped with hip roofs. It is a witty amalgam of vernacular and neo-avant-garde, but the modernist references predominate.[41] The *Transition* portfolio of Half-Time Club buildings for the Public Works Department generally distinguishes itself from the surreal suburban idiom pursued by Edmond and Corrigan and the nineteenth-century historicism of early 1980s Ministry of Housing projects. The Half-Time portfolio can be placed within a broader international recovery of the earlier twentieth-century avant-gardes.

    Although postmodern historicism is often identified with American and Australian vernacular historicism or neoclassical revivals, the recovery and use of modernist avant-gardes was widespread and heterogeneous. A neo-avant-garde historicism spanned from the Russian Constructivism of the AA School tutors (Rem Koolhaas, Bernard Tschumi, and Zaha Hadid), to the Italian rationalists (Peter Eisenman and the *Oppositions* crowd), to the Germanic and Dutch avant-gardes amongst the Neo-Rats and the Melbourne *Transition*/Half-Time axis. These diverse global responses encompass a range of motivations for investigating the resources of the earlier European avant-gardes from redemption to rediscovery to re-dedication to an 'unfinished' modern project. Architecture can be placed within a broader turn to history, remembrance, and the legacy of difficult pasts in the late Twentieth Century.[42]

Four elements of the Melbourne work can be aligned with the influence of the *Tendenza*: the assertion of the built work as the locus of architecture, drawing techniques, stylistic resources, and the centrality of typological analysis. Manfredo Tafuri denigrated the neo-rationalist turn to building design as a return to the "womb of Architecture".[43] The misogynistic metaphor implied infantile regression. In local hands, however, Grassi's call for "attention to the specific conditions of architecture" generated techniques for negotiating the social and political frameworks of projects and patrons. Civics, public agencies, and the public realm were engaged by postmodern architecture.

Postmodernism, in its many manifestations, was marked by a return to historical sources. *Transition*'s 1986 folio of the Half-Time Club Public Works Department projects displayed a fairly consistent set of interests in the Neo-Rationalists; the modernist Dutch, Austrian, and Germanic avant-gardes; and the historical continuities of typology. Murray's rejection of a "bland domestic vernacular" did not foreclose the use of regional elements. Compositions mixed the local vernacular of industrial and suburban (or regional) architectural forms with neo-rationalist and modernist sources. The expression of the institutional character of the buildings was often asserted through European avant-garde and neo-rationalist elements.

Designs could be organised around contrasting binaries of style, form, or spaces so that formal and spatial oppositions expressed the irreconcilable aims of the welfare state's managerial liberalism. Aspirations for nurturance and civic cohesion could operate hand-in-glove with regulation and discipline.

This chapter, and the book in which it is included, should prompt a widening of the field of postmodernism to include a broader geography of postmodern architecture beyond the central case studies of Britain and North America. In Victoria, varieties of postmodernism—from vernacular to Neo-Rationalism and Classicism—were used to publicly assert the renewal of welfare state agencies in housing and public works. At home and abroad, a strident 1970s discourse had conflated Modernism with welfare state buildings and corporate architecture to assert an opposition to industrialised building systems, to organisations and designs structured by hierarchy, and to bureaucratic or managerial relations between architects and users. postmodern historicism would counter architect and client alienation with buildings founded in an intimate past. Historical references would be drawn from individual memories of neighbourhoods or the social memory of cities and civilisations. In the vision of Melbourne's welfare state *Tendenza*, domestic vernacular architectural forms had refused to assert the material presence of the 'institution' and its civic and governmental demands. This second *Tendenza* redeemed architecture from an alienation from itself.[44]

1
Hal Foster, "Postmodernism: A Preface" in *The Anti-Aesthetic: Essays on Postmodern Culture*, ed. Hal Foster (Port Townsend, Washington: Bay Press, 1983), ix.

2
Ibid., ix.

3
My art history lecturer at Monash University, Conrad Hamann, introduced me to the "Neo-Rats". His 1983 reading list covered Tafuri, Rob and Léon Krier, Demitri Porphyrios, Colin Rowe/Fred Koetter and Peter Eisenman's work on Terragni.

4
Malcolm MacEwan, *Crisis in Architecture*, South Melbourne: Royal Australian Institute of Architects Practice Division, 1979, 16–17: "The adoption of brutalist techniques and aesthetics (particularly in the use of concrete) in the massive developments of the 1960s contributed substantially to the development of the feeling that modern architecture was inhuman". John F.C. Turner and Robert Fichter, *Freedom To Build: Dweller Control of the Housing Process*, London/New York: The Macmillan Company, 1972, vii, x: they declare their opposition to "contractor-oriented bureaucratic systems" and proclaim that "the provision of housing for low income people through direct government action has generally been a failure". The British *Architects Journal* published a "Radical Alternatives" issue in October 1977, which included an extensive diagrammatic analysis of managerialism in architectural government offices. Charles Jencks's comments on public architecture are cited and referred to in footnote 15. Local battles with the Victorian Housing Commission and other public bodies are detailed in: *The Displaced: A Study of Housing Conflict in Melbourne's Inner City*, Melbourne: Centre for Urban Research and Action, April 1977 and in Renate Howe, David Nichols, and Graeme Davison, *Trendyville: The Battle for Australia's Inner Cities*, Clayton, Vic.: Monash University Publishing, 2014.

5
For recent work on late welfare state architectural experiments, see Mark Swenarton, "Reforming the Welfare State, Camden 1965–1973," *Footprint* 5/2, 2011, 41–48; and Karen Burns and Paul Walker, "Publicly Postmodern: Media, Image and the New Social Housing Institution in 1980s Melbourne" in *Proceedings of the Society of Architectural Historians of Australia and New Zealand* 32, Architecture, Institutions, and Change, eds. Paul Hogben and Judith O'Callaghan, Sydney: SAHANZ, 2015, 68–81.

6
Manfredo Tafuri, *History of Italian Architecture, 1944–1985*, trans. Jessica Levine, Cambridge, Massachusetts: The MIT Press, 1989, 143.

7
Rafael Moneo, "Aldo Rossi: The Idea of Architecture and the Modena Cemetery," *Oppositions* 5 (1976), reprinted in *Oppositions Reader*, 107.

8
Jacques Derrida writes of the work as "a fabric of traces" rather than a strongly demarcated corpus. See Jacques Derrida, "Living On – Border Lines", *A Derrida Reader: Between the Blinds*, ed. Peggy Kamuf, New York: Harvester Wheatsheaf, 1991, 257.

9
This is a play, of course, on Derrida's "Des Tours de Babel" in *A Derrida Reader: Between the Blinds*, 244.

10 For architecture and the Australia Council, see Paul Walker and Karen Burns, "Architecture and the Australia Council in the 1980s," in *Proceedings of the Society of Architectural Historians of Australia and New Zealand* 32, Architecture, Institutions and Change, eds. Paul Hogben and Judith O'Callaghan, Sydney: SAHANZ, 2015, 688–700; and Karen Burns and Paul Walker, "'Ciao Australia', Postmodern Australian and Italian Exchanges, 1978–1991, from Domus to the Venice Biennale," *Proceedings of the Fourth International Conference of the European Architectural History Network*, ed. Kathleen James-Chakraborty, Dublin: University College Dublin School of Art History and Cultural Policy, 2016, 285–294.

11 For the Victorian context, see Howe et al, *Trendyville*; Renate Howe, ed., *New Housing For Old: Fifty Years of Public Housing in Victoria 1938–1988*, Melbourne: Ministry of Housing and Construction, 1986; and Burns and Walker, "Publicly Postmodern". For Britain, see John Grindrod, *Concretopia: A Journey around the rebuilding of post-war Britain*, Brecon, England: Old Street Publishing, 2013, 323–379. For North America, there are separate city studies such as Anthony Flint, *Wrestling With Moses: How Jane Jacobs Took on New York's Master Builder and Transformed the American City*, New York: Random House, 2013; and Jeffrey Craig Saunders, *Seattle & The Roots of Urban Sustainability: Inventing Ecotopia*, Pittsburgh: University of Pittsburgh Press, 2010.

12 See Fredric Jameson, "Postmodernism, or the Cultural Logic of Late Capitalism," *New Left Review*, 146 (1984): 54–92; and Reinhold Martin, *Utopia's Ghost: Architecture and Postmodernism, Again*, Minnesota: University of Minnesota Press, 2010.

13 The Royal Victorian Architecture Medal; see also Philip Goad, ed., *Judging Architecture: issues, divisions, triumphs, Victorian Architecture Awards 1929–2003*, Melbourne: Royal Australian Institute of Architects, 2003.

14 Peter Corrigan, "Bronze medal and brute steel: BHP building," *Meanjin Quarterly*, Autumn 35, 1 (April 1976), 34.

15 "AA Interview Charles Jencks," *Architecture Australia*, 64, 1 (January 1975), 51.

16 Ibid.

17 Ibid., 52, 55.

18 MacEwan, *Crisis in Architecture*, 8

19 "AA Interview Charles Jencks," 55.

20 MacEwan, *Crisis in Architecture*, 7.

21 Corrigan, "Bronze medal," 34–41.

22 Corrigan, "Bronze Medal," 41; MacEwan, *Crisis in Architecture*, 33, 48. Like Corrigan, MacEwan argued for a reassertion of the value of creativity and foregrounded the architect's alienation. Numerous phrases of MacEwan's are used in the Jencks interview to describe a gap between architects and users, which Jencks reformulates as a communication gap; the idea of the building as a mode of communication finds its way into Corrigan's essay.

23 Deborah White, "Women and Architecture: A personal observation," *Meanjin Quarterly*, Summer 34, 4 (December 1975), 399–404.

24 Ibid., 404.

25 Ibid., 403.

26 Dennis Carter, "Revolutionaries Invade the Public Works," *The Age*, 29 October 1985, 21.

27 Ivan Rijavec, "Victorian Coronial Services Centre," *Transition* 18 and 19 (September 1986), 33.

28 Michel Foucault, *The Birth of Biopolitics: Lectures at the College de France 1978–1979*, New York: Picador, 2008.

29 Michel Foucault, "Governmentality" in *The Foucault Effect: Studies in Governmentality*, eds. Graham Burchell, Colin Gordon, and Peter Miller, Chicago: University of Chicago Press, 1991, 100.

30 Moneo, "Aldo Rossi", 100.

31 Ibid., 110.

32 Shane Murray, "McKinnon High School Music Complex", *Transition* 18 and 19 (September 1986), 31.

33 Sociologist Irving Goffman proposed the idea of the asylum as a "total institution" in his 1961 book *Asylums: Essays on the Social Situation of Mental Patients and Other Inmates*, Harmondsworth, Middlesex: Penguin, 1968, 11. For the international movement to de-institutionalise, see Walid Fakhoury and Stefan Priebe, "The process of de-institutionalisation: an international overview," *Current Opinion in Psychiatry*, 15 (2000), 187–192.

34 Murray, "McKinnon High School Music Complex".

35 Ibid.

36 Ibid.

37 Giorgio Grassi, "Avant-garde and continuity" in *Oppositions Reader: Selected Readings from a Journal for Ideas and Criticism in Architecture, 1973-1984*, ed. K. Michael Hays, New York: Princeton Architectural Press, 1998, 392.

38 Grassi, "Avant-garde and Continuity," 396–397.

39 Murray, "McKinnon High School Music Complex," 31.

40 Mary McLeod, "Architecture and Ideology: Proceedings of the Symposium Introduction" in *Architecture Criticism Ideology*, ed. Joan Ockman, Princeton, New Jersey: Princeton Architectural Press, 1985, 10.

41 The South Yarra House is illustrated in *Domus* 663 (1985), the antipodean issue, and the Community Health Centre is illustrated in Jennifer Taylor, "The Pleasures of Architecture," 219.

42 See Beverley Butler, "Heritage and the Present Past" in *Handbook of Material Culture*, ed. Chris Tilley et al., (New York, London, New Delhi: SAGE, 2008, 463–479.

43 Tafuri, *History of Italian Architecture*, 142.

44 Alienation is a foundational theme in the persistent criticism of modernity and the search for solutions from the nineteenth century onwards. Marshall Berman's book *All That is Solid Melts into Air* writes of the two kinds of 1960s modernity that opposed each other—the freeway and the street. But, through a new synthesis, "a new mode of modernity' might be born, through "which we all could harmoniously move, in which we could all feel at home". See Marshall Berman, *All that is solid melts into air: The experience of Modernity*, New York: Verso, 1982, 329–330.

Exhibiting Scarpa: Transcriptions of the Narrative Detail in Queensland

Antony Moulis and Elizabeth Musgrave

The circumstances by which the work of Italian architect Carlo Scarpa (1906–1978) came to influence a group of architects who began practising in Brisbane in the early 1990s can be traced directly to their educational experiences at The University of Queensland (UQ) in the 1980s and an exhibition detailing Scarpa's work, which was organised by UQ architecture students and graduates and held at Old Government House on the Gardens Point campus of the Queensland University of Technology (QUT) in Brisbane in July 1991. The exhibition showed measured drawings of Carlo Scarpa's remodelling of the Castelvecchio Museum at Verona, offering close documentation of work the Italian architect had originally undertaken in four phases between 1957 and 1973. Brought to Queensland as part of the Biennial Oceanic Architectural Education Conference CIRCUS, the exhibit was accompanied by a keynote talk by its convenor, Edinburgh-based British architect Richard Murphy, an event which itself had significant impact.

Italian Architecture: Ideas and Influences

Within the Queensland context, a distinct interest in Italian architecture and Scarpa's work in particular, emerged in the mid-1960s through architects and educators who were, or would become, Brisbane-based. This interest ran counter to prevailing views, which placed London and the US as the centres of global architectural thinking; Archigram, James Stirling, Peter, and Alison Smithson were notable on one side of the Atlantic and Robert Venturi, Charles Moore, and Peter Eisenman on the other. Young architects working in local practices that subscribed to the Italian journals *Domus* and *Casabella-continuità* during the 1950s and 1960s became aware of good design as being inclusive of all dimensions of life. Ernesto Rogers' editorials in *Casabella* focused on *le preesistenze ambientali* [the pre-existing environment], the notion that 'continuity' is an inclusive concept extending to cultural and historical settings in addition to physical settings. It is unsurprising then that the Queensland Architectural Students Association invited an ageing Gio Ponti, at that time editor of *Domus*, to address students at the 1967 Australasian Architecture Student Association (AASA) Conference, "City-Synthesis", in Brisbane. Inspired by this conference, one young student, Paul Moroney, followed Ponti to Italy but was unsuccessful in landing employment with the architect. Another, Rex Addison, who studied at The University of Queensland from 1965 to 1970, took in the Italian cities Trieste, Udine, Venice, Rome, and Milan on a transcontinental road trip to London in the year after completing his degree. In search of ideas that could inform his practice back in an Australian circumstance, Addison recalls that the work of Gino Valle at Udine stood out for illustrating how "to turn vernacular elements into new design solutions".[1] On his return to practice in Brisbane, Addison married an appreciation of the architecture of Valle with an interest in the work of Robert Venturi and his thinking about ways of recovering elements of vernacular architecture, an issue also relevant in Queensland, with its own tradition of timber building poised for architectural reinvention. Architect and lecturer at UQ Ian Sinnamon may have encountered Scarpa's work directly while touring following his 1958–59 Borsa di Studio Academia Scholarship to Rome for he included images in his 1970s lectures for students.[2]

Addison's interest focused on form and its addition and subtraction, which differed from that of the subsequent generation of students, who were driven by a concern with occupation and tectonic qualities. Nevertheless, such lessons provided a foundation on which—with the arrival at UQ of architect/lecturers such as Sinnamon, Bill Carr, Patrick Moroney, and Peter O'Gorman in the early 1970s (and Brit Andresen later in 1977)—it was possible to claim new starting points for contemporary architecture beyond the type of mainstream Modernism then dominant in Queensland.[3]

It was architect Brit Andresen in particular who brought a strong and abiding interest in Scarpa's work to her practice and then to her teaching at the Department of Architecture at UQ. In 1971, Andresen collaborated with Barry Gasson on the competition-winning scheme for the Burrell Museum in Glasgow. In researching their design proposal, they were alerted to Scarpa's work through Michael Brawne's 1965 publication *The New Museum: Architecture and Display* and earlier abridged accounts in *Architectural Review*.[4] During a hiatus between stages of work on the Burrell competition project, Andresen sought advice from Brawne and the Italian consulate and, armed with Scarpa's contact details, visited Castelvecchio and the library, Querini Stampalia, in Venice in late 1972. She recognised in Scarpa's work the key to several issues that their competition-winning scheme had yet to address, particularly concerning the placement of a vast number of items of varied scales and their meaningful display. In particular, in "looking with the eyes of a designer of architecture for galleries and museums," she was struck by the validation of art with architecture and the relationship to a person.[5], she was struck by the validation of art with architecture and the relationship to a person. On this and subsequent visits, Andresen studied the "deliberate staging of light with artefacts, the way in which you moved led you to see things in a certain perspective […] the invitation to a body to the artefacts […] [for example] the stand that supported, say a bowl, [such] that if you took the bowl away you could see underneath that it was like a pair of hands—but abstracted—that holding towards you so that you could reach".[6] The nature of an architectural approach focused on strong humanist principles meant that Scarpa, considered alongside architects such as Alvar Aalto and Sigurd Lewerentz, would not sit neatly within the modernist cannon. For Andresen, the work of these architects embodied an approach that could be drawn into dialogue with specific circumstances such as those she encountered in Queensland, taking architecture beyond the formalist and self-referential tendencies evident in late Modernism into a new postmodern phase.

Despite a growing interest in Scarpa's work amongst aficionados, access to it through architectural publications remained limited. Apart from the inclusion of Scarpa's work by Michael Brawne in his book *The New Museum* (1965) and occasional articles in *Domus*, publications focusing on Scarpa's intricate marrying of new with existing built fabric did not begin to appear in the UQ Department of Architecture library until after his death. *Global Architecture* published its first issue on Scarpa in 1979.[7] This was followed by Francesco Dal Co and Giuseppe Mazzariol's *Carlo Scarpa: The Complete Works* (1985) and later monographs by Richard Murphy on Castelvecchio and Fondazione Querini Stampalia.[8] With the mounting of the Scarpa Exhibition in Brisbane in 1991, came the opportunity for students to experience the power of the architect's work, not first hand but *in absentia*.

The Scarpa Exhibition and CIRCUS

The events that preceded the arrival of the Scarpa exhibition go back to architect Richard Murphy's initial conception of the idea and an unlikely Queensland connection that soon emerged.

According to Murphy, his original interest in the Castelvecchio came about fortuitously in 1982, when the architect encountered an exhibition of Scarpa's drawings convened by the Verona museum's director, Licisco Magagnato. Deeply intrigued by Scarpa's work, Murphy returned to Verona the following year to meet Magagnato and, in discovering that no final 'as built' drawings of the Castelvecchio existed, seeded the idea of creating a comprehensive survey of the work. Murphy returned to Verona in 1986 with students from Edinburgh University, a trip from which the exhibition "Carlo Scarpa at the Castelvecchio: Survey of a Journey" was created, shown at Edinburgh University from December 1987 to January 1988 and subsequently at the Building Centre, London, in May 1988.[9]

The circumstances through which Murphy's drawings of the Castelvecchio came to Brisbane three years later were equally fortuitous. Earlier in the 1980s, Rod Bligh, an engineer from Brisbane who was working with Arup in Edinburgh, answered an advertisement in a local newspaper and joined a share house with the architect Murphy. The two became friends and Bligh accompanied Murphy on the cycling trip to Italy during which they visited the Castelvecchio at Verona, and the architect conceived the idea to undertake the measured drawings of Scarpa's work. Rod is the son of Graham Bligh, then director of Bligh Voller Architects, a well-known Queensland practice, and Rod's brother Chris, studying to be an architect, was on his "year out" in London in 1988 when he assisted Murphy in the mounting of the Scarpa exhibition there.[10]

After his return to Brisbane in 1990 to resume his studies at the University of Queensland, Chris became a member of the CIRCUS organising committee, which invited Murphy and his exhibition to Brisbane the following year.

Most of the students from the CIRCUS Conference committee had graduated from the Bachelor of Architecture by the time the conference actually came to pass. They included Sheona Thomson, Richard Kirk, Peter Besley, Jo Besley, Louisa Carter, Julia Capp, Brian Bass, and Rachel Doherty. Introduced to Scarpa's work through the Italian journal *Domus* to which she held a subscription, Alice Hampson was invited to work with the committee, particularly on the convening of the Scarpa exhibition.[11] Hampson, who had visited Castelvecchio in 1985, joined Sheona Thomson and this author (Antony Moulis), who had both visited the building in 1987, to prepare the opening and organise the mounting of the show.

CIRCUS was held on 8–12 July 1991 across a number of historic venues in Brisbane's inner city, including the City Hall Auditorium, St Andrews Uniting Church, the School of Arts, and Old Government House, where the Scarpa exhibition was housed. In the evenings, students bunkered down at the old Petrie Terrace Police Barracks, making the city a site of both dwelling and discourse. Writing the "Welcome" to students in the conference program, the Head of The University of Queensland's Department of Architecture, Michael Keniger, noted how the choice of such public city venues was a means of claiming the rich network of space that the city provides, a deliberate distancing of students from beaches, rural retreats and the comfort of the suburbs.[12] Reinforcing this attention to the city as frame and object was the mounting of the "Companion City" urban design competition exhibition, convened by the Melbourne-based journal *Transition* and shown over the course of the conference at the Metro Arts Gallery in Edward Street.

The decision of the students to 'occupy' the city also reflected the recent political situation, lending a genuinely liberating quality to the event. The fallout from the Fitzgerald Inquiry into Queensland police corruption (1987–89) was ongoing, with key figures of the previous National Party government, including the former Premier and some of his ministers, on trial for perjury and criminal misconduct. Students, who had only three years earlier risked arrest by gathering in groups of three or more in the city's streets, were now free to wander together between the venues along Ann Street, one of Brisbane's main thoroughfares that linked many of the key venues.[13] Although heritage protection legislation had yet to be enacted in Queensland (it was eventually passed in 1992), there was a sense that Brisbane's historic fabric was now more likely to survive the spate of unfettered development that had seen the destruction of popular landmarks, often in the dead of night, including the Bellevue Hotel and the Cloudland Ballroom (demolished in 1979 and 1982, respectively). Such high-profile demolitions had reinforced the view that the State wilfully disregarded Queensland's civic and social past, a narrative that architecture was inevitably drawn into. The preferred architecture of the ruling National Party was emphatically late modern, used as a sign of economic and social progress at a state level. Within a context of architectural patronage that favoured modernist forms, practice in Brisbane remained largely blind to critique or shifts in the discipline taking place internationally, which were nonetheless taking hold in architectural education.

With the demise of the conservative government in 1989 and despite the ongoing recession and cuts to education spending, there was an air of renewal and optimism—a feeling that change was possible for Queensland as it emerged from its tenure as a 'police state'. In a cheeky move indicative of their cognisance of this new open society, students invited the Deen Brothers—Brisbane's most obliging building demolition firm, responsible for the removal of the Bellevue Hotel and the Cloudland Ballroom—to be amongst the major sponsors of CIRCUS events. Indeed, the Deen Brothers' sponsorship of a Heritage Walk that also had the support of the National Trust caused a full public controversy, fuelled by the appearance of the company's infamous motto, "All we leave behind are memories", on the walk flyer.[14]

The diverse range of speakers at the conference reflected this optimistic outwardly directed view. The international speakers included Sarah Bonnemaison and Christine Macy from Canada; Chris Macdonald, then in Austin, Texas; Pascal Chossegros from Paris; Andrew Holmes and Jeanne Sillett of the Architectural Association London; William Mitchell, then at Harvard; Nimish Patel and Parul Zaveri from India; and Richard Murphy from Edinburgh. A host of local speakers reflected the full range of architecture's interests and included established and emerging architects, academics and critics, and sociologists and environmentalists. Workshops, exhibitions, and other fringe entertainments accompanied the lecture series, and the week culminated with the CIRCUS Ball at the historic Smellie & Co building on Edward Street and its near-accidental destruction by fire during a band performance.

Into this mix arrived the Scarpa exhibition featuring 53 measured drawings of the Castelvecchio accompanied by a slide presentation "Spazio, Tempo e Luce" [Space, time and light] with audio commentary by the architect—a window into an architecture located half a world away that seemed nonetheless vitally present.

For local students, Murphy's talk on Scarpa was the most anticipated of the conference. On the evening of Wednesday, 10 July 1991, over a period of nearly two hours, the Edinburgh-based architect led a packed audience in St Andrews Uniting Church on a virtual tour of Castelvecchio revealing his wonder at the work, using both photographs and the measured drawings to unfold, step by step, its spatial, experiential and tectonic assemblage.[15]

Murphy took time to demonstrate what he understood as the key thematic devices in Scarpa's work. Some were formal preoccupations: a like of asymmetry resolved in balanced compositions; the revelation of layers in 'retreating planes' from solid forms; the dissolution of corners;

the careful separation of the new from existing elements; and an interest in syncopated rhythms in the compilation of structural forms. There were also manifest tectonic concerns—the idea that "materials acknowledge each other when they meet" and that the manner of their joining be expressed and elaborated—such that different "actions" in the transfer of load be addressed separately. Connected to this was the concept that the act of support involved (in tectonic terms) the construal of two parts 'cleft' from a whole; a separation that required an articulated re-joining. The experiential dimension of Scarpa's architecture was revealed in Murphy's description of the sequence of rooms of the museum, an itinerary of movement and visual glimpses with a sustained cumulative effect. Describing each room in turn, Murphy dwelt on Scarpa's presentation of the museum's objects to the viewer—sculptural elements, figures and paintings—and the way in which their setting enhanced their individual character as it produced a narrative-in-miniature of the object's use and meaning. How objects were lit and held in place, how light and shadow changed with movement and with time became, for Murphy, part of an interplay that drew visitors into a self-constructed experience of architecture.

    The culmination of the museum, and of Murphy's description, was the triple height space housing the Cangrande Statue located in the gap between the main wing of the museum and the castle wall, a space only comprehended through multiple viewpoints.

    For Murphy, Scarpa's architecture was not about symbols or referents—in a conventional postmodern sense. It was about material presence, the very fact of built form, read through experience. This included direct experience, an invitation to a heightened awareness of one's surroundings, and also experience gathered through time—the presence of history—its material form seen in the contemporary moment. Important to the latter was Scarpa's tactic to "expose the layers of history by selective excavation and creative demolition", which meant that "the building itself becomes a giant exhibit revealing its growth and change in nature".[16]

    The exhibited drawings manifested this condition, laying bare, in a graphic form, the material facts of Scarpa's architecture as an authentic reading of work. Line-work delineated matter straightforwardly, conveying without sentiment the outline, texture, height, depth, volume, and mass of elements—their fittings and the manner of their fixings. The drawings in their tectonic verisimilitude established a relationship to building that was, in a sense, hyper-real. Here registered were the intentional relationships between artefacts and elements experienced by an imagined body, just as one might find them in-situ, with the sectional drawings most clearly providing the opportunity to project that imagined body into the spaces of the work.

Educational Experiences

Both the exhibition and Murphy's presentation made a deep impression. After the exhibition's dismantling, the drawings were 'gifted' to The University of Queensland's Department of Architecture and became a resource to be consulted within design studios, where the role and meaning of architectural space and its detail became a locus of exploration and discussion. Andresen used the work to present a set of themes to her students, largely in the form of observations, that could make a basis, individually or collectively, for their architectural thinking.[17] For example, she described how Scarpa had found "opportunities to make relationships with near landscape [and] not so much the larger landscape" at Castelvecchio; that is, between the exhibition rooms, with their objects of display, and the courtyard space.[18] Relatedly, the remaking of edges—such as that between the museum's interior and the space housing the Cangrande statue, through the layering of sliding screens, walls, doorways, bridges and stairs—brings attention to elements and their contingent relations, the assemblage of extended threshold spaces. This making of space at close range is the constructed "near landscape" to which Andresen refers.[19]

As an educator, Andresen saw lessons for students from Scarpa's work in terms of "what it was you could do between the building and the garden".[20] The particular setting of inside to outside, as captured again and again in Scarpa's architecture, suggested new possibilities for the configuration of that same setting when translated to the local conditions of Brisbane, with its benign climate and fecund nature. In tandem with Murphy, Andresen was also greatly excited by the idea that Scarpa's work activated the past in the present moment—the possibility of experiencing both continuity and difference through the orchestration of architecture's material fabric—a concept that resonated with postmodern thinking. Andresen framed the design studio tasks for her students through reference to the writings of Colin St John Wilson and Demetri Porphyrios, whose humanist attitudes and conscious address to history she deeply shared, particularly the idea that projecting architecture towards the future could only occur through a meaningful engagement with the past rather than a rejection of it. Andresen's view, for herself and her students, was "to learn to bring things with us".[21] It was an approach that Scarpa exemplified through work that negotiated the specific circumstances of a locale, famously, in Scarpa's case, that of his birthplace, Venice, and the surrounding province of Veneto, where he undertook the bulk of his architectural work.

Another touchstone for students of the 1980s at UQ was the elaborately drawn unbuilt works of Chris Macdonald and Peter Salter, who Andresen had encountered through the Architectural Association in London, where they were Studio Unit Masters. Macdonald participated in design studios at UQ, invited by Andresen, on two occasions in the 1980s prior to his return as a guest speaker at the CIRCUS conference. The drawn projects he completed with Peter Salter between 1982 and 1986 projected similar intricate tectonic qualities to those apparent in Scarpa's architecture as witnessed in Murphy's drawings. Their intricate Oriental Museum competition entry for Durham was already a well-thumbed favourite amongst the student body, with its highly mannered bent shapes in plan appearing as palimsest-like tracings of the extant form of the Castelvecchio.[22] Through design studio projects instigated by Andresen and Macdonald, as well as local architect/academics Peter O'Gorman and Max Horner, students were encouraged to develop an acumen for reading and imagining architecture through design and drawing, skills also put to work in apprehending Murphy's measured drawings of Scarpa's strongly narrative work. Drawings were not seen in the manner of spectacle but as texts to be carefully constructed and from which the lessons of architecture might be patiently read and revealed to the imagination. Andresen recalls thinking at the time of the Castelvecchio exhibition how "terrific [it was] students could see the actual drawings, knowing in a funny way [that] many students design drawings rather than buildings" during their university studies.[23] Nonetheless, she saw they "would be reignited with enthusiasm for the work of Scarpa [...] for the work as drawings and the importance of visiting the buildings".[24]

Building upon Scarpa

In the early 1990s, Brisbane's inner-city detached housing stock remained under threat of demolition and redevelopment permitted by the 1987 Town Plan. This moment coincided with renewed disciplinary interest in matters contextual amongst architecture students, deepened by the almost universal experience of share-housing in old Queenslanders.[25] These houses, as sites of investigation and experimentation, provided young architecture graduates schooled in Scarpa-esque thinking with rich material for testing ways of building in the manner of the architect, both temporally (in linking the past to the present) and spatially (through strategies of narrative).[26] Out of this milieu, there appeared two striking instances of domestic work by young practitioners, which bore the mark of such ideas and experiences translated into the locale of Brisbane.

In the early work of Donovan Hill, the architectural office set up by UQ graduates Timothy Hill and Brian Donovan in 1992, formal and thematic references to the work of Scarpa are clearly evident. Between 1984 and 1986, Timothy Hill worked with Brit Andresen on a bathhouse and tower extension to a 1950s beach shack on Stradbroke Island, a project that was subsequently exhibited at the Venice Biennale.[27] The HH House, completed in 1993, involved the renovation of a Queenslander in Brisbane's inner-city suburbs, the kind of rear deck and kitchen extension that provided a typical 'first project' for new graduates. Yet Timothy Hill's reimagining of the simple brief is entire. The rear of the house, refashioned from re-used VJ boards, timber sections, and off-form concrete, is like the space of the Cangrande in miniature.

The emphasis on the vertical volume is deliberately contrasted to the horizontal raised platform of the house, creating a strong spatial connection to the garden, which is marked out within the site boundary as a discrete territory in the manner of Scarpa's Querini Stampalia. The concrete stairs provide housing for objects and sculptures, again in the manner of Scarpa, with an early image of the project showing the figure of mother and child by Queensland sculptor, Catharina Hampson-Brans, on a tower-like plinth.

The familiar square rooms of the plan are broken out into a sequence culminating in the large rear volume, with its sculptural centrepiece acting as a conceptual underlay to its entire architectural schema, indicating how directly Scarpa's Castelvecchio operates as a source. The sculpture, critically positioned on a sightline from the interior, has an animate quality, like a figure strolling across the view, framed by a vertical window deeply thresholded. Directly called to mind are the "body to artefact" relations in Scarpa's work, to which both Andresen and Murphy separately referred.

The presentation of the HH House in a sectional drawing, which shows a cut through the rear volume and its kitchen window, stages architecture both formally and conceptually like Murphy's drawings of Castelvecchio—as evidence of material fact to be read 'text like' as experience of, and for, the body. Reference to the body is not only present in the outline of the figure but also in the form of the window as a liminal extension of the body. The scene of a familiar domesticity is monumentalised by its architectural surrounds, a deliberate juxtaposition of the high and the everyday, relating the project back to local proclivities both cultural and social with ambiguous intent.

Donovan Hill used the formal and conceptual frame of Scarpa's work to engage with Brisbane as a context defined by pre-existences—matters particular and local. Their unstated aim was to depart from then conventional responses to the Queensland house as a vernacular form. The underlying simplicity of the house's form is overwritten, with the built addition appearing as a patient but complex assembly of fragments, an outcome inclined towards excess. As seen in the HH House, rear elevation and familiar elements—batten skirtings, windows, doors and VJ walls—are defamiliarised and re-presented through a collage-like technique. The reinvention of the latent order of the Queenslander—taken up in the 1980s work of architects such as Rex Addison and Russell Hall, who directly re-interpreted its vernacular form and construction—is not the architects' ambition. The relation to the vernacular is otherwise understood as curation of artefacts including the house itself and the objects contained. In re-presenting elements of building usually cast away such as pieces of old painted VJ housed within the new structure, the architects sought a self-conscious play with history.

It was an open reflection on the Queensland house as both form and experience (the extant condition of the 'share house'); a dimension that was, in this instance, not to be overlooked or erased. In seeking to engage with memory and the presence of history, its material form seen in the contemporary moment—Scarpa's work had provided another vital cue.

A similar set of preoccupations is evident in the work of Alice Hampson, an earlier collaborator of Donovan Hill, who first met Timothy Hill in the office of Brisbane-based architects Denham and Munro in 1981. In a staged process that involved carving out and shaping unoccupied spaces in and around a 1930s Mervyn Rylance house, Hampson explored the affinity of sequence for display and narrative.[28]

In structuring two discrete routes to her studio—a secret internal one and a more public descent through a series of garden courtyards—Hampson deploys a Scarparesque game involving the manipulation of scale to appropriate [in her own words] "more than [she] deserved", both physically and figuratively.[29]

The act of joining materials, of attaching, hanging, buckling, or layering elements is, through its assemblage, made expressive of different 'actions' and 'operations' and infused with additional meaning through reference to metaphor. As with Scarpa, motifs abound. In the studio, it is the consistent use of timber battens in articulating an internal landscape, edging delicate screens, and establishing datum and objets d'art that unifies and ties a series of events to an overarching idea.

The careful positioning of delicately battened lamps within the space and in the large picture window resonates with vertical garden structures in the courtyard outside and the towers of the distant city beyond, conflating space and drawing the cityscape in—a constructed 'near landscape' appropriating elements that are afar. Through their placement and contextualisation, each object becomes a "narrative-in-miniature" in its own right, part of a bigger story that references the individual to the city seen beyond the domestic space.

The assemblage of fragments and the crafting of material fabric, space, and landscape informed many other early works by members of the CIRCUS cohort. The potential of domestic space to be extended and episodic was further explored by Timothy Hill in two houses for the Noble family in New Farm, Brisbane (1991) and Stradbroke Island (1991).[30] Architects Lambert and Smith deployed the strategy of promenade to order the entry sequence for the CSIRO's Queensland Centre for Advanced Technologies at Pinjarra Hills (1990–93).[31] In a project to extend an existing garage to provide additional space for a growing family in 1993, Alice Hampson, in partnership with Julie Borgelt and Sheona Thomson of Also Architects, stitched a sequence of distinct, carefully articulated territories into a "tapestry of rich experiences".[32] A strategy of promenade was also deployed by John Price Architects to link two interventions in a Queensland bungalow with interior and exterior landscapes to construct a narrative linking cellar and garret (1991 and 1998).[33]

Brit Andresen notes that these 1980s graduates had to rely on "ingenuity to make the most of tight budgets and pragmatic clients", but they also engaged with a range of concerns including "the nature of enclosure, the disregarded realm of the interiority, sequential/simultaneous spatial experience, relations between representational and abstract form, and the influence of materials/light/construction in particularising the experience of time and space".[34] The works they made flourished as economic, social, and political conditions improved up to the 1997 Asian Financial Crisis, which effected another downturn in Queensland's economy.

Postmodernism in Brisbane

The 1980s had seen an explosion in the publication of critical theories in architecture: the expressive potential of tectonics and the mythologising of detail; contextualism and the idea of architecture as an urban artefact; phenomenology and the body in place; critical regionalism; and the architecture of disjunction. It was a minefield of material, illuminating and complexifying the terms of the discipline of architecture from which students could select in fox-like fashion.

Into this mix arrived Carlo Scarpa's work as an influence on the Brisbane architectural scene, interpreted in postmodern terms. This was unusual, given his place in the Italian context. Scarpa was known as a post-war architect not as a postmodernist. His work, according to Manfredo Tafuri, needed to be understood in its "isolation and uniqueness".[35] Scarpa certainly did not fit with the received view of Italian postmodernism abroad, exemplified in Aldo Rossi's interest in models and archetypes. Nor were Rossi's ideas adopted as strongly in the Brisbane context, where "discontinuous form, the praise of the fragment and the intense fashioning of materials"—all traits of Scarpa's work—held greater fascination in looking beyond the dominant modernist agenda, which the city imbibed for reasons both cultural and political until the late 1980s.[36]

For those local students at CIRCUS, who were just embarking on their careers in 1991, theoretical stances were less ideological than practical and architectural, and, in their journey into the practice of architecture, Scarpa's work resonated. There was no lengthy apprenticeship beginning with the presentation of theories through speculative design works on paper, the familiar route to practice of postmodern contemporaries elsewhere. Despite the recession, there were opportunities to build in Queensland, and choices of theoretical approach looked towards those that celebrated the fact of building. Drawing was understood as a re-presentation of architecture in its forensic verisimilitude, with the existing to be excavated, edited, and augmented with layers of structure and material fabric, space and light. The Castelvecchio measured drawings, brought to Queensland from half a world away, provided a model for ways of testing the imagination. Scarpa's ideas had shown how, in a local circumstance, architects might learn "to bring things with them"—and give presence to the past—capturing what Tafuri termed "the experience of discontinuous historical space".[37]

1
Silvia Micheli and Andrew Wilson, "International influences in Post-War Queensland: Protagonists, Destinations and Models" in *Hot Modernism: Queensland Architecture 1945–1975*, eds. John Macacathur, Deborah van der Plaat, Janina Gosseye, and Andrew Wilson, London: Artifice, 2015, 130.

2
See the interview of Ian Sinnamon by John Macarthur and Deborah van der Plaat, School of Architecture, The University of Queensland, 06 June 2012, https://goo.gl/8dCym3.

3
Janina Gosseye and John Macarthur, "Angry Young Architects: Counterculture and the Critique of Modernism in Brisbane 1967–1972" in *Hot Modernism: Queensland Architecture 1945–1975*, eds. John Macarthur, Deborah van der Plaat, Janina Gosseye, and Andrew Wilson London: Artifice, 2015, 41.

4
Michael Brawne, *The New Museum: Architecture and Display*, New York: Praeger, 1965; Michael Brawne, "Object on View," *The Architectural Review* 126, 753 (1 November 1959), 242–254; Michael Brawne, "The Picture Wall," *The Architectural Review* 125, 748 (1 May 1959), 314–325.

5
Brit Andresen, in discussion with the authors, 12 August 2016. Andresen also recalls a text by Roberto Aloi, *Musei Architecture Technica*, 1962, as significant. Andresen recorded texts, meetings, and dates in her notebook dated 1972.

6
Brit Andresen, in discussion with the authors.

7
See Yukio Futagawa, ed., *GA Global Architecture*, 51 (1979), including the Showroom of Olivetti, S. Marco, Venice, Italy (1957–58); Querini Stampalia, Venice, Italy (1961–63); and Castelvecchio Museum, Verona, Italy (1958–64).

8
Francesco Dal Co and Giuseppe Mazzariol, *Carlo Scarpa: The Complete Works*, New York: Rizzoli, 1985; Richard Murphy, *Carlo Scarpa and the Castelvecchio*, London, Boston, and Sydney: Butterworth Architecture, 1990; Richard Murphy, *Querini Stampalia Foundation: Carlo Scarpa*, London: Phaidon, 1993.

9
Richard Murphy, *Carlo Scarpa and the Castelvecchio*, London and Boston: Butterworth Architecture, 1990, vi.

10
Rod Bligh, in discussion with the authors, 25 August 2015.

11
Alice L.T. Hampson, in discussion with the authors, 26 October 2015.

12
Michael Keniger, "Welcome," CIRCUS Conference Program, 8–12 July 1991, Brisbane, Australia.

13
Amendments to the Traffic Act banning street marches came into effect on 4 September 1977. Legislation was prompted by the threat of protests against uranium mining and was met with strong opposition from some within the Liberal party, church leaders, trade unionists, civil libertarians, academics, and many members of the general public. See "Traffic Amendment Bill" in *Queensland Legislative-ly Assembly Hansard* (1977), 599, https://www.parliament. qld.gov.au/documents/hansard/1977/1977_09_14.pdf.

14
Dean Brothers' promotional flyer from the CIRCUS Conference Program, 8–12 July 1991, Brisbane, Australia.

15
The lecture was taped on cassette and is held by Dr Antony Moulis.

16
Murphy, *Carlo Scarpa and the Castelvecchio*, 4.

17
In her teaching practice, Andresen also referred to Canova Museum and Plaster Cast Gallery (1957), Possagno; Querini Stampalia (1961–1963), Venice; and Brion Tomb and Sanctuary (1969–1978), San Vito d'Alitcole; all by Scarpa.

18 Brit Andresen, in discussion with the authors.

19 Ibid.

20 Ibid.

21 Ibid.

22 Christopher Macdonald and Peter Salter, *Macdonald and Salter: building projects 1982–1986*, London: Architectural Association, 1987.

23 Brit Andresen, in discussion with the authors.

24 Ibid.

25 Brisbane share house experiences are recalled in the work of young contemporary writers. Andrew McGahan's *Praise* (1991 Australian/Vogel Literary Award) and *1988* (1995) are both semi-autobiographical novels drawing from the author's life as a young adult in Brisbane. Nick Earls' novels *Zigzag Street* (1996), *Bachelor Kisses* (1998), and *48 Shades of Brown* (1999) chronicle his life as a medical student share-housing in inner city Brisbane.

26 The rate of development after the implementation of the 1987 Brisbane Town Plan prompted its amendment to include provisions for Character Housing and Demolition Control in 1995.

27 Reported as "News" in *Architecture Australia* (August 1991), 13.

28 Peter O'Gorman, "Studio Vista," *Architecture Australia* 85, 1 (January 1996), 48-53; Peter O'Gorman, "Courtyard Collage," *Architecture Australia* 87, 4 (July 1998), 52–57.

29 Alice Hampson, in discussion with the authors, 26 October 2015.

30 Ian McDougall, "Fortitude Valley House Additions: Lambert and Smith," *Architecture Australia* 80, 7 (1991), 42; Brit Andresen, "Queensland Dynamics: Eighties Graduates on the Way Up," *Architecture Australia* 73, 5 (1984), 62.

31 The project architects were Antony Moulis, Timothy Hill, and John Price. The project was awarded a Commendation in the RAIA Queensland Chapter FDG Stanley Award.

32 Andresen, "Queensland Dynamics," 65.

33 Elizabeth Musgrave, "From Cellar to Garret: Extending the Poetic Range of the Bungalow" in *AASA Refereed Design Scheme*, eds. Bill Busfield and Patrick Beale, Perth: Faculty of Architecture, Landscape and Visual Arts, University of Western Australia, 2003. The project Architects were John Price and Elizabeth Musgrave.

34 Andresen, "Queensland Dynamics," 60.

35 Manfredo Tafuri, *History of Italian Architecture 1944–1985*, Cambridge Massachusetts: MIT Press, 1989, 111.

36 Ibid., 114.

37 Ibid.

Learning from Kahn and Scarpa: Rigour and Ornament in the Ana Kindergarten

Peter Kohane

Fig. 24—29

Swetik Korzeniewski and Paul Desney's Ana Kindergarten (Auburn, Sydney, 1979–82) was conceived as a didactic statement: it had the role of outlining an alternative to currently held design strategies in Australia.[1] The architects believed that practice was diminished by an uncritical acceptance of themes such as universal space, the free plan, and the notion that particular functions determine spatial settings. In specific terms, Korzeniewski and Desney were troubled by a prevailing approach in the design of schools within New South Wales, where emphasis is placed on a simplistic conception of the plan as a circulation system, along which various uses are placed, each dedicated to a particular purpose. The architects focused instead on the plan as an interwoven arrangement of room-like settings, including a colonnade, porch, courtyard, and playrooms.

Ideas developed in the works of American Louis Kahn (1901–74) and Italian Carlo Scarpa (1906–78) were brought together in the scheme for the kindergarten. This analysis of Korzeniewski and Desney's design will take into consideration Kahn's distinction between 'served' and 'servant' spaces, as well as his regard for the 'form' of an 'institution'. The latter prompted Korzeniewski to claim that an architect's questioning of the design brief may be necessary for an institution to flourish. He focused on a child's delight in the kindergarten's served spaces, which comprise an entrance courtyard and two playrooms. These accommodate activities that cannot be categorised or predicted. Scarpa's work was recalled in the ornament of the building's external and internal rooms, as well as the garden front.

The United States and Italy: Working with Kahn and Scarpa
Any inquiry into the sources of inspiration for the Ana Kindergarten should begin with Korzeniewski's work under the guidance of Kahn in Philadelphia and Scarpa in Vicenza. When enrolled as a student of architecture at the University of Sydney in the late 1960s, Korzeniewski attended lectures on modern architecture by Arthur Baldwinson.[2] During these lectures, Kahn's buildings were illustrated, with emphasis placed on the composition of the Bath House (1955) in Trenton. At this time, Korzeniewski also admired Robert Venturi's *Complexity and Contradiction in Architecture*, particularly its references to Italian buildings and their settings of streets and squares.[3] The lecture series at the University of Sydney and Venturi's book played a part in Korzeniewski's decision to enter the Master program at the University of Pennsylvania in Philadelphia. His studies in 1969 and 1970 included participating in two studios run by Kahn, which turned out to be decisive for Korzeniewski's formulation of the principles that would shape his practice.

After leaving Philadelphia in 1971, Korzeniewski worked in Denys Lasdun's London architectural office and was deeply involved in the competition for Glasgow's Burrell Art Museum. While the firm was one of the five second-stage finalists, its scheme was unsuccessful.

Korzeniewski's contribution to the development of the design involved research into books and journals documenting past and recent galleries. This inevitably included works by Carlo Scarpa, at the time a little-known architect outside Italy.[4]

Upon his return to Sydney in 1972 to teach architecture at the University of Sydney, Korzeniewski emphasised past and present Italian buildings and towns in his courses. A sabbatical in 1976 provided an opportunity to travel to Europe and meet Scarpa in Venice. A discussion between them led to Korzeniewski working for six weeks in the master's Vicenza office. The Australian architect learnt that invention and skill are essential to the making of all kinds of objects, including buildings. Scarpa and Korzeniewski discussed aspects of recently completed and current projects, including the Brion Vega Cemetery (1970–72) at San Vito d'Altivole, Italy. The master's major works in the north of Italy were also studied by Korzeniewski, who was fascinated by the relationship between water and built forms in the Querini Stampalia Library (1961–63) in Venice and the Brion Vega Cemetery (1969–78), in San Vito d'Altivole. With the master's achievements in mind, Korzeniewski left Vicenza to travel to Carrara, where he designed and contributed to the carving of a marble fountain. This was shipped to Australia and installed in the garden of his residence at Whale Beach in Sydney. Scarpa was recalled in Korzeniewski's ensuing work on his Whale Beach house, as well as the adjacent one that has a bath house (1981–82), enriched by the innovative use of concrete and added ornament.

Meeting of the Masters

Kahn and Scarpa were each highly influential in showing ways out of the modernist dogma in the second half of the twentieth century. The relevance of these two architects for the design of the Ana Kindergarten, as well as its wide reception, offers insight into the implications of international trends for architectural discourse during the 1980s in Australia.

Kahn and Scarpa were aware of the complementarity of their thought. Kahn's commission in 1968 to design a Congress Hall for Venice (1968–74) provided an opportunity to meet Scarpa.[5] The architects could discuss their approaches to design. These involved Kahn accentuating the order of a building, where rooms are discrete yet interconnected. Scarpa focused instead on the vitalising effects of fragments. However, the two architects also shared ways of designing. For example, solutions emerged through the constant reworking of sketches. Kahn drew with a charcoal pencil on a series of sheets of tracing paper, while Scarpa built up images, often on a single thick piece of cardboard. Both architects recognised the importance of unfolding explorations. In more specific terms, Kahn and Scarpa stressed the relationship of light and materials in the making of spaces and exteriors. They also respected a principle, according to which connections between structural elements are not concealed but honoured through the addition of ornament.

Kahn wrote a poem about Scarpa that accompanied an exhibition on his work.[6] Published just after Kahn died in 1974, it referred to the Italian master's achievements, including his interpretation of structure and its embellishment:

> In the work of Carlo Scarpa
> "Beauty"
> the first sense
> Art
> the first word
> then Wonder
> Then the inner realization of "Form"
> The sense of the wholeness of inseparable elements.
> Design consults Nature
> to give presence to the elements
> A work of art makes manifest the wholeness of the "Form"
> a symphony of the selected shapes of the elements.
> In the elements
> the joint inspires ornament, its celebration.
> The detail is the adoration of Nature.

Two years after the poem was published, Scarpa welcomed Korzeniewski into his office. Scarpa was keen to engage with a young architect who had participated in Kahn's studios. Korzeniewski benefited from working with the Italian master, particularly as his ideas complemented those of Kahn.

With two of the most significant architects of the twentieth century mentoring Korzeniewski, his scheme with Paul Desney for the Ana Kindergarten is founded on a regard for the order of the plan, the idea of the institution, and the enlivening role of ornament. In 1982, the building was opened and received a Royal Australian Institute of Architects (NSW) Merit Award. The scheme was published in 1983, with a generously illustrated essay for the architectural journal *Transition*. The scheme subsequently appeared in *A+U*, *L'Architecture d'Aujourd'hui*, and *International Architect*.[7] The kindergarten demonstrated for the first time that the works of Kahn and Scarpa are relevant to contemporary architecture in Australia.

The Project of the Ana Kindergarten

The Ana Kindergarten in Auburn was part of an initiative of Gough Whitlam's Labor government, which funded kindergartens for several ethnic groups. Auburn at the time had a sizeable Turkish population. The building accommodates forty children, aged between three and five years. The kindergarten was constructed on a street with low-scaled detached houses. A suitable site was chosen: it runs on a west–east axis and comprises two blocks of land.

A single-storey cottage is on the southern one. Korzeniewski and Desney retained this west-facing building, with its width respected in the new structures. The architects integrated the existing house into a scheme that extends towards the eastern boundary of the site.

According to Korzeniewski and Desney's plan, the domestic building that addresses the street is linked to the kindergarten, which is composed of two parts. The back of the house is connected to the first of these, which is a place of invitation to the kindergarten. Its composition involves outer spaces, primarily for services and circulation, surrounding the significant one of an entrance courtyard conceived as an external room. The second part of the kindergarten, which is the main wing for children, continues the theme of peripheral and central spaces. However, the latter are two relatively large settings, each conceived as a top-lit enclosed room. The two new parts of the project conform to a strategy, in which narrow and ample rooms interlock. Further, the kindergarten comprises the impressive courtyard and the two playrooms, which are configured in unique ways to accommodate varied activities.

The Courtyard

As shown in the plan, access from the street to the kindergarten is facilitated by an open space to the north of the existing cottage and the adjacent new wing with the courtyard. Carers and children walk beside the house while looking ahead to a pergola and low fence, as well as to a gate, the slender wrought iron forms of which have the shape of leaves. The adjacent northern grassed area for children to play can therefore be glimpsed. However, before reaching the pergola and the gate, individuals turn to make their way into the courtyard. This is where carers and children part in the morning and meet at the end of the day.

The influence of Kahn and Scarpa on the Ana Kindergarten is introduced by focusing on the external room of the courtyard. Three themes are addressed. The first concerns Kahn's account of served and servant spaces. In the second, his definition of the form of an institution is linked to Korzeniewski and Desney's statements about the idea of the kindergarten. The third pertains to Scarpa's esteem for ornament. By discussing each in relation to the courtyard, a foundation is created for understanding the entire kindergarten, which incorporates the two playrooms and the imposing north front.

Kahn's Distinction between Served and Servant Spaces

The distinction between served and servant spaces in Kahn's architecture contributed to Korzeniewski and Desney's kindergarten, particularly its geometric rigour involving the conjunction of wide and narrow bays. In the first part of the building, the square-planned served space of the courtyard is bounded by the servant ones of a kitchen to the south and covered circulation volumes on the three other sides. Carers and children who have walked by the existing house therefore do not enter the courtyard directly. They can move within the narrow volume located between the back of the house and the courtyard. Having changed direction, individuals descend steps into the external room. Alternatively, they move along an axis that links the two northern spaces to the courtyard. In this instance, people can pause to sit on benches on opposite sides of the setting that is adjacent to the main courtyard. Whether entering the courtyard from its east or north sides, carers and children pass through one or two covered spaces to arrive in the ample room that is open to the sky.

Kahn's Theory of an Institution

The second theme was addressed in Kahn's theoretical statements, including an essay from 1961 titled "Form and Design".[8] He claimed that an architect must fathom the form of the institution, which can be defined in terms of relationships pertaining to individuals and spaces. This ideal remains intact when an architect proceeds to develop a design that responds to particular concerns such as the site, the client's requirements, and the budget. A respect for form, however, sanctions a designer's authority to cast doubt on the brief by addressing overlooked activities and spaces.

Kahn's theory was invoked in Korzeniewski and Desney's statements about the kindergarten. Their text in *Transition* explained that the building's courtyard is "a village square in miniature, where all arrivals, departures and non-exclusive activities occur, maximising social contact".[9] The significance of the master was subsequently conceded by Korzeniewski, who stressed that:

> the idea of what's programmed and what isn't is interesting; because one of the things I still remember Kahn saying was that the architect was not a chemist […] he doesn't get a prescription, fill it out, and here's the product, the solved problem. Kahn said no, that's not it, you've got to question the nature of the institution […] the point was that sometimes an architect would find the necessity for a certain space that was not in the program.[10]

Korzeniewski provided an example:

> [The client] wouldn't think of an entrance lobby as being something that people would gather in and say hello and goodbye […] a sliding door would suffice […] so Kahn put the responsibility on the architect to come up with spatial requirements that would allow the institution to flourish in the best possible way. So a building could prevent that

institution from reaching fulfilment; or it could encourage and allow that institution to reach its flowering.

Kahn's teachings contributed to Korzeniewski and Desney's realisation that the kindergarten should include a courtyard that accommodates several activities, including meeting with staff and a carer saying goodbye to a child. The worthy setting is a suitably scaled and adorned external room.

Scarpa's Integration of Architecture and Ornament

Scarpa's Brion Vega Cemetery was a source of inspiration for the ornament of the kindergarten's courtyard. When visiting the master's recently completed project in 1976, Korzeniewski was impressed by the exterior of the chapel, which is enriched by the connection with water, the detailing of the concrete, and the added ornaments. These qualities were invoked in the kindergarten's initial served room of the courtyard.

Carers and children enter this external room to appreciate its salient element, which Korzeniewski and Desney described as a "little pond" for fish.[11] It is set into the courtyard's northwest corner. Individuals who pass into the courtyard by descending the stairs on the west side look from above into the pond. For those proceeding through the two spaces to the north, the fishpond marks the beginning of the courtyard. When standing within the external space, children are also enchanted by the fall of rainwater into the pool. This water passes through two prominent spouts, which project from the upstands of the trough roofs of the circulation spaces to the west and north of the courtyard.[12] With Scarpa's chapel recalled, Korzeniewski recognised that a child in the kindergarten will delight in the view of fish in the pool, as well as the play of water.

Scarpa was also a guide for additional details animating the courtyard. One of these involves the formwork for each of the concrete cantilevered spouts, which determines its ornamental character. A form shaped as a *cyma reversa* projects from the block. This classical moulding is suited to the nature of a spout because, unlike a bracket, it does not support a load from above. The spout also has a coloured ceramic tile set into its outer face. In a second enrichment to the courtyard, the significance of the pool is conveyed by the detailing of its concrete walls. Scarpa's chapel of the Brion Vega Cemetery was recalled in the construction of the kindergarten's fishpond, where the plywood sheet formwork generated its rough texture and accentuated horizontal lines. The Italian master's regard for the integration of architecture and ornament also contributed to the courtyard. While working on the site, Korzeniewski adorned the fishpond's north side with a bas relief ornament in cement of a fish. The courtyard is further enlivened by the brick wall of the kitchen, which includes another bas relief ornament, in this case of flowers.

The kindergarten's entrance courtyard was enriched by themes that remain pertinent to the wider composition. Kahn's distinction between served and servant spaces contributes to an interpretation of Korzeniewski and Desney's building, which emphasises the significant square-planned volumes, as well as the subordinate concrete roofed ones that are primarily for circulation. Kahn's account of the form of an institution is then considered in relation to the kindergarten's two playrooms. Scarpa's lessons are related to the building's richly adorned north front.

The Playrooms

With Kahn's concept of served and servant spaces endorsed in Korzeniewski and Desney's design for the kindergarten, children move through rigorously connected volumes. Having left the served room of the entrance courtyard, they proceed into the circulation space on its east side. Children continue to the north before turning once more, in this case to pass into the second and main part of the kindergarten. The transition is marked by an iron gate that opens on to the colonnade, which is the longest of the building's servant spaces. This provides protection from the summer sun. Moreover, the north side of the colonnade is defined by stocky paired columns that determine the human scale and rhythmic order of the space, while offering views of the garden. The middle of the colonnade is marked by a connection with another circulation volume, which incorporates a porch opening onto the garden and a gallery extending to the back of the building. Spaces running along the south side accommodate toilets and storerooms. However, children initially move from the colonnade into the servant space of the gallery to pass through doors on both sides that open onto the served spaces of the luminous top-lit playrooms.

Kahn's account of the form of an institution was invoked in Korzeniewski and Desney's discussion of the kindergarten, which accentuates a child's delight in the varied qualities of the two playrooms. The architects introduced their theory by referring to "a diversity of [...] places – each providing different experiences".[13] This entailed a critique of dominant themes in current practice: "To the 'open' plan we propose an alternative: distinct interiors related to gardens by means of porches, galleries or colonnades. To the proposition of stringing uses along a circulation system we propose an alternative: the gathering of rooms around gardens, courts or squares, defined places for which 'uses' can only be partially listed but never exhausted".[14] The kindergarten's internal and external spaces "would stimulate and sustain the natural curiosity of the child".[15] The theory was especially relevant to the inimitable and complementary natures of the two playrooms. With Kahn as a guide, Korzeniewski and Desney encapsulated their theory by noting: "Our decision to explore the theme of two [...] rooms of differing characters was the major architectural idea of the project".[16]

These interiors have particular spatial qualities that are not tied to functions. The architects distinguished between the playrooms opening from the west and east sides of the gallery, when noting: "One room is made predominantly of linear elements, the other of planar elements".[17] While each interior has small clerestory windows cut into the brick walls, its quality of light stems from the higher source of a lantern, which is integral to the timber forms deployed to support or construct the roof. A comparative analysis of the playrooms involves their central apertures and timber forms.

The Western Playroom: Structure and Bright Light

Korzeniewski and Desney explained that the western playroom "has a central timber structure, which in part rises through the roof to make a lantern".[18] A person appreciates the high openings because their light fills the interior. The composition is enriched by the timber forms, which frame intimate settings for play. One such space is at floor level, while another is raised above like a tree house.

The principle of structural rationalism offers insight into Korzeniewski and Desney's design for the western playroom, where timber forms are embellished and add to the quality of light. Rationalism informed the works of Eugène Emmanuel Viollet-le-Duc, as well as Kahn and Scarpa.[19] For Viollet-le-Duc, the logic of a Gothic or nineteenth century building is enhanced by diagonal forms transmitting forces to the ground. A related theme is the connection between structure and ornament. This was addressed in Kahn's poem from 1974 about Scarpa's work, in which the final two lines refer to the joint as the foundation for embellishment. The influence of structural rationalism is evident in the timber motif's vertical and diagonal members, which are slender yet resist the forces from the pyramidal roof and the lantern. The connections between the timber forms are celebrated through imposing brackets, conceived as ornaments that explain the workings of the structural system. Moreover, the principle of structural rationalism was critical to the luminosity of the playroom. This involved the logic of the timber elements, which are thin and therefore support the lantern without obstructing and diffusing its light. The room is therefore brightly lit.

The Eastern Playroom: Planar Surfaces and Diffused Light

Two themes in Kahn's work informed the design of the kindergarten's eastern playroom; rooms within a room and an interior's structure revealing light. The master's concern for interconnected rooms was relevant to Korzeniewski and Desney's account of the interior's "four corner alcoves", which are composed of brick piers and their concrete roofs.[20] These peripheral rooms are located within the encompassing room. Kahn's fascination with interplay between light and matter underpinned Korzeniewski and Desney's statement that the playroom's "brick piers support an ascending plywood structure which carries the central lantern".[21] Light within the playroom is not strident but is softened by contact with the forms of the roof.

Kahn's Bath House introduced the theme of interconnected rooms.[22] His overall building comprises four rooms, two of which are entirely enclosed because they accommodate bathers, who change into swimming attire before entering the pool. In each changing room, concrete blocks are deployed to construct the walls, as well as corner hollow columns that support a timber pyramidal roof. The columns are small-scaled habitable rooms with concrete roofs. A changing room is distinguished by robust walls and hollow columns, as well as a light timber canopy with a square oculus. The roof's structural members are configured as intersecting squares.

A changing room within the Bath House contributed to Korzeniewski and Desney's design for the kindergarten. Kahn's hollow columns were adapted for the eastern playroom, where brick alcoves with concrete roofs are conducive for varied activities, including a teacher interacting with a small group of children. Moreover, these four rooms are set into the larger room with its timber roof. The canopy is not heavy because it is constructed with timber forms, arrayed according to the geometric theme of rotated squares.

Yet Kahn's Phillips Exeter Academy Library (Exeter, New Hampshire, 1966–72), rather than the Bath House, was invoked in the diffused light of the eastern playroom.[23] The central hall of the library is enriched by light from its clerestories, which is revealed by the concrete cross that supports the roof. This link between light and structure influenced Korzeniewski and Desney's design for the kindergarten. The playroom's lantern admits light that falls onto the canopy's deep vertical planes made of plywood. The structural forms thereby assume the role of illuminating the interior. This room is a vessel of diffused light. The light is not strident but has assumed a textural character.

Kahn's theory of form was reconsidered when Korzeniewski and Desney referred to the idea of the kindergarten. They stated that the "various rooms with their different characters will suggest activities appropriate to them. Some activities will be better in one room than another".[24] This is especially relevant to both playrooms. The circulation space between them is significant because it is low and dim and therefore adds to a child's perception of the impressive scale of each top-lit interior. The distinction between the two playrooms stems from the architects' interpretations of structure and light. In the western room, light from the lantern is not subdued by contact with the linear elements of the tectonic motif. This interior therefore contains intense light. When walking back to the gallery and then into the eastern playroom, a child experiences a different but equally imposing interior. It is enriched by peripheral rooms within the overall room. Moreover, light from the lantern is moderated by striking the forms of the canopy.

A child may therefore move between the playrooms, to appreciate particular kinds of spaces that intimate varied activities.

The North Front: Formality and Ornament

Schemes by Kahn and Scarpa were relevant to Korzeniewski and Desney's design for the kindergarten's north front, which serves as an appropriate backdrop for dignified events and everyday activities. Special occasions included the opening of the kindergarten in 1982. The esteemed Labor politician, Tom Uren, stood within the porch to deliver the speech. His height demonstrated that the north front is scaled for children, not adults. Nonetheless, the brick piers and the concrete forms of the porch created an imposing frame for the ceremony. In everyday terms, the playground is for children, who are impressed by the north front of the kindergarten. The composition is imposing and ordered but not overbearing because it is enlivened by ornament.

According to Korzeniewski and Desney's composition, a child walks from a playroom into the gallery, proceeding within this circulation space towards the north. He or she pauses at a privileged place in the building, which the architects identified by noting that the gallery "becomes a porch facing the garden".[25] The child proceeds down steps to reach this enclosed communal space. The north side is articulated by the long front of the kindergarten, which is augmented by the colonnade with its small-scaled coupled columns, as well as the centrally located porch.

Kahn's concern for the relationship between the exterior and the interior of an edifice was relevant to Korzeniewski and Desney's design of the kindergarten's north front. The master explored alternatives to a theme in modern architecture, where the glazed walls link the exterior and the interior. By focusing instead on the traditional themes of the monumentality and order of a building, Kahn's projects demonstrated that an exterior can mask or allude to an interior comprised of discrete rooms. With this endorsed in the design for the kindergarten, Korzeniewski and Desney stressed "the robust appearance of the exterior, which [contrasts] with the relatively delicate interior".[26] Moreover, the two unique playrooms are "free to rise up and gain light from over the roofs of the servant spaces".[27] Because the differences between these playrooms are largely concealed, a beholder appreciates the monumentality of the building's garden front, which derives from the disposition of the colonnade and the porch, as well as the two large rooms that are characterised by their pyramidal roofs and lanterns. Kahn's understanding of a building's exterior and interior was pertinent to the design for the kindergarten, which is distinguished by the formality of the main front.

With Scarpa's buildings also recalled by Korzeniewski and Desney, the scheme for the kindergarten is enhanced by ornament. The Italian architect's influence was critical to the north front's colonnade and porch. As seen from the garden, the building is animated by the detailing of concrete forms, the inclusion of decorative tiles, and the shapes of the brick piers.

The chapel of Scarpa's Brion Vega Cemetery, where shadows are an attribute of the concrete forms, was a source for the kindergarten's upstands of the roof slabs. These forms cover the circulation spaces, including those surrounding the courtyard. The same roof is deployed for the long colonnade and the gallery, as well as the porch. Korzeniewski noted that, "the builder made the formwork out of plywood but I came in afterwards and built in all the mouldings".[28] These included a scotia. When the formwork was removed, the convex shape of the scotia produced the quarter round that runs along the bottom edges of each upstand of a roof segment. This is evident in the roofs of the colonnade and the porch. The latter's concrete form is more imposing, as it is wider and incorporates a centrally located recessed strip. Korzeniewski explained that the curves and indentations in the concrete forms add to the "play of light and shade".[29] For him, "the sharp crisp edges and shadow lines [...] give the concrete a precision and delicacy otherwise lacking".[30]

The influence of Scarpa can also be discerned in the polychromatic tiles, which are bedded into the concrete and brick forms of the colonnade and porch. While the projects by the Italian master are all enriched by elaborate details, Korzeniewski especially valued the chapel of the Brion Vega Cemetery. Its concrete forms are adorned with small rectangular ornaments, one of which is positioned above the door approached directly from the street entrance. This motif, which is a bas relief highlighted with gold leaf, was recalled when Korzeniewski worked on the main front of the kindergarten. He set tiles into the upstands of the concrete roof of the colonnade. The building has a columnar order, which is established by the even rhythm set out by paired pillars and tiles located directly above, in the roof. The height of this roof determines the location of the lintel belonging to the porch. This concrete form is adorned with two tiles, positioned at the edges.

Scarpa's work contributed to the kindergarten's brick forms. This is evident on the north front, where tiles are placed in the bases of the piers. Moreover, shaped bricks are used for these bases, as well as the capitals above. Various kinds of bricks are also deployed to construct the sills of the building and the capping of its walls. Korzeniewski stressed that "lessons from Scarpa [were vital to] the kindergarten, particularly the detailing of the concrete and brick forms, as well as the inclusion of tiles".[31] Korzeniewski conceded, "If I'd never seen Scarpa I'd never have thought of any of this".[32]

Korzeniewski and Desney's Ana Kindergarten contributes to an understanding of postmodern architecture during the late 1970s and 1980s, specifically a triangulation between the United States, Italy and Australia. Having graduated from the University of Sydney, Korzeniewski was dismayed by the current state of architecture in Australia and particularly technocratic planning techniques in which various spaces, each with a particular use, are placed along a circulation system, indifferent to the cultural role of architecture and the social institutions that it houses. In the first of two life-changing encounters, he participated in Kahn's studio at the University of Pennsylvania. The second significant experience involved working with Scarpa in Vicenza. These aspects of Korzeniewski's early career provided a foundation for his designs, which prioritised the room as a spatial and social setting that could interpret the institution, and celebrated spatial and constructional articulation with ornament. With qualities of buildings by two of the most significant masters of the twentieth century amalgamated in Korzeniewski and Desney's work, their Ana Kindergarten is characterised by the attributes of compositional rigour, clarity of structure, and enlivening ornament.

1
Swetik collaborated on several projects with Paul Desney, a fellow student at both Sydney University and Harrington Street studio. They gained local and international recognition.

2
Arthur Baldwinson (1908–69) was one of the first Australian modernist architects to bring his European professional experience into his local designs. From 1953, Baldwinson was senior lecturer in town and country planning at the University of Sydney.

3
See Robert Venturi, *Complexity and Contradiction in Architecture*, New York: The Museum of Modern Art, 1966; Swetik Korzenwieski in discussion with the author and Mark Stiles, Ultimo, Sydney, January 2015.

4
Swetik Korzenwieski in discussion with the author and Mark Stiles.

5
For Kahn's Venice project, see Elice Vider, "Palazzo dei Congressi" in David Brownlee and David De Long, *Louis I. Kahn: In the Realm of Architecture*, New York: Rizzoli, 1991, 404–409.

6
Robert McCarter, *Carlo Scarpa*, London: Phaidon, 2013, 272.

7
See Richard Munday, "New Work Review: Kindergarten at Auburn by Swetik Korzeniewski," *Transition* 3, 2 (February 1983), 37–40; Richard Munday "Ana Kindergarten, Swetik Korzeniewski and Paul Desney," *Architecture and Urbanism* 158 (November 1983), 91–95; Richard Munday, "Korzeniewski and Desney, Kindergarten, Sydney, NSW (1982)," *International Architect* 4 (October 1984), 48–49; and Rory Spence, "Korzenwieski and Desney. Kindergarten, Sydney," *Architectural Review* 1066 (December 1985), 52–53.

8
See Louis Kahn, "Form and Design" in *Louis Kahn: Essential Texts*, ed. Robert C. Twombly. New York and London: W.W. Norton, 2003, 62–74.

9
Swetik Korzeniewski and Paul Desney, *Transition* 3: 2 (1983).

10
Swetik Korzenwieski in discussion with the author and Mark Stiles.

11
Korzeniewski and Desney, *Transition* 3: 2 (1983).

12
This type of construction is called a concrete slab with an upstand. The upstands around the slab form a trough, which catches the water. The slabs fall slightly toward the end, where spouts are located.

13
See Swetik Korzenwieski and Paul Desney's theoretical statement in Munday, "New Work Review" *Transition* 3, 2 (February 1983), 38.

14
Ibid., 39.

15
Ibid.

16
Ibid.

17
Ibid.

18
Ibid., 38.

19
For rationalism in twentieth-century architecture, see Kenneth Frampton, *Studies in tectonic culture: The poetics of construction in nineteenth and twentieth century architecture*, Cambridge, Massachusetts, and London: MIT Press, 1995.

20
Munday, "New Work Review".

21
Ibid.

22
For the Bath House, see Susan Solomon, "Jewish Community Center" in David Brownlee and David De Long, *Louis I Kahn: in the Realm of Architecture*, New York: Rizzoli, 1991, 318–323.

23
For Exeter Library, see Peter Kohane, "Library and Dining Hall, Phillips Exeter Academy" in David Brownlee and David De Long, *Louis I Kahn: in the Realm of Architecture*, New York: Rizzoli, 1991, 390–396.

24
Munday, "New Work Review".

25
Ibid., 39.

26
Frampton, *Studies in tectonic culture*.

27
Munday, "New Work Review", 38.

28
Swetik Korzenwieski in conversation with the author and Mark Stiles.

29
Munday, "New Work Review: Kindergarten".

30
Ibid.

31
Swetik Korzenwieski in discussion with the author and Mark Stiles.

32
Ibid.

Romaldo Giurgola:
From America with Po-Mo

Gevork Hartoonian

The modern/postmodern debate, so clarifying and important in the 1970s and 1980s, has been undone in part by the success of the postmodernist critique.[1] — Jacques Rancière

I

The commissioning of Italo-American architect Romaldo Giurgola to design the Parliament House of the Australian Commonwealth links Australian architectural history into the main international debates of the time, driven by the American reception of Italian thought and the concept of the post-modern. To begin considering this link, I will start with two proclamations. First, that the transaction between Italian architecture and Australian architecture should be plotted from a critical perspective, the index of which is centred on the dialectics between modernity and capitalism. Second, that any discussion concerning external influences on Australian architecture is a matter of history, even though the investigation of the subject could shed a new light on the historicity of Australian architecture. I say this because the globalisation of capital and information, the global commodification of cultural products (including architecture), and, most importantly, the prevailing state of digital reproducibility have accelerated the temporal experience of space beyond that with which Modernism was identified. As a result of this unfolding, Modernism seems to us as antiquity did to the moderns.[2] The historical development briefly plotted here allowed Fredric Jameson to formulate postmodernism as the cultural logic of late capitalism.[3] Jameson does not discuss postmodern architecture as a style issue but rather maps postmodernism in the dialectics of the Real and history. Nevertheless, the attention he gives to the spatial, compositional, and, most importantly, aesthetic aspects of postmodernism should be historicised in the context of architectural historiography. This means that, their origins now disregarded, all past architectural languages, including modern architecture itself, operate today like weightless particles floating in the imagination of architects and in the virtual space of networks.

That modernity was bound to particular historical conditions unravelling in Europe in the late eighteenth century is obvious. What needs to be reiterated here is that beside geographic proximity, the driving force of modernity in different countries was the appropriation of technology as an absolute reflection of the zeitgeist. If technical innovations lent new tools and objects, time remained the spectre of modernity to be captured and sublated in art and architecture. This much is evident from the work produced by Italian futurists and Russian constructivists and in various interpretations of the *Neue Sachlichkeit* [New Objectivity], let alone the British rear-guard assimilation of modernity through the hegemonic discourse of the arts and crafts movement. Unfolding these issues goes beyond the objectives of this essay. Yet it is useful to say that the Deutscher Werkbund debate had critical implications for the move from *Sachlich* [realistic/objective] to *Neue Sachlichkeit*, a transformation through which architecture lost something analogous to the aura that permeated early photography.[4] According to Walter Benjamin, because of longer exposure to natural light, the face of a person captured in early photographs possessed a halo that disappeared as technical innovation shortened the time exposure of the camera.[5] A similar comparison can be made between the cool and attractive images of contemporary, digitally reproduced architecture and the look of early modern architecture. For example, once the harbinger of the modernist obsession with the new, Villa Savoye today looks like an innocent object compared to the spectacular look of contemporary architecture.

This brief and comparative analysis of various manifestations of objectivity aims to posit two things. Firstly, that the temporal distance of postmodernism from early modern architecture did not give rise to an auratic mystification of the modern. This demonstrates that modernity is an ongoing historical process as capitalism tries to sustain its hegemonic position. Secondly, given this paradoxical temporality, the prefix 'post' is the site of major issues about postmodernism. The implied temporal break, lying over substantive continuity as it does, offers a useful paradigm to assess external influences on Australian architectural praxis. Significant here is the American postmodernism identified with the work of the 'Greys', an architectural group originally comprised of Louis Kahn, Robert Venturi, and Romaldo Giurgola. Associated with the University of Pennsylvania in the late 1950s, these three architects, together with Robert Geddes and George Qualls, were dubbed the "Philadelphia School" by Jan C. Rowan, the editor of *Progressive Architecture*, in 1961.[6] Diverse in their practice, what brought these architects together as a 'school' was their aspiration to reiterate American architectural traditions, "exploring them with innovative élan".[7] Manfredo Tafuri is more precise as far as the architectural ideology of the Greys is concerned. In his seminal essay "The Ashes of Jefferson", he wrote: "Both the Whites and the Greys attempt to come to grips with an intentionally paradoxical assumption: for both camps, the theme of 'resemanticisation' is central; only the instruments employed to reach such an objective vary".[8] Interestingly enough, Kahn and Venturi were both exposed to Italian architecture and had written about or incorporated aspects of it in their praxis, Giurgola included. Harry Francis Mallgrave reminds us that a 1953 publication by Venturi was a short excerpt on "Campidoglio, the Roman senatorial complex recast into a mannerist vocabulary by Michelangelo".[9] However, as we will see shortly, each of these three architects used the mannerist tools popular among postmodernists for different ends.

II

Among the protagonists of the 'Philadelphia School', Giurgola is particularly relevant to the objectives of this essay, not only because he was born and received his architectural education in Rome, but also because of his timely mediation between postmodern simulation of historical forms and his love affair with and recollection of architectural principles of fifteenth-century Rome, in particular its unique use of the element of wall and geometry. In the limited historicist atmosphere energised by the architects associated with the Greys, Giurgola felt at home, to say the least. Caught between Venturi's mannerist and Kahn's neo-rationalist interpretations of the both-and design strategy, Giurgola felt closer to Kahn, even though most of his American work does not subscribe to Kahn's notion of monumentality, which is purchased at the expense of the extensive use of the element of wall and a vigorous appropriation of geometry. Paradoxically, however, most of Giurgola's later work, produced on both sides of the Atlantic, does subscribe to the aesthetic of the 'ordinary' as formulated by Venturi. That said, I should add that Giurgola faced new challenges in Australia, where the intensity of architectural debates was subdued, and the nation's capital Canberra, where Giurgola was principal architect for the New Parliament House (1979–88), did not offer the level of historical and formal complexity of Rome or even Philadelphia, the city where his best built-work is located.

Most famous architects in post-war America were, in one way or another, exposed to the theoretical debates taking place at schools of architecture, and Giurgola was no exception. Having a close rapport with Kahn, and teaching at both the University of Pennsylvania (1954–1967) and Columbia University (1967–1991), Giurgola's discourse was influenced by the turn to phenomenology and the general implications of Rudolf Wittkower's *Architectural Principles in the Age of Humanism* (1949).[10] In her review of Wittkower's book, Alina Payne wrote "the argument presented here proposes a deeper cultural continuity between the discourse of modernist architecture in the 1940s and 1950s and the readings of history that were conceived at the same time".[11] In retrospect, we can say that Wittkower's discourse precipitated the esteem for 'continuity', framed either in terms of formal compositions or the phenomenological universalisation of the experience of the body, which had particular influence on the architectural praxis of the post-war era.

The notion of continuity, however, was challenged by the relativistic understanding of the relationship between sign and signifier advocated by the linguistic theories of the time. On the other hand, facing the eclipse of the political project of modernity, 'geometric games' were now being played using the theoretical tools laid out by phenomenology, semiology, and the humanist worldview of the return of the same. These developments found their ways into architectural theories under the rubric of 'fragment' and 'partial vision'. We will examine the implications of these two concepts in the work of Giurgola shortly. For now, it is important to recall what Manfredo Tafuri had to say about these theoretical turns that marked the period from

1951 to 1967. Reflecting on the competition entries for the offices of the Chamber of Deputies in Rome (1967), Tafuri wrote that, in the "whirl of formal ideas emerging from the many projects submitted to the competition, it became evident that the lessons of Louis Kahn, Giurgola and Paul Rudolph had been assimilated".[12] He continued, "if nothing else, Italian architectural culture was now more astute and more enlightened on the formal level".[13] Even though Giurgola never formulated his work strictly in these terms, he remained sympathetic to Kahn's notion of 'room' as the sole compositional element, whatever the scale of the given project. Interestingly enough, in an article written in 1967, Denise Scott Brown wrote that the present debate on architectural theory provides critical reflections of the work and ideas of Giurgola. Dubbing the Italian architect a follower of Kahn, Scott Brown highlighted the pragmatic dimension of Giurgola's own theoretical writings, in particular the concept of 'partial vision'. According to her, Giurgola's buildings do not necessarily follow his own advice, particularly the smaller projects that "may be too frail to take the weight of so much philosophy".[14] For Giurgola, instead, the architect has limited knowledge of the abstract world and should therefore design based on what he or she can know of a given situation with measurable dimensions and an understandable context. As Giurgola noted, a partial vision, speaking in phenomenological terms, "is sensitive to movements, orientations, directions, light, colour, recollections and symbols—in a word to all phenomena that are the expressions of life".[15]

Considering the fact that Kahn's early work followed a fairly orthodox version of the international style architecture and that his work changed considerably after his return to the USA from Italy—where he was an architect in residence at the American Academy in Rome in 1950—it can be inferred that Giurgola's interest in Kahn was based on a mutual comprehension of the principles of Roman architecture, in particular the singular geometric role of 'room' and the form-giving potentialities of the element of wall. What does play out in Kahn's formal and surface research, wrote Aldo Rossi, is Roman-ness as a "model" for "half stylistic and half functional elements".[16] Therefore, as far as the notion of 'influence' is concerned, Tafuri's assessment of late 1950s Italian architecture should be understood dialectically; meaning that the influences of Roman architecture on both Kahn and Giurgola were later returned to Italy after being decoded in the context of post-war America and the formal games established by postmodernism. In the third part of this essay, I posit that the absence of a dialectical understanding of Italian influences in Australian architecture might indeed exemplify the singularity of Australian architecture within a *longue durée* understanding of the historiography of Modernism.

Even though there are similarities between Kahn's and Giurgola's architecture at a compositional level, the Italian architect never became fixated on 'repetition' of the kind evident in Kahn's and Mies van der

Rohe's later work. While Giurgola did subscribe to Kahn's dictum of form and order, most of his work avoids uniformity achieved through repetition. Instead, he gives priority to site and the demands of the program. Giurgola wrote:

> Order must not be confused with theory elaboration and its consequence: visual formalism. Order comes, rather, from a realistic apprehension of the facts that make the city—facts that extend from the historical experiences of human events to the functional logic of its structures.[17]

There is a sense of pragmatism implicit in the way Giurgola formulates his design strategy. In an essay for Mitchell/Giurgola Architects' 1983 monograph, Giurgola underlined four 'constants' central to a comprehensive understanding of his work. These are: (1) the definition of a place through a sequence of rooms as constituent parts; (2) the language of space understood as an internal or external definition in the formulation of an itinerary; (3) resonance as an essential quality of architecture; and, finally, (4) the development of an architectural aesthetic based on a building's accessibility, clarity, and power to elucidate its meaning and relationships.[18] However, the architect's use of architectonic elements from the past and recent past, including those of Modernism, demonstrates, according to Paul Goldberger, the "firm's flexibility and pragmatism, as well as their postmodern approach".[19] An extreme example of eclecticism is evident in the Kasperson Residence Conestoga Pennsylvania, where the external volume is a pastiche of two fragments: one piece is finished with white cladding that looks decidedly 'modern', while the other uses traditional domestic materials and architectonic elements popular in American shingle-style houses such as clapboard siding and a brick hearth and chimney.

The use of pastiche as a design strategy attains a high level of sophistication in the Penn Mutual Tower (1975), an addition to a neoclassical building dating from 1913. Finely embellished with an exposed concrete structure and glass, the twelve-storey tower is charged with the scale of the street-level pedestrian by incorporating part of the façade of the old building into its frontal façade. Of the challenges architects faced during the postmodernist turn to humanism, Giurgola noted "our challenges are much vaster, much more comprehensive how we humanize what the environment is in terms of both the city and the country, how we make the scale at which man is participant and an indispensible but not the dominating element".[20] He continued that, even in the Parliament House, "I tried desperately not to fall into the trap of making a glorious building".[21] Detached from the body of the office tower, the marble wall of the Mutual Tower, with its revivalist surface articulations and openings, serves "as a screen or an art object rather than deceptively historic front to a modern building".[22] In this particular project, the wall reverses the Albertian dictum that the column is an ornament to the wall. The idea of wall freed from its historical rapport with the column alludes to Giurgola's fascination with Baroque architecture, which became a strong form-giving but also expressionistic element throughout his major work carried out both in the United States and in Australia.

Consider the addition to St Patrick's Cathedral (1996–2003) in Parramatta, New South Wales, a project that provided Giurgola with an opportunity to conjugate the two ideas of wall as an ornament and 'realism'. Out of the intellectual milieu of the United States in the late 1960s, realism was now reproached as a strategy to finalise the design process pragmatically and in collaboration with the client, the engineers, and the artists. This much is evident in the main gathering space of the building: a rectangular space enclosed with two parallel white-plastered walls directing the spectator's attention to a third wall, the alter wall, panelled in Tasmanian timber from inside. Clad in copper from outside, this third and seemingly freestanding wall with its theatrical figuration—perhaps symbolically in reference to the wings of an angel—recalls the undulating entry façade of Saint Carlo in Rome, itself a Borrominian bricolage. However, built in a steel frame structure and clad in polished precast concrete panels from outside, Giurgola's design looks, from both inside and outside, as if it is held together by three walls. Significant to this tectonic figuration is the interior space, where the aforementioned two walls are horizontally extended and punctuated by load-bearing piers with concealed steel columns that support the beams and are all painted in white again.

Two additional traditions inform Giurgola's design in St Patrick's Cathedral: the building's three independent walls are a reminder of Adolf Loos' suggestion that the first task of the architect is to erect four carpets and the second task is to think how to hold up the four carpets. Giurgola recodes the Loosian axiom in reference to Frank L. Wright's notion of 'breaking the box', though interpreted in reference to the two aforementioned theoretical unfoldings of post-war American architecture, the fragment and the partial vision. Facing the situation caused by the incompleteness of the project of modernity and the structuralist association between meaning and its referent, Giurgola chose to use the element of wall to deconstruct and animate the platonic geometry of the square, at least in the planimetric organisation of a number of his successful projects.

The implied square shape geometry of the plan of the residence for Mr and Mrs Otto Patazau (1963), for example, is intruded upon by a diagonal wall that, interestingly enough, ends in re-emphasising the square as the principal form-giving element of the plan. This extrusion can also be pursued in Giurgola's idea of partial view, which can be seen here in reference to the fragment of a pre-existing complete geometry, the square. Giurgola's formal play takes on added significance when one considers the central square space of the house, which is surrounded by various rooms, a reminder of Kahn's design in Goldenberg House (1959), Pennsylvania, USA. The difference between these two designs, as far as the use of the diagonal and the central room is concerned, is Kahn's strict play of geometrical game and monumentality, which contrasts with Giurgola's use of the diagonal to open and orient the design towards the landscape and natural light. Similar observations about the animation induced by the diagonal wall and the strategy of surrounding a centralised space with several rooms can also be made about Giurgola's Newman Residence (1979), Bedford, New York, and Kahn's Jewish Bath House, New Jersey, USA.

Instead, I would like to focus on another work by Giurgola, the Administration Building at the Academy of the New Church, Pennsylvania (1963), the plan of which not only emulates the notion of 'partial view' but also closely follows Kahn's Goldenberg House, mentioned earlier. Here, too, the spatial organisation of both designs is centred on the horizontal and vertical axis of an implied square. A central room, typical of Palladian villa typology, dominates both designs. As for the diagonal, the difference between the two buildings is suggestive of two different philosophical approaches to design. Whereas in both cases the inclusion (intrusion?) of diagonal walls animates the design, in Giurgola's plan, the diagonal wall opens the design into the landscape while retaining the classical notion of frontality, a theme that did not seem to interest Kahn, at least not in the Goldenberg House. To complete this list of geometrical permutations, I must bring to my reader's attention Giurgola's design for the Acadia National Park Headquarters (1965), Maine. Here, by converting the triangular profile of the section into a plan, a Corbusian technique, Giurgola reiterates the notion of fragment, the geometric strength of which is sustained by a circular shaped metal screen, placed where the axes of the triangle meet each other. Furthermore, the slant roof of the building is extended to meet the ground in a highly-detailed manner, providing natural light for the rooms located on the lower floor. This esteem for making the building part of the landscape is what Giurgola learned during his visit to Gunnar Asplund's house, where the wooden floor extends the interior spaces to "the paths outside, towards a distant meadow, meeting with the intense blue of the sea".[23] To create continuity between the roof and the landscape, the design tries to decode the idea of fragment as a disenchanted object torn between "the wish to adhere with enthusiasm to the multiple pressures of urban reality and, at the same time, to introduce in it architectural events and fragments which might force the entire meaning of that reality".[24] In retrospect, Giurgola's use of strategies such as fragment and partial view were aimed at distancing his work from Kahn's notion of monumentality and from Venturi's idea of the 'ordinary'.

In one of his famous articles published in *Perspecta* in 1965, Giurgola underlines the importance of architecture's rapport with landscape in terms of the nature of space in Renaissance and Baroque architecture. He wrote: "Responding to this mutual space relationship, the interior spaces of the Baroque organism are extended outside, to make from that released energy the piazzas, streets, and gardens".[25] This understanding of the Baroque sense of spatiality put next to the geometric interplay between circle and square noted earlier are the principles followed to the highest degree in Australian Parliament House (A.P.H., 1979–88) in Canberra. Noteworthy is the expressive and organisational role of the wall and the way it integrates the design with the adjacent streets and the fabric of Canberra beyond.

But first, and to further underline the Italian influences on Giurgola's mature work, we should recall the centrality of classical typologies in the design of A.P.H., which, according to Kenneth Frampton, appear in a "reduced trabeated manner with strong affinities for the Italian Tendenza".[26] And second, following James Ackerman's brilliant reading of Michelangelo's work, I would like to highlight the change in the perception of wall induced by the Baroque perception of space, structure, and form. Discussing Bramante's design for St. Peter's, Ackerman acknowledges the architect's "handling of the wall as a malleable body" inspired by Roman architecture, especially the great baths, the form of which "could not be revived without the technique that made it possible".[27] He continues, the "structural basis of the baths was brick-faced concrete, the most plastic material available to builders".[28] There is no need to remind the reader here of the centrality of the concrete structural frame or brick-clad wall to the aesthetics of the best work produced by Kahn and Giurgola. Related to my discussion here, however, are corollaries that Ackerman establishes between space and time in reference to Renaissance and modern architecture. To achieve equilibrium between space and expression without debunking the space and structure rapport, Baroque architecture departed from "the fifteenth-century concept of the wall as a plane, because the goal of the architect is no longer to produce an abstract harmony but rather a sequence of purely visual (as opposed to intellectual) experiences of spatial volumes".[29] A similar persuasion of visual effect (theatricalisation) is evident from the free-standing undulating walls of the A.P.H., the main purpose of which is to energise a design otherwise fixated on a square centred in a circle (a Vitruvian compositional order). The wall here tries to define a territory that had yet to decide between the politics of modern secularism and the spiritual, not only in reference to the traditions of humanism but, more importantly, in reference to the native residents of Australia. The historicity of this contradiction, if you wish, is subdued by the wall's overwhelming presence, seen from four corners as well as from the bird's eye view of the complex. In addition to their formal allusion to the colonnade of St. Peter's, the position of the two walls in Giurgola's design frames a horizontal axis, the vista of which aligns the citadel with the old Parliament House, the War Memorial Building, and then Mount Ainslie. Thus, the primary task of the design, the architect wrote, "has been the search for a relationship of balance and reciprocity between imposition of government and the natural state from which government evolves".[30] Furthermore, the dichotomy between secularisation and the mystics of nature is not the design's main paradox. There is also paradox in the way the design intentionally projects a totality out of a number of ideologically charged sequential 'places', as noted above, and in the architect's discourse on fragments and partial vision. To this end, it is worthwhile to recall Giurgola's biographic recollections, one of his best poetic moments. In a text entitled "The Producing Moment", he wrote:

> The anxiety of reading about ourselves, reading Kierkegaard, Heidegger, Sartre became part of the magic, and of my maturity. We learned to look at the action and the existence of our city as we learned about the tormented Rome of all times, the interrupted events, the unfinished buildings, the ruins, the fragments with new eyes. There was the talk of an imperial Rome. But where? My Rome was all pieces and fragments, beautiful that way. And nothing else could express its life, as I was coming to share that life, nothing else but architecture.[31]

Therefore, Giurgola used the design of A.P.H. to re-energise the pleasure of life and architecture in reference to the notion of an 'incomplete Rome', and the ways that architecture might substitute the desire for a lost dream. Clearly, wrote Frampton, "Griffin's proposal for crowning the hill with Humanist dome has been deliberately abandoned here in favour of dematerialised superstructure".[32] In the A.P.H., war, death and sacrifice are celebrated in an ahistorical understanding of the ethos of the nation-state at a historical juncture when Modernism was taken over by late capitalism and a path was opened for the wall-to-wall dissemination of the post-war mass culture. This much is clear from the mast placed at the centre of the A.P.H. complex; it holds up the country's flag high enough to be seen from the four corners of the city, a populist sign reminiscent of Venturi's use of the same rhetorical language in his design for the Civic Center, Thousand Oaks, California (1969).

III

The above pages were written to underline the significance of Kahn, Venturi, and Giurgola for any scholarly investigation of post-war American architecture and for the reception of postmodernism in Australia. More than any contemporary historian, Tafuri has made critical remarks on the work of these architects, assessing the American contribution to the formation of post-war architecture in conjunction with the debates and the work produced in Italy. This might be music to ears familiar with the work of Tafuri. However, after the rise of postmodernism, any discussion concerning the theme of influence must be gauged in reference to themes that ideologically underpin the formation of individuals as both subjects and objects of an era of capitalism, the presence of which is felt, not in factories alone, but everywhere, in the city, in the street, and in the room, a compositional tool dear to Kahn and Giurgola.[33]

Sympathetic to the dissemination of various discourses of post-war 'realism', a victorious America turned its attention instead to converting military industries into a means for re-producing a culture, the various consumer brands of which would soon initiate a sense of 'identity' even before its products had reached beyond American borders. The realism of American mass-culture obviously differed from the Italian post-war movement of *realismo*.[34] It also differed from the British post-war new-empiricism. I have no intention of exploring this subject in relation to the three mentioned countries, each of which had distinctive contributions to the formation of post-war architecture. Instead, what I want to pursue here is the way realism was appropriated by Giurgola. This raises questions concerning architecture's relation to the Real, the symbolized given wherein architects/artists produce meaningful work if only to "legitimize the dominant political power".[35] Consider Venturi's famous book, *Complexity and Contradiction in Architecture* (1966). Drawing on the traditions of art history, Venturi theorised architecture as a continuum of the received traditions of Modernism and the disciplinary history of architecture, which together (contradiction) had to express the actuality of the present conditions (complexity). In her thoughtful review of the book, Deborah Fausch suggests that, similar to Michelangelo's Porta Pia, the main façade of Vanna Venturi House (1962) "spread wide to demonstrate a shift from one social realm to another".[36] In retrospect, we can say that Kahn and Giurgola both subscribed to the Venturiesque notion of realism but used it differently.

Instead of following the strand of postmodernism that gave huge attention to the surface, Kahn and Giurgola tried to follow both modern and pre-modern traditions exemplified in the idea of room as discussed in the second part of this essay. What needs further attention here is their difference on this matter. In a footnote explaining the ways that a few Italian architects tried to de-form the "meaning of American rigorism", Tafuri includes Giurgola's criticism of Kahn.[37] Giurgola wrote that Kahn has

> used the fragment of the Euclidean geometry, as probably a new geometry will be formulated in order to translate those simple postulates he proposed – postulates which became lost both in the stylistic sterility and in the avant-garde ventures as well. But in those broken crystals are the signs of our reality, a contradictory world where the contradictions give the time measure of our situation but where a coherent architectural dimension is maintained.[38]

It is a brilliant observation by an optimistic Giurgola, who, in line with his reflections on 'his' Rome, as cited above, tried to subdue Kahn's rigorism by an inclusive approach to, not only nature and landscape, but also the cliental and programmatic needs of the brief. Caught between Kahn's rigorism and Venturi's idea of 'ordinary' and in the pursuit of the fragment, Giurgola did indeed design a couple of projects, including the United Fund Building and the Walnut Street Garage, both in Philadelphia, that brought him international fame. Again, to benefit from Tafuri's criticism, Giurgola's Walnut Street Garage is more than a fragment. Its tectonics leads the "spectator into a symbolic maze representing a sort of emblematic summary of the ground covered by modern architecture".[39]

In one of the highly significant chapters "Modern Architecture and the Eclipse of History" in his aforementioned book, *Theories and History of Architecture*, Tafuri critically maps the situation of post-war architecture in a retrospective criticism.[40] He reproaches the realism of the Tuscan humanists of the Quattrocento, wherein contradictions do not end up in a Hegelian synthesis; rather, in their approximation to the Real, these contradictions are considered as ideological constructs waiting to be decoded. I am also reminded of a few American artists of the 1950s who emulated the landscape of consumer goods as subject matter for their work. This rather controversial analogy can be explained in the following words: whereas 1950s artwork was criticised in the light of the contesting project launched by the historical avant-garde, the political dimension of the work produced by Andy Warhol and others, paradoxically, could not have been recognised today without the work's direct encounter with the culture industry.[41] Only in this line of criticism can we posit that Kahn's rigorism was a timely strategy of resistance against realism, one consequence of which was an inclination towards the aesthetics of 'ordinary' formulated by Venturi. Ironically enough, neither Kahn's juxtaposition of room with monumentality, nor Giurgola's fascination with fragment, nor the postmodern garment tailored according to the Venturi-esque collage of both, and could stand up to the emerging agile capitalism, the architectonic implications of which can be mapped today in the landscape of globalisation and a state of objectivity that is indexed by digital reproducibility.

Having established this critical perspective, the fact that, today, geographic differences are re-territorialised, and that 'delay', central to the post-war debate on centre and periphery, is suspended, I hope my argument has demonstrated how the decoding of received traditions worked in the architecture of Kahn, Venturi and Giurgola. I also tried to map the historicity of late 1950s architecture, leading to a historical criticism of the idea of influence. However, having discussed this, it is not farfetched to say that, as a young nation, Australia has not been able to pursue the American path, a young nation operating on the fringes of rich European architectural traditions that has been able to decode and then recode received influences from European architecture to the extent that the decoded object does not at all resemble its origin.[42] Most received influences, regardless of their form (narrative or formal), are recoded in Australia, more often than not in reference to the available techniques and skills, and thus they remain as fragments without radical consequences, except to be catalogued for historians interested in archival studies. As stated at the beginning of this essay, in the present age of globalisation, the situation is rather changed in favour of Australian architecture. In the present situation, where "everything solid melts into the air",[43] as Marx rightly observed at the dawn of modernisation, both ideas and forms formative for the contemporaneity of architecture are there, floating like weightless particles in the Internet and available with the click of a button. Without dismissing the criticality of "agonistic dialectics" and its implications for critical praxis, the commodification of cultural products at a global scale offers an opening, wherein Australian architecture could remain modern forever.[44] But any serious investigation of past influences must probe the Real, the historicity of contemporary architecture marked by the contradictions central to the historical unfolding of capitalism.

1
Alexander Nagel, *Medieval Modernism: Art Out of Time,* London: Thames & Hudson, 2012, 12.

2
See Fredric Jameson, *The Ancients and the Postmoderns: On the Historicity of Forms,* London: Verso Books, 2015.

3
In "Postmodernism and Consumer Culture", Fredric Jameson's primary focus is the breakdown between language and time that ended in the contemporary investment in image and its subsequent transformation into spectacle. See Frederic Jameson, "Postmodernism and Consumer Culture" in *The Anti-Aesthetic: Essays on Postmodern Culture,* ed. Hal Foster, Port Townsend, WA: Bay Press, 1983, 11–125.

4
On this subject, see Harry F. Mallgrave, ed., *Otto Wagner: Reflections on the Raiment of Modernity,* Santa Monica: The Getty Center for the History of Arts and Humanities, 1988.

5
Howard Eiland and Michael W. Jennings, *Walter Benjamin: A Critical Life,* Cambridge, Massachusetts: Harvard University Press, 2014, 364.

6
J. C. Rowan, "Wanting to Be: The Philadelphia School," *Progressive Architecture* 42 (April 1961): 131–63.

7
Harry Francis Mallgrave, *Modern Architectural Theory: A Historical Survey, 1673–1968,* Cambridge: Cambridge University Press, 2005, 400.

8
Manfredo Tafuri, *The Sphere and the Labyrinth,* Cambridge, Massachusetts: MIT Press, 1987, 298.

9
Mallgrave, *Modern Architectural Theory,* 400.

10
See Jorge Otero-Pailos, *Architecture's Historical Turn: Phenomenology and the Rise of the Postmodern,* Minnesota: University of Minnesota Press, 2010.

11
Alina Payne, "Architectural Principles in the Age of Humanism," *Journal of the Society of Architectural Historians,* 53: 3 (September 1994).

12
Manfredo Tafuri, *History of Italian Architecture, 1944–1985,* Cambridge, Massachusetts: MIT Press, 1989, 94.

13
Ibid.

14
Quoted in Brendan R. Beier, "Preserving the Work of Mitchell/Giurgola Associates," unpublished thesis, University of Pennsylvania, 2006, 18.

15 Romaldo Giurgola, "Reflections on Buildings and the City: The Realism of the Partial Vision," *Perspecta* 9/10 (1965): 107–130.

16 From Aldo Rossi's introduction to Boullee Architecture, quoted in Manfredo Tafuri, *Theories and History of Architecture*, trans. Giorgio Verrecchia, New York: Harper & Rowe, 1979; Italian edition, 1968, 55.

17 Giurgola quoted in Beier, "Preserving the Work of Mitchell/Giurgola Associates," 45.

18 Romaldo Giurgola, "Constants," *Mitchell/Giurgola Architects*, New York: Rizzoli, 1983, 16.

19 Paul Goldberger, "Works of Mitchell/Giurgola," *Architecture + Urbanism* (December 1975): 121–123.

20 Maitiu Ward, "Interview: Romaldo Giurgola", *Australian Design Review*, 6 May 2011, https://www.australiandesignreview.com/architecture/interview-romaldo-giurgola/.

21 Ibid.

22 Beier, "Preserving the Work of Mitchell/Giurgola Associates," 36.

23 Romaldo Giurgola, "The Producing Moment," *Inland Architect* January–February, (1981): 39–40.

24 Tafuri, *Theories and History of Architecture*, 130.

25 Giurgola, "Reflections on Buildings and the City: The Realism of the Partial Vision", 107–130. In the same issue of the magazine, Robert Venturi published selections from his forthcoming book, *Complexity and Contradiction in Architecture*. See Robert Venturi, "Complexity and Contradiction in Architecture: Selections from a Forthcoming Book," *Perspecta* 9/10 (1965): 17–56.

26 *Mitchell/Giurgola Architects*, New York: Rizzoli, 1983, 11.

27 James S. Ackerman, *The Architecture of Michelangelo*, Chicago: University of Chicago Press, 1986, 28.

28 Ibid.

29 Ackerman, *The Architecture of Michelangelo*, 28.

30 Quoted in Frampton, "Forward," 12.

31 Giurgola, "The Producing Moment," 39.

32 Frampton, "Forward," 13.

33 On Louis Kahn's concept of 'room', see Peter Kohane, "Louis Kahn and the Art of Drawing a Room," *Houses by Louis I. Kahn: Architecture + Urbanism*, ed. Noriko Tsukui, 461 (February 2009): 171–174.

34 See Tafuri, *History of Italian Architecture*.

35 Slavoj Žižek, "Introduction," *Mapping Ideology* (London: Verso Books, 1994): 4.

36 Deborah Fausch, "Complexity and Contradiction in Architecture," *Journal of Architectural Education* 66:1 (2012): 31–32.

37 Tafuri, *Theories and History of Architecture*, 75.

38 Tafuri, *Theories and History of Architecture*, 75. Giurgola's statement is part of his article "On Louis Kahn," *Zodiac* 17 (1967): 119.

39 Tafuri, *Theories and History of Architecture*, 128.

40 Tafuri, *Theories and History of Architecture*, 14.

41 I am making these claims in reference to two retrospective exhibitions I visited in 2012. These were: *Regarding Warhol: Sixty Artists, Fifty Years*, The Metropolitan Museum of Art, New York, 18 September 31 December 2012 and *Roy Lichtenstein: A Retrospective*, National Gallery of Art, Washington DC, 14 October–6 January 2012. I have discussed this issue in Gevork Hartoonian, "Capitalism and the Politics of Autonomy" in *Architecture Against the Post-Political: Essays in Reclaiming the Critical Project*, ed. Nadir Lahiji (London: Routledge, 2014): 69–83.

42 Against this, we can agree with Panofsky and Saxl, who claim that "rebirth" is one of the essential characteristics of the European culture in which "breaking with tradition" is an excuse "to go back to it from a brand-new stand point". Quoted in Tafuri, *Theories and History of Architecture*, 66.

43 Karl Marx, Manifesto of the Communist Party, 1848, chapter 1, checked Sept.14, 2017. https://www.marxists.org/archive/marx/works/1848/communist-manifesto/ch01.htm

44 See Chantal Mouffe, "Agonistic Politics and Artistic Practices" in *Agonistics: Thinking the World Politically*, London: Verso Books, 2013, 85–105. Also see Kenneth Frampton, "Towards an Agonistic Architecture," *Domus* 972 (October 2013): 1–13.

Fig. 1—7
Colonne e una Torre: Italian
Designs for Melbourne 1978

Fig. 8—11
Ciao Australia:
Domus Looks to the Antipodes

Fig. 12—14
The Architecture of the City:
An American Rossi in Australia

Fig. 15—17
A Welfare State: *Tendenza*
in 1980s Melbourne

Fig. 18—23
Exhibiting Scarpa: Transcriptions of
the Narrative Detail in Queensland

Fig. 24—29
Learning from Kahn and Scarpa:
Rigour and Ornament in the
Ana Kindergarten

Fig. 30—33
Romaldo Giurgola:
From America with Po-Mo

Fig. 34—37
Culture Mining

Fig. 38—41
Thinking about Gino Valle and a Few
Others in My Small Italian Pool

Fig. 42—45
Between La Tendenza and
Neoliberty: Mauro Baracco Goes
to Australia

Fig. 46
Encountering Italian Architectural
Culture via USA and Australia

Fig. 47—50
Canberra: The Invisible City

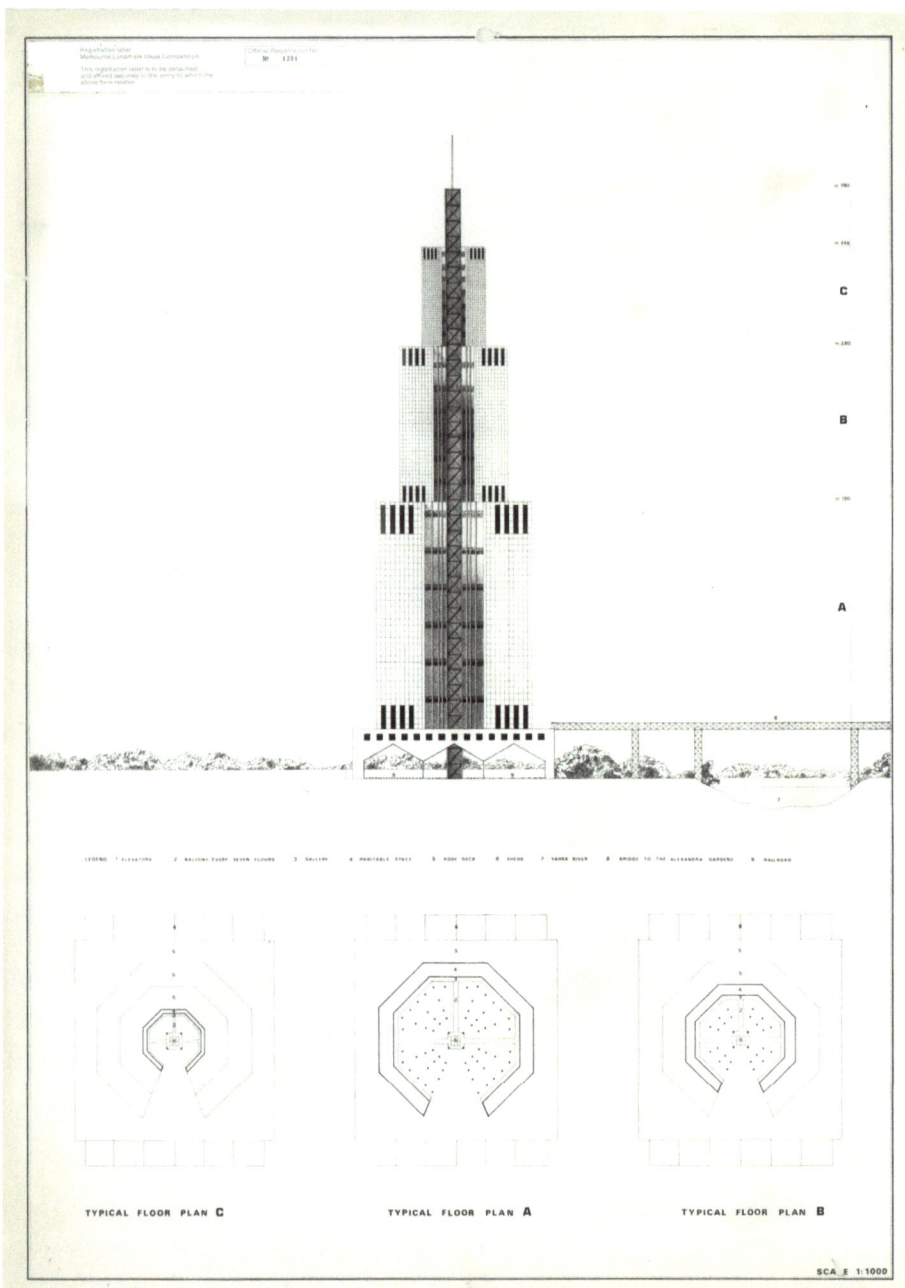

Fig. 1 Plans and elevation (Sheet 1), "Stepped Tower", entry #1251, Melbourne Landmark Ideas Competition (1979), by Aldo Rossi and Gianni Braghieri, with Stefano Getzel. Image courtesy of Public Records of Victoria.

Fig. 2 Isometric view (Sheet 2), "Stepped Tower", entry #1251, Melbourne Landmark Ideas Competition (1979), by Aldo Rossi and Gianni Braghieri, with Stefano Getzel. Image courtesy of Public Records of Victoria.

Fig. 3 Rendering (Sheet 4), "Stepped Tower", entry #1251, Melbourne Landmark Ideas Competition (1979), by Aldo Rossi and Gianni Braghieri, with Stefano Getzel. Image courtesy of Public Records of Victoria.

Fig. 4 Rendering (Sheet 5), "Stepped Tower", entry #1251, Melbourne Landmark Ideas Competition (1979), by Aldo Rossi and Gianni Braghieri, with Stefano Getzel. Image courtesy of Public Records of Victoria.

Fig. 5 "Melbourne Banqueting Hall and Ballroom", detail from entry #465, Melbourne Landmark Ideas Competition (1979), by Peter Wilson and Jenny Lowe. Image courtesy of Public Rectords of Victoria.

Fig. 6 "The Pillars of Melbourne", detail from entry #3143, Melbourne Landmark Ideas Competition (1979), by Adolfo Natalini, Superstudio. Image courtesy of Public Records of Victoria.

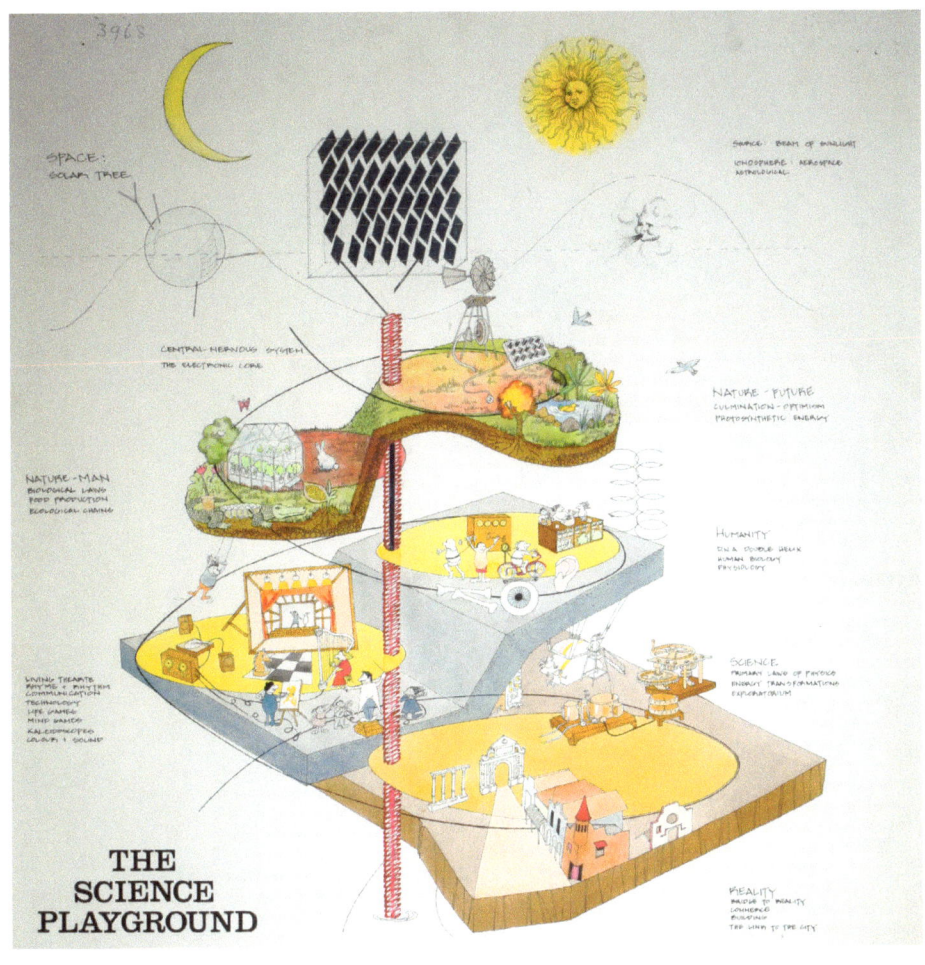

Fig. 7 "The Science Playground", detail of entry #3968, Melbourne Landmark Ideas Competition (1979), by Kevin Greenhatch, Ian McDougall, George Hatzisavis and Betty Greenhatch. Image courtesy of Public Records of Victoria.

Fig. 8   Domus Cover, issue 663.

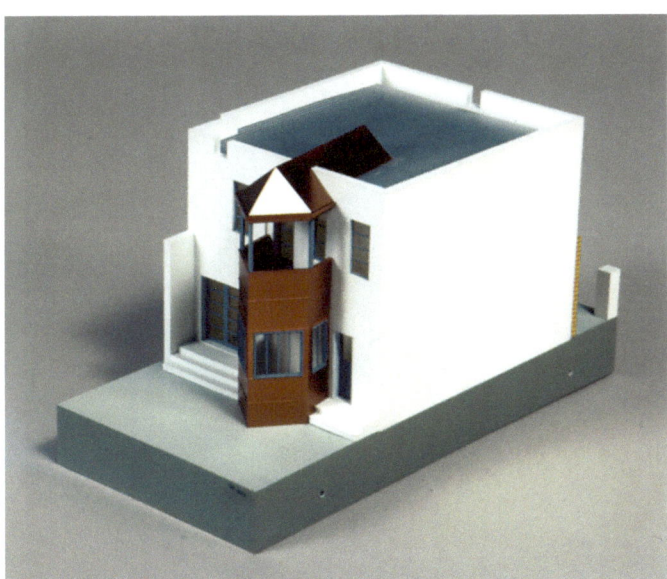

Fig. 9 Norman Day Architect, Public Houses (1983), Northcote, Melbourne, as published in *Domus,* issue 663 (1985), 24. Image courtesy of John Gollings.

Fig. 10 Architectural model of McDougall House (1983), South Yarra, Melbourne, as published in *Domus,* issue 663, (1985), 26. Copyright Museums Victoria.

Fig. 11 Edmond & Corrigan, Kay Street Infill Houses (1983–84), **Melbourne,** as published in *Domus,* issue 663, (1985), 28. Image courtesy of John Gollings.

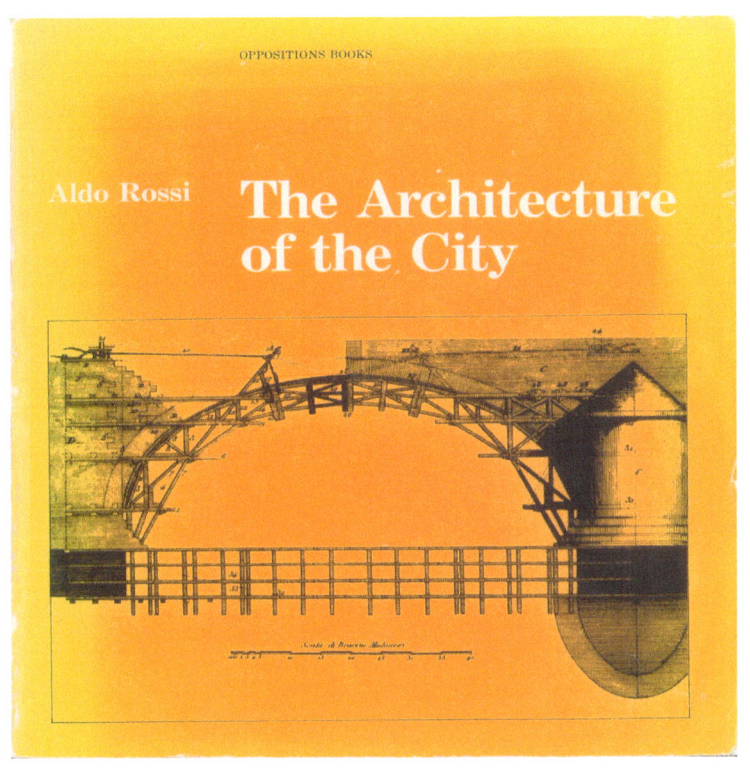

Fig. 12 Cover of the American edition of The Architecture of the City (published in 1982 by MIT Press on behalf of the Institute of Architecture and Urban Studies and the Graham Foundation).

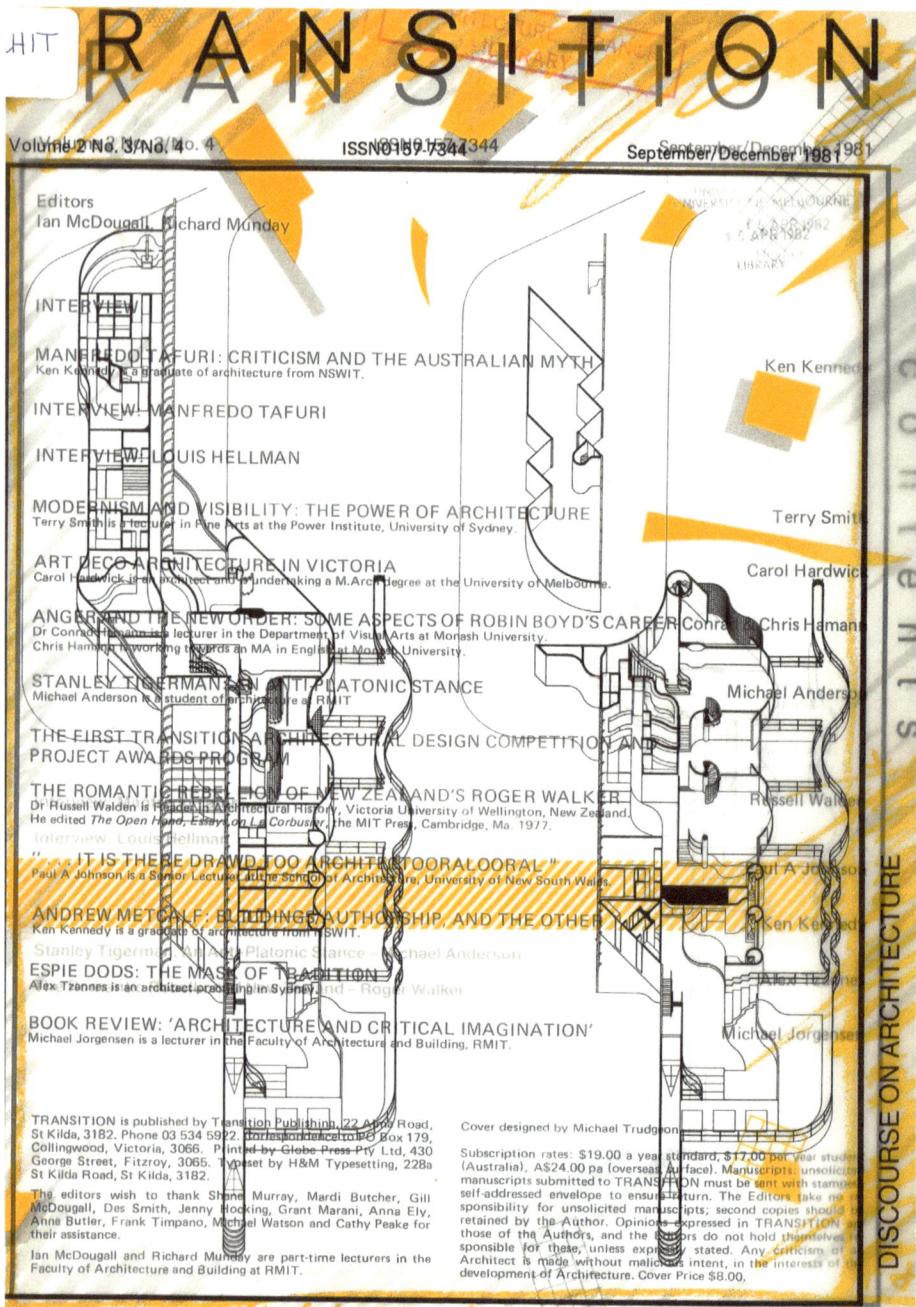

Fig. 13 Cover of Transition 2: 3-4 (1989). This issue featured the journal's interview with Manfredo Tafuri and an article on Tafuri by Ken Kennedy.

FASHION AND CONSUMPTION: Notes on Aldo Rossi

— Micha Bandini

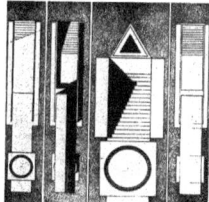 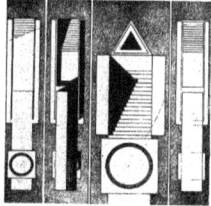

MICHA W BANDINI, Dott. Arch. (Rome), M.T.C.P. (Sydney). Born in Rome where she graduated and started to teach both in Design and History of Architecture. She later went to Australia where she spent a few years teaching, practicing and consulting on environmental problems. For the last 3 years she has been based at the Architectural Association Graduate School, where she has been involved in the co-ordination of a newly formed department of Theory and History.

A. Rossi: Monument to the partisans at Segrate, 1965.

A quick scan over the last decade of architecture would probably suggest that one of the few agreements that could be reached concerning contemporary architecture is that there has been a common search for a raison d'etre. Paradoxically, the more the disagreement spreads about the means of overcoming present difficulties and finding fruitful directions for the future, the more the debate becomes circumscribed by the same themes, and the more the protagonists find themselves repeating, more or less, the same well-rehearsed lines.

While it is true nowadays that architectural ideas circulate more easily than ever with the help of the media, it is also true that all kinds of design projects, and even those with difficult content, are instantly digested and quickly converted into easily imitable models. Magazines adroitly reshuffle projects, art galleries — some of which now specialise in the merchandising of costly original architect-drawn projects — have begun to create a lucrative secondary market, and the student public, especially in these days of uncertain employment, seems the natural target for a consummerist sale where originality, creativity, polemics and history is the name of the game.

But the architectural game is only played by a small esoteric community. The powerful economic forces which allow the destruction of our cities do not need either creativity or originality to trample on history, and that sector of the architectural community which uses polemic in tackling the paramount problems of land rights and use does not seem to be using either creativity or originality to its best advantage.

Fig. 14 First page of Micha Bandini's article "Fashion and Consumption: Notes on Aldo Rossi", Transition 3:1 (1982).

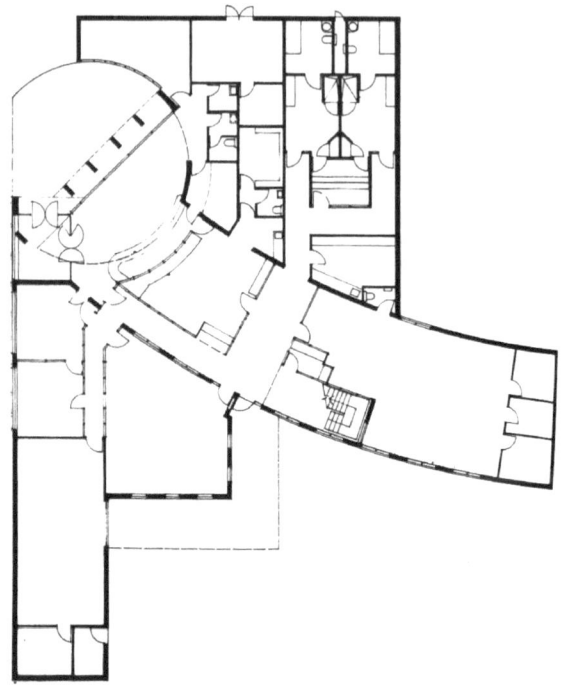

Fig. 15 Andrew Hutson, Gisborne 24 Hour Police Station. Ground floor plan, as published in Transition (September 1986), 30.

Fig. 16 Bill Goodwin, Campbellfield 24 Hour Police Station. Elevations, as published in Transition. (September 1986), 32.

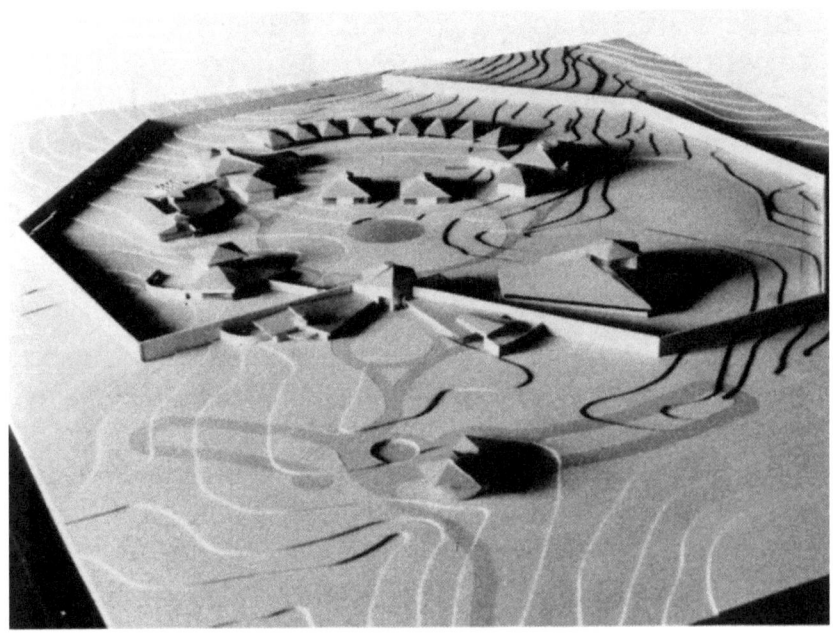

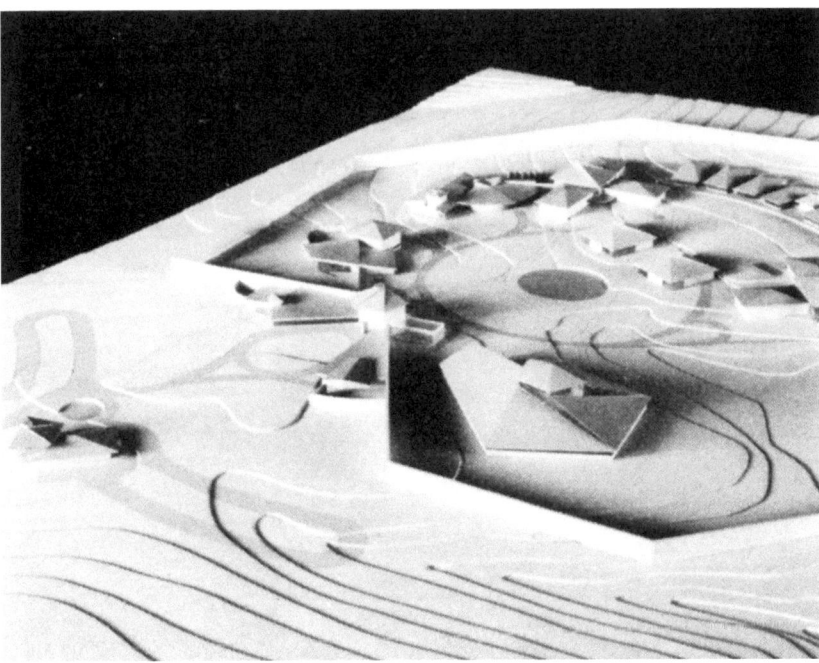

Fig. 17 Francesco Timpano and Alex Selenitsch, Regional Prison, Castlemaine. Model, as published in Transition (September 1986), 34.

Fig. 18 Pedro Guedes, Competition drawing (1972) of the Burrell Museum, Glasgow. Image courtesy of the architect.

Fig. 19 Heritage Walk Flyer, CIRCUS conference (1991). Image courtesy of the University of Queensland, Department of Architecture Archive.

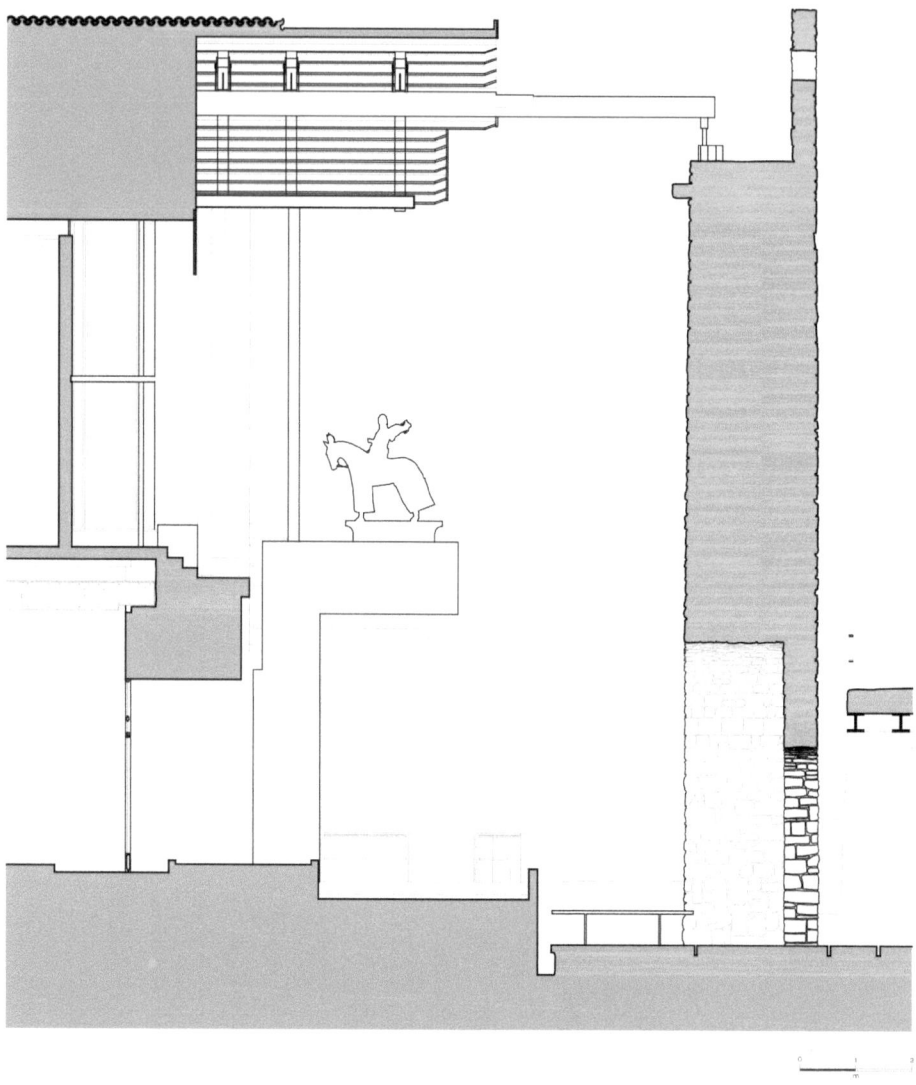

Fig. 20 Castelvecchio, Verona. Section drawn by Jeremy Sherring. Image courtesy of Richard Murphy Architecture.

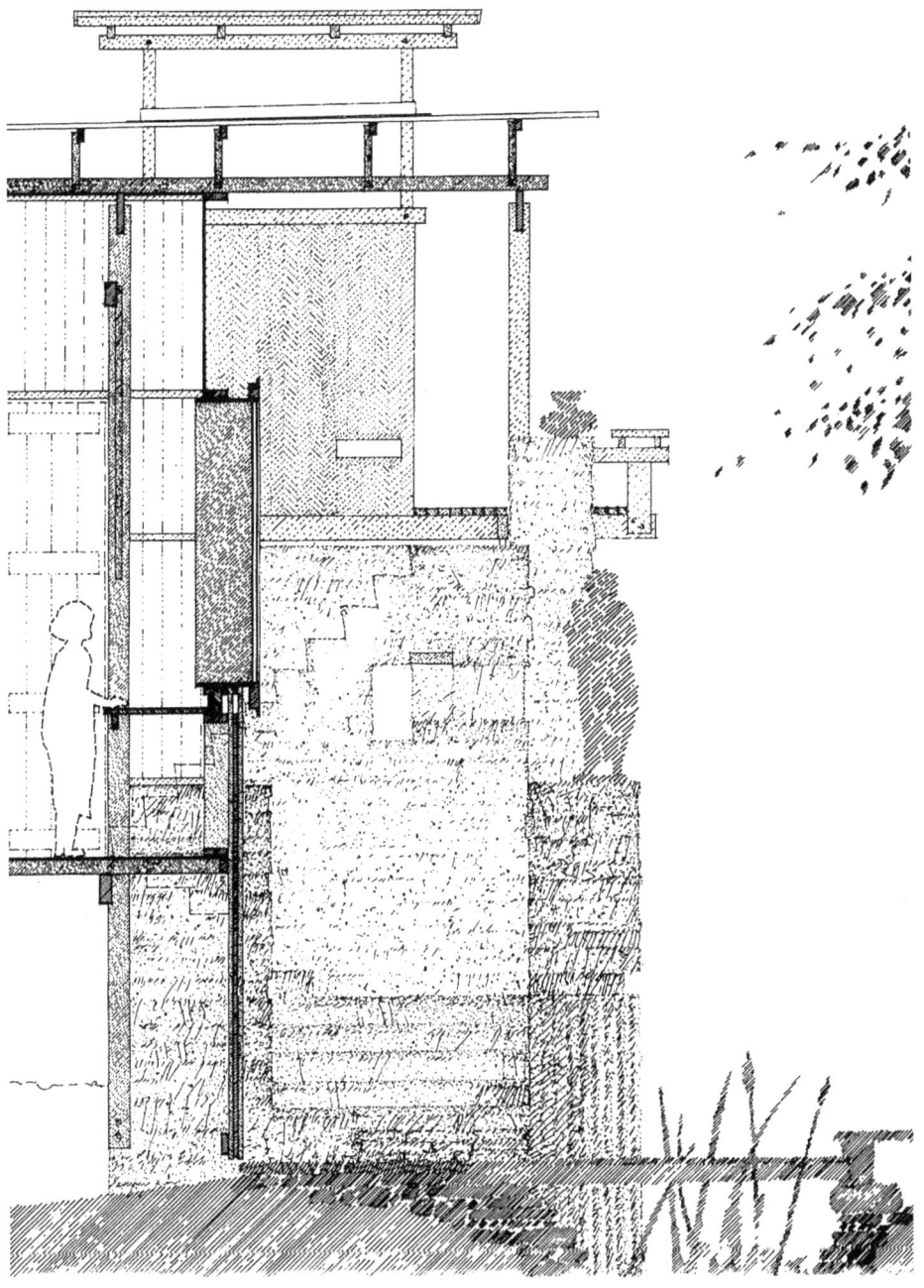

Fig. 21 Donovan Hill, HH House (1993) Brisbane.
Section. Image courtesy of the architects.

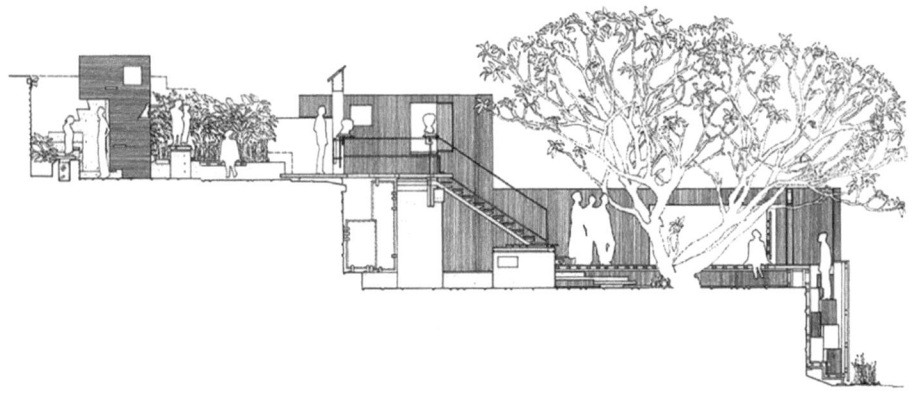

Fig. 22 Alice Hampson, Residence (1998) Hamilton, Brisbane. Section. Image courtesy of the architect.

Fig. 23 Donovan Hill, HH House, (1993) Brisbane. Detail. Image courtesy Jon Linkins.

Fig. 24 Swetik Korzeneiski with Paul Desney, Ana Kindergarten, (1979–1982) Auburn, Sydney. Exterior detail. Image courtesy of the architect.

Fig. 25 Swetik Korzeneiski with Paul Desney,
Ana Kindergarten, (1979–1982) Auburn, Sydney.
Exterior detail. Image courtesy of the architect.

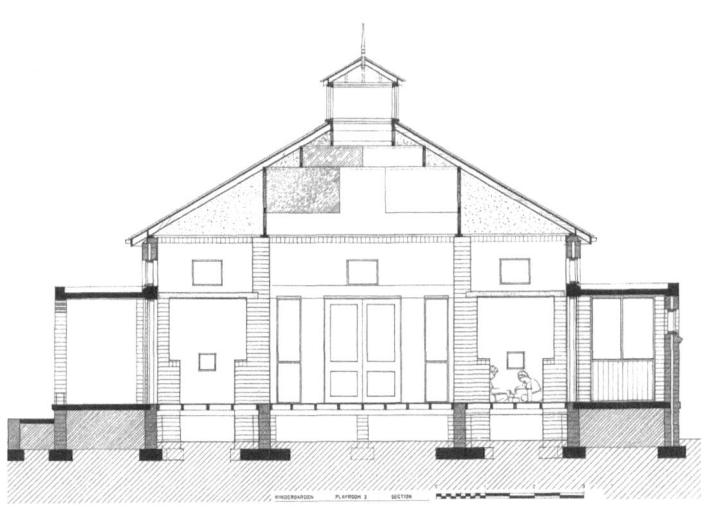

Fig. 26 Swetik Korzeneiski with Paul Desney, Ana Kindergarten, (1979–1982) Auburn, Sydney. Garden front. Image courtesy of the estate of Max Dupain.

Fig. 27 Swetik Korzeneiski with Paul Desney, Ana Kindergarten, (1979–1982) Auburn, Sydney. Section of playroom. Image courtesy of the architect.

Fig. 28 Swetik Korzeneiski with Paul Desney, Ana Kindergarten, (1979–1982) Auburn, Sydney. Detail of the playroom. Image courtesy of the estate of Max Dupain.

Fig. 29 Swetik Korzeneiski with Paul Desney, Ana Kindergarten, (1979–1982) Auburn, Sydney. Playroom. Image courtesy of the estate of Max Dupain.

Fig. 30 Romaldo Giurgola, St Patrick's Cathedral (1996–2003), Parramatta, New South Wales. View of the front. Image courtesy of Hal Guida Architects and John Gollings.

Fig. 31 Romaldo Giurgola, St Patrick's Cathedral (1996–2003), Parramatta, New South Wales. View of the side. Image courtesy of Hal Guida Architects and John Gollings.

Fig. 32 Mitchel/Giurgola Associates, The Penn Mutual Tower (1975), Philadelphia. Photo by Rollin La France. Image courtesy of the Architectural Archives, University of Pennsylvania.

Fig. 33 Romaldo Giurgola on the lawns of the Parliament House, Canberra, 2011. Photo by Neil Fenelon, National Library of Australia.

Fig. 34 ARM, Geelong Library and Heritage Centre (2013–15). Image courtesy of John Gollings.

Fig. 35 ARM, Extension (1994) of the St Kilda Library (1972), Melborune, by Enrico Taglietti. Image courtesy of John Macarthur.

Fig. 36 ARM, Australian Institute of Aboriginal and Torres Strait Islander Studies Centre (1999–2001), National Museum of Australia, Canberra. Image courtesy of John Gollings.

Fig. 37 ARM, St Kilda Town Hall (1991–94), Melbourne. Image courtesy of John Gollings.

Fig. 38 Rex Addison, Linocut print "Over the Lines" (2005). Image courtesy of the architect.

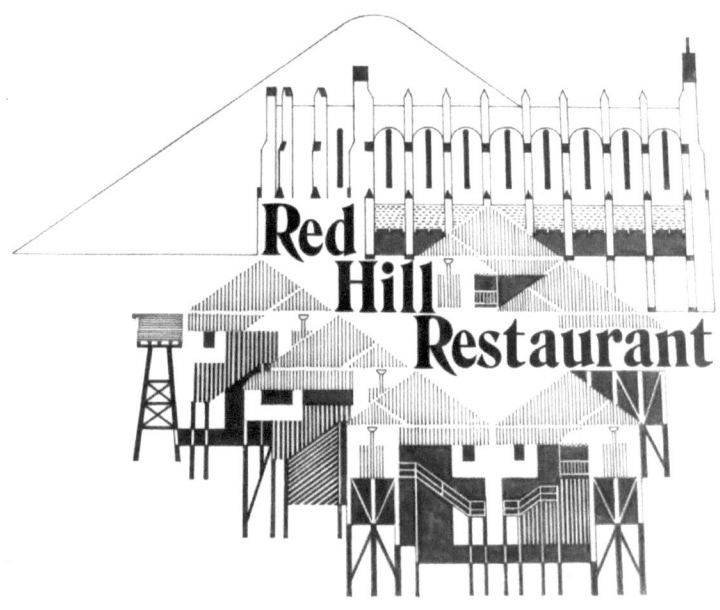

Fig. 39 Rex Addison, Red Hill Restaurant graphic (1976). Image courtesy of the architect.

Fig. 40 Rex Addison, The Nerang Post Office (1983–85). North face. Image courtesy of the architect.

Fig. 41 Rex Addison, Burrundulla Garden Housing (1987), Kambah, Canberra. Image courtesy of John Macarthur.

Fig. 42 Edmond and Corrigan, Athan House (1986–88), Monbulk. Rear. Image courtesy of John Gollings.

Fig. 43 Edmond and Corrigan, Athan House (1986–88), Monbulk. Front. Image courtesy of John Gollings.

Fig. 44 Edmond and Corrigan, Chapel of St Joseph (1976–78), Box Hill. Image courtesy of John Gollings.

Fig. 45 Baracco+Wright Architects,
Garden House (2013–15), Western Port Bay.
Image courtesy of Erieta Attali.

Fig. 46 Roy Grounds, Medley Towers (1968–70), University of Melbourne. Image courtesy of Conrad Hamann.

Fig. 47 Enrico Taglietti, Giralang Primary School (1974), ACT. Photo Max Dupain. Image courtesy of the architect.

Fig. 48 Enrico Taglietti, St Anthony Parish Church (1968), Marsfield, NSW. Photo Max Dupain. Image courtesy of the architect.

Fig. 49 Enrico Taglietti, St Kilda Library (1971), Victoria. Photo John Edson Assoc. Image courtesy of the architect.

Fig. 50 Enrico Taglietti, Australian War Memorial Annex (1977), ACT. Photo Enrico Taglietti. Image courtesy of the architect.

Culture Mining

Ian McDougall

in conversation with

John Macarthur and Silvia Micheli

Ian McDougall is a founding director of ARM (Ashton Raggatt McDougall), an Australian practice with an international reputation, which has substantially contributed to the making of national postmodern architecture. Ian studied architecture at The University of Adelaide in the early 1970s, completing his degree in Melbourne. He was co-founder and long-term editor of Transition magazine, a major architectural venue for the promotion of postmodern culture in Australia.

John Macarthur

Ian, ARM has been a proponent of 'the local': of Melbourne architectural discourse and the particularities of Australian cultural memory. At the same time, you are greatly informed by the international discourse on architecture. How do you position yourselves?

Ian McDougall

The generation before us seemed to be happy with not having any architectural culture. For them, architecture was future directed. But there was a time in the 1970s when we decided collectively that you couldn't have architecture without a tradition. The question that confronted us was where that tradition came from: is it England, America, or Italy, or is it what's around you? The early years of ARM were characterised by the search for a meaningful architectural language that somehow captured our own experiences, and so we lurched between international influence that was in the air at the time to art theory and also to the work of local heroes. And we are still doing that!

The mining—and undermining—of historical prototypes was a primary focus for us. We got interested in the copy and 'variations-on-a-theme' and what was happening in music with sampling. Some local artists were doing tape work by essentially splicing together other people's work and then putting noise over it. So, there was this sort of mood of iconoclasm to the whole of creative activity, which also had a very serious undertone of cultural mining. I think really, at that time, there were two main aspects: one was the cultural mining, and the other was us being at the edges of culture. Living in Australia, we felt that we needed validation that we were good enough in the eyes of world culture.

Around the same time, there was the growing influence of new technology, computer-aided design, and a new ease and recklessness in the copy and paste function. I got into early computer drafting in 1984, and, by the time we teamed up as ARM in 1986, the issues of technological change had taken over the whole discipline. The interest in digital space and the impact of that, the feeling of a new world that was anti-drawing, traditionalists' antagonism to anti-drawing, all started to grow at that time. It was also the start of that tendency where everyone was scanning everybody else's images you know, paintings and whatever. People would say: "Hey, wait a minute, you're supposed to get copyright release to use those famous images, to publish them". And others would just go ahead, appropriating imagery: publications, T-shirts. We had something of this attitude to the international canon. It was an attempt to create a language not by formal replication but by working within a cultural framework that was shared but also disrespected. It was almost like play acting within the global cultural structures and seeing what these acts of borrowing revealed from our own mongrel upbringing in Australia.

Our influences were not only global. We were interested in the way our own cities and the buildings that surrounded us, buildings that we held dear, might re-emerge in our new work. In hindsight, we were not interested in a normalising straightjacket answer to the usual question: 'What is an Australian architecture?' Our search was about the capacity to mine aspects of local experience that which is familiar and that which is often ignored or denied. But, at the same time, as we were analysing ways of dealing with being in this place, we would also attempt to engage in an exchange with the rest of the world. We would do this without denying our own obsessions, wit, and experience. Part of the tactic for global exchange comprised critique and contrarianism. We researched the writings of the touring gurus of the time as they paraded through our city at the International Series of Architects run by the RAIA, and we would confront them with their own rhetoric, point out contradictions or flaws in their thought—challenge their arrogance!

It is interesting to muse on how difficult it still is to have a global to local exchange. At the 2015 National Architecture Conference in Melbourne, I shared a panel session with Deborah Saunt, a British architect who has done a concrete and glass pavilion called Covert and put garden beds in the streets to make pedestrian malls in Camden. She made the point that we live in a world where social media is the driver of the new, where global access to information is so amazingly easy and how wonderful it all is. I made the point that this may be true if you want to find out about the wonders of London— it is not true if you seek esoteric historical information about Bendigo or the mid-century modern architecture of Caulfield. "Rubbish," she said. She had found out a lot about Aino Aalto from the web. I incautiously said "Who cares about Aino Aalto, how do I find out about the life of Beverley Ussher?" What is the point of this story? If we listen to the superficial prophets of elsewhere, it all seems so easy somewhere else. Our work is displaced from 'there'; it is always an 'exotica' or a 'copy' or both.

Silvia Micheli
In terms of what you were copying, was it Aldo Rossi? Anyone different? Was it just the centre, or was there any particular status to Italian architecture because of the urbanistic aspects of the book *The Architecture of the City*?

IM   Let me start by saying we have been persistent champions of the Baroque as inspiration for a contemporary architecture. Our work recalls earlier traditions of allegorical components of architecture; the cave, the ruin, the garden, the maze, the folly. Needless to say, we have been long intrigued by projects like the Gardens of Bomarzo, near Viterbo (Italy). Our recent Geelong Library and Heritage Centre (2014–15) recalls and intertwines the elements of garden, of grotto, and ruin. In explaining the work to the public, we have chosen to use Piranesi's drawing of Tempio di Minerva Medica in

Rome to encapsulate the building's character. Perhaps we are reflecting Aldo Rossi's theory of Permanence and the immutability of monuments. When we read Rossi's *The Architecture of the City*, we identified a statement that resonated with our own desire to understand the nature of our city:

> A city is a collective memory of its people, and like memory it is associated with objects and places. The city is locus of collective memory. This relationship between locus and citizenry then becomes a city's predominant image, a great shape history moulds its future to.

The idea that the city was an ongoing project, identified by enduring ideas, became a persistent roadmap for us. For me, Melbourne comprises three major architectural flowerings, which describe its cultural being. First, there is the nineteenth century boom of Marvellous Melbourne; second, there is the post-war boom of Melbourne Modern; and, finally, we have the post-1990s growth of Postcode 3000/Melbourne Design City.

JM Your early polemical project of an upside-down monument for the show *New Classicism* seems to have aspects of La Tendenza, of Rossi, and Giorgio Grassi…

IM Yes, but it's also a crossover into the commercial classicism of those years, combined with a vaguely constructivist heroic. So, it was a mining of that proposition and against the sort of rustic, arcadian Aussie stuff. But it's also a bit of artist Tony Clark, who was one of those Fitzroy artists who was doing those tapes I mentioned earlier but also quasi-classical landscapes around the same time as the show. There is a duality in our taking up international discourse of the time. Through repeating the rhetoric, we also set out to somehow undermine it, by showing it in the local context. Maybe not undermine it, but certainly question, throw it open to the questions, questions about its validity.

SM There was a lot of Rossi in *Transition*, the journal you founded with Richard Munday and edited in the 1980s.

IM Yes, yes. And also I think that, within Melbourne, there were a lot of people discussing that particular line—was it the allure of a connection between history and practice, or theory and practice, that we longed for? I'm not sure how it arose, other than the fact that we all got interested in Eisenman's publications and then it was also the time when everyone got interested in Tafuri. I can't remember which we read first, Tafuri and Francesco Dal Co's *Modern Architecture* or Tafuri's *Architecture and Utopia*, but we then read right through it. Rossi and Tafuri had a strong presence in the city, not necessarily as an academic study—it was almost absorbed through the air.

Quite a group of people in Melbourne, surprisingly, were interested in the neoliberty architectural movement, and that was reinforced by Conrad Hamann's readings of it, which had a very strong influence on our thought. We felt that really strident difference between the intentions of the Modernism of Italy in the 1950s and the British line. I wasn't really aware of Reyner Banham's article critiquing Neoliberty until later, but early on we were aligned with the Italians and their urbanism, their architectural and philosophical stance, against the Brits and their High Tech and somewhat protestant, fairly dreary, way of looking at the world.

SM   Aldo Rossi was interested in Neoliberty, so it all makes sense.

IM   What interested me in Neoliberty was what I saw as an attempt to localise the work—working from regional history through individual experiences and the rhetoric of the local—into something that seems to be connected to the city: the possibilities within a city, analysing and grabbing them as a cultural connection with the context that it's in, and then using them in a creative and new way. That was probably my take. And I don't think that other Melbourne people were that familiar with Neoliberty. If a colleague stumbled on similar ideas, you said "Oh, that's like the ideas of, say, Ridolfi". And they'd say "Oh yes, I do know that work".

The interest in the Italian argument was stronger when Conrad and Peter Corrigan were around; stronger than another local dialogue back to Finland, which was probably through Kevin Borland, or the dialogue of International Modernism through Boyd, which probably is American. I think our interest in things like Neoliberty was because we reacted against the traditions valorised in Melbourne at that time: either the emerging high tech or a main stream of global Modernism.

SM   So, to clarify, it seems to me that you were looking at the Italians, and in particular Rossi and Grassi, not from a formal point of view, but trying to discover the mechanism to recover local architecture, through addition, memory, all concepts that Rossi and Grassi were using intellectually to beef up their theory and finally their forms. So, I guess though there is a huge difference in forms, there is a similarity in the theoretical approach. Is that the case?

IM   Yes, it was not a formal exploration, it was intellectual.

JM   That's interesting, because when you quote Rossi, Alvar Aalto, Mies van der Rohe, there's a bit of debunking.

IM Oh yeah. Absolutely.

JM But, in fact, your method is a little bit close to Rossi and not at all close to Mies.

IM Yes. That's right. And the debunking is also a kind of bravado, in a way. As if to say "Yeah, okay, let's take that on, if what you say is right, this is what it looks like". And then, for us, it was hilarious; when Jean Nouvel came to Melbourne, he refused to go into Storey Hall, saying "Whoa, that can't be right, that's terrible what you've done there, that's terrible". We say, "No, no, you said we should have a position and that's our position".

So, it was both an uptake of international ideas and a confrontation with those ideas. But it's not serendipitous or even a version of a whimsical selection. We chose parts of the international discourse that have a cogency for us and hence a sense of sharing that idea. You know, the tradition of the bush leftist history in Australia is comparable to the history of the left in Europe, or it can be seen to be. It had shared lines, without it actually looking similar. Maybe that's the political lineage to what we do.

JM So, today postmodernism is groovy again.

IM Groovy again, is it?

JM Oh yeah.

IM Goodness me, when you live long enough!

JM ARM was fairly identified with postmodernism very early on. Does that come through today?

IM Yes, yes, absolutely.

JM But for the period in which ARM has come to prominence, postmodernism has been desperately unfashionable, a no-go area.

IM I've never been uncomfortable with 'postmodern' in philosophical terms. True, in the US, in architecture, it came to mean something that we weren't interested in whatsoever. And Howard Raggatt has often said "No, no, no, we don't like to use that word". Because internationally it aligns you with pretty crappy stuff. But I've never been uncomfortable with it from an intellectual position because all the things that underpin it, if I can understand it, are what we've always believed in; the strategies that involved self-reference, the localisation of language, the way it holds interpretation as not singular, in its contradictions, the surreal and diverse juxtapositional cohesion. These are ideas and attitudes we've always held. I'm quite happy with it as a term.

You know, I do reread some of the analysis of postmodernism, even though sometimes it's so philosophically opaque I can't understand it. Nevertheless, there are parts that constantly strike a chord with me. "Yes, we do believe that." So, I don't have a problem with the term at all.

JM So, it's no mistake you invited Charles Jencks to write in the book *Mongrel Rapture: The Architecture of Ashton Raggatt McDougall*.

IM I don't necessarily share all of Jencks' line, but, you know, I would have thought the whole history of architecture is about being a bearer of ideas, of cultural propositions, and, to some extent, ideas that are iconoclastic or challenging. It is this architectural stance to which ARM is committed and perhaps that aligns us with what the postmodern position is. We've not been interested in a singularity of architecture. When you look at the projects that we've done, they're all over the place. It looks like a complete mess. But this comes to the very point, where it's inescapable that our projects are not about form. They are actually about the proposition, testing the structure of architectural meaning and language and about the ongoing attempt at discovery, embedded within the work, through the mining of the history of architecture and the culture of architecture, the constant allusions. That has been our long-term project.

Thinking about Gino Valle and a Few Others in My Small Italian Pool

Rex Addison

in conversation with

Silvia Micheli and John Macarthur

Rex Addison is a Brisbane-based architect. As a student in the late 1960s, he was interested in the Italian architectural journal, Domus, which gave a European perspective on the architecture of the day. Through Domus, Rex became keen on the work of the Italian architect Gino Valle, his ability to deal with context, and his use of geometry. Rex's architecture, shown in his works in Brisbane, Papua New Guinea and Canberra, takes on and shares the critique of Modernism.

Fig. 38—41

Silvia Micheli

Rex, you have a very peculiar relationship with the Italian architectural culture.

Rex Addison

My Italian pool of influences is small. The architects I was interested in are not many in number, and they occurred at a formative stage of my life in architecture. The group does not include Palladio, for instance.

John Macarthur

Why not Palladio?

RA   Oh, Palladio offered a symmetrical straightjacket: that did not appeal!

SM   Can you tell us about your encounter with Gio Ponti at the Australasian Architecture Student Association (AASA) Conference "City-Synthesis" in 1967?

RA   In 1967, I was in the third and last of my full-time years in Architecture at The University of Queensland. In those days, the last three years were spent working in architects' offices and going to university at night. In May 1967, the annual Architecture Students Convention was held in Brisbane. Most of the formal talks were given at the Astor Theatre in New Farm, an old inner Brisbane suburb. Amongst national and international speakers, Gio Ponti was there, too! In his broken English, he would present his buildings and say time and again as he walked around Brisbane "Is a paradisa [It is a paradise]," while we enjoyed his charming Italian sonic rhythms and ogled at his collarless corduroy yellow ochre suit. Other than that, our lines of communication suffered due to his poor English and our non-existent Italian. However, after Ponti's visit in Brisbane, James Birrell's Union College (1963–74) at The University of Queensland in Brisbane featured in the Italian architectural journal *Domus*.

SM   At that time *Domus* was already internationally recognised. Did you know *Domus*?

RA   Of course, *Domus* was an impressive magazine at the time. In 1968, I worked in Geoffrey Pie's office, which was then at his house, also in the suburb of New Farm. I should say that at that time, New Farm had Brisbane's highest Italian population. Geoffrey was throwing out all his recent *Domus* magazines. I rescued them and kept subscribing for another couple of years. Ponti and his daughter Lisa edited the magazine at the time. *Domus* had ads featuring Ponti's buildings.

SM   What role did *Domus* have in your architectural education?

RA   During the 1960s, before travelling abroad, students were supposed to complete a six-year architectural course (three years full time at university and three years working in an office and attending university at night). International magazines were paramount for Australian students, who were eager to know more about what was going on overseas. Our interests were more focused on European architecture rather than American.

JM   Was Ponti's architecture appealing to you?

RA   I particularly admired the balustrading for the staircase of the auditorium of the Pirelli building (1956–60) in Milan. I saw this detail published in a book of architects working details. I was just finding my way in the architecture course and I was looking for the 'geometric keys' to unlock significant formal solutions. It was clever how the string line of the stair became the diagonal of the truss balustrade. I worked in Jim Birrell's office, and in 1968 I spent a lot of time documenting a multistorey hotel in Port Moresby, Papua New Guinea. My design for the balustrade variations picked up on the geometric lines that the stair can generate, an idea that started with the Pirelli model. The hotel was never built. In the 1970s, back from overseas and working for Goodsir Baker Wilde Architects, I designed a faculty building on the campus of the Papua New Guinea University of Technology in Lae. The stairs to the roof deck were closer to the Ponti model. By that stage, I was aware of similar solutions in the railway footbridges of Queensland, where the string line of the stair became the diagonal chord of the spanning truss. Years later I made a linocut print of a footbridge in a mythical location.

SM   Rex, could you tell us more about your 'small Italian pool'? What other architects were included?

RA   Back at Geoffrey's office in 1968, I first saw the work of Gino Valle in *Domus*. Valle was a practitioner who worked mainly in North-East Italy. The Manzano House (1965–66) in Udine interested me at a number of levels. Some views seemed to reveal the house in section and elevation simultaneously, much as a drawing can. The shots of the building published in *Domus* did not reveal much of the urban context. It mentioned a town called Udine. I was hungry to know more because the house had a distilled language that suggested a precedent. Certainly, the use of the red colour did. I liked the red. We have red buildings in our part of the world that I liked—and still like—a great deal. I did a sketch design for Geoffrey's local Italian house painter, Paul Carbone. My Villa Carbone in New Farm, designed in 1972, is too literal a take on the Valle's Manzano house, but it's interesting to look back on. It never went ahead.

Another job I worked on at the time was relocating a big old Queensland house. The house was so large that it had to be cut up into five pieces, and the segments sat on the new site à la Gino Valle, it seemed to me, revealing itself in section and elevation simultaneously. It made me wonder if you could devise new ways for the parts to relate to one another in a new time and place. The thought remained in my head, although it reinforced my understanding of the formal potential of the section.

At that time, a friend was starting a restaurant in an old shopfront in Red Hill, another old inner Brisbane suburb. Red Hill was indeed a steep hill covered with small timber houses and dominated by Robin Dods' St Brigid's Catholic Church. I did a graphic for the shop window: a notional view of the houses, the church, the hill, and the name. The graphic made me dissect the houses into their component parts. More thoughts…

In 1974, when I designed our first house, the sectional/elevational assemblage of parts finally got an airing. I felt I was adding to an existing building language and changing the syntax. I felt that was a contribution an architect could make to carry the conversation forward.

JM Why do you like Gino Valle's red?

RA Many of the older buildings of Queensland had used powdered ochre colouring in a linseed oil base, both for the timber and the corrugated iron, red being a prominent colour and Dods' belfry at Brisbane's St John's Cathedral being a particularly good example. I like the red colour as it gives a sense of commonality to all the buildings, like the mailboxes and school buses in the US, a sort of language through the country. For the particular red I wanted, I asked Brian Oxlade, a member of an old Brisbane family whose company had supplied house painters and artists for years. I used his recipe on my house. I have used that colour, if not the recipe, many times since, and I am sure that Valle's use of the red, as well as my own experience, has given me the confidence to do so. The red colour provided a common language as well as a regional flavour. Valle was good at reinventing forms that were familiar in the area.

SM Did you ever meet Gino Valle?

RA No, but I had my 'Valle moment' in 1971, after graduation. Four of us, Don Watson, a fellow student at UQ School of Architecture, Ian Sinnamon, one of our lecturers, my wife Susan and I drove overland from India to England, taking six months. You could do that then! In Baghdad, we spotted a Ponti building without knowing about it! I assumed it was 'a Ponti' by the reflectivity of the tiles and the inflections of the rooflines. I had no verification of the author of the building, but I could not imagine who else could have done it. It was the Development Board Building (1956–58), a block of government offices. I noticed that the local police were all driving Holdens! By the time we got to the Mediterranean in Lebanon, our emaciated bodies testified to our travel-weary state. We made our way through the countries that define the north-eastern shores of the Mediterranean till we got to Italy. Streets and laneways in Northern Italy with urbanity on tap. Near Udine, I started to see red…

In Udine, I saw a building whose architect I was sure I knew, although I had never seen that work published. "Gino Valle?" I asked an entering tenant of the building, and he invited us up to his own office on the top floor. I took some shots of his office and views from the roof terrace. Years later I came upon these two views from the major opus on Valle's work, the architect's drawing and a photograph of the same view after completion of the building, showing just how completely their aims of seamless insertion into the town fabric had been achieved. A better reading of the grain of the town I could not imagine! And a fine new building with no historical overtures and in a wholly new material: I thought it was just great!

Capitalism is a difficult paradigm to work under as an architect. There is a notion, these days, that, for a town or city to have an injection of energy, they have to build an icon. Of course, that means economic growth and ultimately money. An icon is what the architectural community can and will supply. We have fed that notion as a profession ourselves of course, post-Bilbao. If you are in Sydney and feeling provincial on the world stage, get Frank Gehry in; if you are in Brisbane and feeling even more provincial, Dame Zaha Hadid perhaps can help. These buildings tell me that there are no local lessons worth listening to. Their insertion could not be more different than Gino Valle's at Udine. His buildings do a lot of listening.

SM   What other cities did you visit during your trip to Italy?

RA   Arriving from the Bosporus, we entered Italy via Trieste and Pordenone without any precise itinerary. From there to Udine was, for me, the highlight of the Italian tour. We visited Rome and its Via Appia, Pisa, the Uffizi Museum in Florence, and the sloping Piazza del Campo in Siena. We were fascinated by the streetscapes of these towns, with buildings hanging over the street and their uniformity of shapes. In Urbino, I visited Giancarlo De Carlo's university buildings on the hill, but they did not appeal to me, as they are fantastically indulgent and very expensive, although theoretically correct. Valle's buildings instead were modest but effective. In Milan, I had a chance to see the contemporary architectures of BBPR, Angelo Mangiarotti, and Franco Albini. I was trying to work out what kind of architect I wanted to be and Gino Valle came across as a great example. I know his architecture didn't relate to Brisbane, but, in a way, he confirmed for me a direction I intended to pursue.

SM   Ponti's *Domus* used to discuss architecture as well as industrial design and art. Did you have any flair for the 'Italian style'?

RA   In the 1960s I convinced Susan (then my girlfriend) that she should purchase an Olivetti Valentine portable typewriter, as advertised in *Domus*. Of course, 'real men' didn't type in those days! Then I moved into an old schoolhouse in New Farm and bought a second-hand Fiat Bambino… Life took on an Italian air. We returned to Australia from our trip in late 1972, and the following year there was a furniture competition. One of the old *Domus* magazines showed an adjustable height table designed by a group of Italians. Its form reminded me of an old family outdoor table, made from hardwood by my carpenter grandfather. That table was as heavy as lead! I thought that the idea could be taken a little further with a few more adjustment options so I designed my own version for this competition. I didn't win but I asked my grandfather to build my design. As its life turned out, the various adjustments were awkward so it just settled in as a normal height table and was in daily use till very recently.

SM   Rex, during the Italian part of your intercontinental trip you had the chance to visit Valle's Zanussi factory too. How did the building affect your design?

RA   Another of the magazine collections Geoffrey was throwing out back in 1968—it was quite a spring clean!—was *AC*, standing for the subsequently dreaded material, *Asbestos Cement*. It featured that material's use in buildings and was quite a lively international magazine at the time. It was in the January 1967 issue that I first saw Gino Valle's Zanussi Headquarters in Porcia, Pordenone (1959–61). I saw it 'in the flesh' on the Italian leg of our big overland trip but on a day teeming with rain. It was impressive from the highway. I liked the way the upper floor overlapped the lower, giving protection and a formal opportunity for the space to spill down the stairway and into the floor below. I felt it was fluid and eloquent. American architect Robert Venturi would say he was using a "circumstantial diagonal in an otherwise rectangular order". Venturi was another postmodern architect I really enjoyed, having read his book, *Complexity and Contradiction in Architecture* (1966).

Of course, I had come across these circumstantial diagonals before. The houses of my region usually had expressed back stairs, defining them in one sort of lattice or another. Like Valle's Zanussi stairs, they held on to the top level with one of their defining lines while descending to another with the diagonal of the string line. I loved the way this technique worked spatially; dropping from the upper level, you are at first enclosed with the memory of that level and then released to the new line and view from the lower level. It creates a narrative about the descent, which enriches the journey through the building. Dods uses this geometry often, and he would have seen it in the work of Mackintosh and Voysey, as would have Valle, although much later. I have used it often in timber houses, and, at the back of the Nerang Post Office (1983–85), I came as close as I ever did to Valle's Zanussi Headquarters type.

JM   Can you tell more about your interest in Robert Venturi?

RA   Yes, Venturi somehow interested me. In particular, his Beach House from 1959 always impressed me in section. It was quite small and with a roof whose geometry was quite sophisticated.

SM   Rex, while you are talking you use a very specific vocabulary, including words such as 'geometry', 'abstraction', and 'pop'. They are all notions that belong to the postmodern tradition. What was your position in regards to postmodernism?

RA   Postmodernism is a swear word now!

JM   It is coming back!

RA   Yes, it is true! It was a hot topic, and it became clear to me when I started working in Papua New Guinea that I did not agree with the stylistic dictates of Modernism. I believed that Modernism deserved a critique. It was just that I did not agree with Le Corbusier's five points! I also used vernacular elements, which were meant to be recognisable. For instance, I am thinking of the pyramidal roofs, chimneys, bricks, and letterboxes that I used in the Burrundulla Garden Housing at Kambah, Canberra that I designed in 1987.

Between La Tendenza and Neoliberty: Mauro Baracco Goes to Australia

Mauro Baracco

in conversation with

John Macarthur and Silvia Micheli

Mauro Baracco moved from Italy to Australia in 1995, following several years of sole practice in parallel with employment as a design architect in Gianni Braghieri's studio, where he had been involved with projects in collaboration with Aldo Rossi. In Melbourne, Mauro found a very vital architectural environment, with a community of architects deeply interested in Italian postmodernism. In turn, Mauro become keen in the typology of the Australian suburban house. Mauro's interest soon focused on Robin Boyd's work, to which he dedicated his PhD studies and a more recent book.

Silvia Micheli
Mauro, how was your recent trip to Italy?

Mauro Baracco
Well, you know Italy: it is a nice place to go for holidays but… You wouldn't want to live there. It's pretty decadent. Actually, I found all Europe pretty much decadent, but Italy even more.

SM   I know, it's all so complicated. That's Italy! With this conversation, we aim to know more about the architectural community of Melbourne and its engagement with Italian postmodern architecture through your particular experience in moving to Australia. But let's start a bit earlier, with your education in Italy, your understanding of postmodern architecture, and, in particular, postmodern architecture in Italy, which is fairly difficult when you are embedded in that very cultural environment. You have probably had the opportunity to reflect back on that while living and working in Australia.

MB   A key moment of my education was in 1980, visiting the first Venice Biennale of Architecture curated by Paolo Portoghesi. His exhibition *La Strada Novissima* was the celebration of postmodernism at an international level. I was only a second-year student then. You know, when you are a second-year student, you are not very conscious of what is happening around you, but you realise that there is something going on. During the following few years, I was particularly interested in understanding what this postmodernism was. And, mind you, at the time I wasn't even particularly conscious of what Modernism had been!
    I became more conscious about the reason for my confusion a few years later, when I came to Australia. I realised then that studying at the Turin Polytechnic and graduating there with mentors such as Roberto Gabetti, I was never really taught about international figures such as Le Corbusier or Mies van der Rohe. Gabetti used to advise his students— I was originally one of them before becoming a tutor in his architectural design courses after my graduation—to not even look at Le Corbusier! So, I self-educated myself by looking at architectural magazines and reading history books to prepare for history courses that I used to run at the European Institute of Design in Milan, the city where I moved after my graduation. Tafuri became an essential reference. While still a student, I was also particularly interested in *Domus* from the 1980s onwards, when it was directed by Alessandro Mendini. He set up a great series of issues—I still remember the exciting colourful covers and, of course, many articles on postmodern design.

SM   I love those covers with the drawings of the celebrity architects!

MB   That was a very important moment for me. Not that I necessarily embraced postmodernism in a formalistic or stylistic way, like some architects exhibiting at the Venice Biennale did—I'm thinking of the Americans Robert Stern and Michael Graves, for example.

I realise that some of my Melbourne colleagues such as Conrad Hamann are more inclined to establish architectural formal relationships, whereas to me postmodernism was, in a way, a broader idea related to the revisitation of the past. And this also explains why later I became more interested in Robin Boyd than 'postmodern' Melburnian architects. Here, I have to acknowledge Peter Corrigan, mentor and inspiring figure to many of these architects. I was very fond of Peter. Among other things, we taught History of Architecture together at RMIT for many years, and I consider him a great mentor of mine as he has been deeply and constantly generous in introducing me to certain ideas of Australianness and Melburnianness. But then he also generously accepted the fact that my sensibility was different from a formal and aesthetic point of view. Having said so, I like many of Edmond and Corrigan's works, in particular the ones informed by a certain 'brutality' and 'straightforwardness' in the use of shapes and colours. I think they are intellectually highly sophisticated and compelling, somehow much more than the works by Boyd, who was not interested in metaphorical or symbolic forms. Boyd can be considered a 'postmodern' architect, to whom the term 'post' is associated with the notions of 'shift' and 'recalibration' in regard to Modernism, also including a reappropriated relationship with landscape spaces. He was never driven by a desire to be subversive towards Modernism through symbolism, pastiche, or colourfulness. postmodernism as the re-representation of 'repressed memories'—I remember these terms from an Ian McDougall's lecture of many years ago—is something that never really interested Boyd, and this is why Boyd is of interest to me.

SM   If we could linger for a while in the period of your education in Italy and your introduction to the profession, what did you make of postmodern architecture and what kind of method did you learn?

MB   As a student, I became really interested in architecture probably in my last years. The 1980 Venice Biennale of Architecture must have triggered something that only a few years later I became conscious of. I started my studies in Genoa, but Genoa is too beautiful. Often—too often!—I used to enjoy its weather and beaches. So, I moved to the more rigorous and less tempting environment of Turin Polytechnic, where I graduated in 1985. A key moment of my education among the many courses I undertook there was the design studio coordinated by Roberto Gabetti, a collaborative design course also including professors Lorenzo Mamino and Sisto Giriodi as co-studio leaders. I loved Gabetti's highly humanist approach as an academic and practitioner. His lectures were rich with references and personal accounts related to the world of literature, landscape architecture, philosophy, art, even botany. He wrote beautifully and taught us the value of reading.

SM   When you were working with him, did he ever mention the controversial article written by Reyner Banham about Gabetti and Isola's Bottega d'Erasmo in Turin and his attack on the Italian Neoliberty?

MB   No, he didn't. He may have done this in an indirect way, through his continuous referral to the role of the 'local' in relation to the world. He never used to give descriptive lectures on his own work. He would let others do so, such as me, Mamino, Giriodi, and other tutors involved in his extended design studio course. He would intervene in the discussion to mention external references in relationship to his design and life approach; I remember comments and stories about Italo Calvino, Umberto Eco, Gianni Vattimo, and Marcel Proust, just to name a few. Only later I came to know that article, which became very important to me; my history lectures at RMIT on Italian Neoliberty were based on a counter-critique of Banham's critique. Back to Gabetti's lectures, I remember being introduced to the idea of regionalism through his remarks, sometimes ironic and a little polemic, in regard to the difference between the 'international' milieu of Milan and the 'peripheral' one of Turin.

SM   Would you call it 'localism' instead of 'regionalism'?

MB   The term 'localism' sounds appropriate. Keep in mind that Gabetti used to discourage students from learning English, his argument being that Turin and the Piedmont region which, by the way, is my original region—have strong affiliations with French culture, traditions, and landscape. The idea of localism was consistently re-affirmed through his many publications. One of these, for example, was on the work of Giovanni Battista Schellino, an architect operating in the small town of Dogliani and the surrounding Langhe region in the second half of the Nineteenth Century. It celebrates the sense of local reinterpretation, somehow the 'misreading' of a canon, in this case the Gothic style, that Schellino himself could only learn from publications since he never travelled outside his provincial rural world.

John Macarthur

Ian McDougall has written a piece on localism, which is published in his *Mongrel Rapture* book. In that essay, he describes a very similar attitude to Melbourne, which he says comes to him from Corrigan, who inspired him and his generation to have the same insistence on the value of local things. Is that sympathetic with the kind of discourse in Gabetti's design studios?

MB   Very much so. The day I announced to Gabetti I intended to move to Australia, he shared an insightful thought: "Wherever you are in the world, always try to relate to the local. I don't know what the local would be for you in Australia, but try to embrace and interpret it, because it's only by relating to the local that you can really find the language and the ground to understand the culture in which you are operating." And that's how, retrospectively thinking, I have become interested in Boyd when working in Australia.

JM   It's so interesting that you say that Gabetti was somehow already postmodernist without the label because he was telling you not to look at Le Corbusier. You didn't know about Modernism so you didn't know what postmodernism was, but in fact your education was already beyond Modernism, cut off from Modernism. And then you went to the Venice Biennale in 1980, and, thinking about that in subsequent years, you reflected on what a postmodernism would be as a kind of architecture rather than just being opposed to Le Corbusier and Mies van der Rohe.

MB   That's exactly right, yes.

JM   Can we talk about your years between Italy and Australia?

MB   I travelled in Australia for the first time in 1988. At that time, I was working in Gianni Braghieri's office on projects by Rossi and Braghieri.

SM   Why did you choose to work with them?

MB   That was not a totally conscious choice: it's somehow indicative of a kind of drifting path that has been driving my life, especially in early years. Upon graduating, I wanted to work with someone prominent. Extending from my continuous reading of *Domus* issues and more magazines and journals and wanting to leave my original provincial place, a beautiful but very secluded town on the border between Italy and France, I intended to be where interesting architecture was happening. I remember I travelled to Amsterdam for a few days with the idea to work for a Dutch architect, having in mind Theo Bosch and Aldo van Eyck. I visited a friend of mine, an Italian cultural attaché based in Amsterdam, who at the time was organising an exhibition on Aldo Rossi there. He introduced me to some of Rossi's collaborators involved with the exhibition, who advised me of some potential forthcoming job opportunities as Braghieri was in the process of opening a new office in Milan, still with strong affiliations to Rossi. Following this and a few more conversations between the Rossian Dutch group and Gianni Braghieri, I rang Gianni in Milan, and a few weeks later I was hired! I guess I was in the right place at the right time.

JM   Can you tell us about the Rossi office? What was the business? And what was the atmosphere in the studio?

MB   When I started working at Braghieri's office, we would often have collaborative sessions in Rossi's office, which was only a few hundred metres away, and sometimes Rossi himself would come to Gianni's office. At the time, Rossi was consolidating his 'international star' profile, following from the success of his early Berlinese work, among other projects in Italy. He preferred being involved with many small offices instead of managing a large one. Morris Adjmi was in charge of an office in New York, from which he was managing a few works with Aldo, including the project of the Architecture School on the Miami University campus. Then there was one small base in Tokyo—these were also the years of the Hotel Il Palazzo in Fukuoka (1987–89) and another one in the Netherlands with Umberto Barbieri in charge. Also, the main office in Milan was not that large; apart from Aldo, there were no more than six staff. He didn't like to act as 'principal director' of the office, with all the typical managerial tasks and activities that come with this role. He preferred to rely on trustworthy and efficient staff, 'loyal soldiers' ready to do everything for him. Also, he used to avoid project contracts that included the construction supervision job. In the office, there was a strong sense of loyalty, at every level: formal, ethical, and intellectual. It was difficult to have critical conversations about the work that was produced there. I remember some of the staff, probably the most loyal, were from Switzerland, ensuring that the office was marching on solidly and impeccably.

JM   What was the conversation in the office? Did they talk about postmodernism? Did they use the term?

MB   Not really.

SM   They were doing it!

MB   There was not so much conversation, not much criticism either. Rossi was a strong intellectual, but he was never really able to open up the discourse in his office. I think this was somehow his own fault, as he was inclined to employ loyal soldiers to do the job, rather than being surrounded by theoretical minds, thus also potential critics. After all, he had many other opportunities to be intellectually engaged outside his office!

One day I asked him to have one hour of his time in preparation of a review of the Molteni Family Tomb (1980–87) in Giussano that I was writing for *Domus* magazine. He opened up totally. It was great to realise how he really liked to be engaged intellectually. This is something that could happen, I guess, with staff who may have been more critically engaged and maybe a bit less 'loyal', staff like me and a few others. I remember, for example, John Sandell and Claude Zuber, who were kind of 'outsider' figures in the office.

SM   So, concepts like memory, localism, tradition were not debated in the office?

MB   Not really.

JM   Did you read Rossi's theoretical works?

MB   Yes, of course.

JM   Were you expected to know Rossi's *The Architecture of the City* (1966) and *A Scientific Autobiography* (1981) while collaborating with his office?

MB   I did know these books. I'm not sure that it was definitely expected to know these, but certainly everyone in the office was familiar with them—the problem is that many of the staff were unfamiliar with much of everything else!

JM   Was there a sense in the office about a distinct difference from American postmodernism, from Robert Stern and Michael Graves and so on? Was there a way of making those differences sharper? What were the concerns?

MB   No, not really. Rossi and Braghieri were just marching on with their beliefs, with their way of designing, and there was never really a moment where they were talking or discussing or being critical or in favour of other architects. Rossi was normally referring to architects such as Karl Friedrich Schinkel and Étienne-Louis Boullée; he was beyond his contemporaries.

SM   Tell us about coming to Australia and what people made of you as a 'product of Rossi's office' and what people made of Italian architecture in Australia. How did you negotiate that?

MB   When I came to Australia, I ended up in Melbourne as a consequence of Leon van Schaik's invitation to be involved with short intensive teaching at RMIT. When I first met Leon, he invited me to run intensive studios for the Masters course, which I did a couple of times, coming temporarily for a few weeks to Melbourne through the European summer. This was between the end of the 1980s and early 1990s. When I came to Melbourne for my first teaching experience in 1989, I also met Peter Corrigan. I was aware of Peter's work because this had been published in *Domus*.

SM The monographic issue of *Domus*, *Ciao Australia*, published in 1985, yeah?

MB Yes, *Ciao Australia*, that one. I was pretty taken when at the end of the first of a series of lectures I gave in conjunction with the intensive design studio, Peter came to me, introduced himself, and invited me out for dinner. Following this, through the next couple of weeks, he took me to visit many places, including the NGV (National Gallery of Victoria), where an exhibition of the Angry Penguins was on, and the MCG (Melbourne Cricket Ground), where he was a member. He also gave me tickets for Circus Oz. What a generosity! I couldn't have received a better introduction to fundamental aspects of Australian culture! That's when I started thinking and further speculating about possible analogies between the peripheral conditions—in terms of geography, but also culture and traditions—of Melbourne, Victoria and Turin, Piedmont. This is also why I invited Peter to be a visiting professor at Turin Polytechnic a couple of years later. He came in 1991.

SM Do you think you were received this way because you were Italian, so there was a very good understanding of what you could bring in?

MB Yes, possibly so. I think Peter liked Italians and related well with Italian culture. It seems that Italians have been pretty influential here in Melbourne.

JM Even in Brisbane. I think everyone in Australia thought that the leading architectural culture in the postmodern period was Italian in the same way it later became Spanish and then Dutch. That was like a national idea. Was it surprising to you that all Australian architects were interested in Italy?

MB Probably not. This was also because my direct experience in discussing Italian architecture occurred by being interviewed for a couple of magazines—*Transition* and *Pataphysics*—where the majority of the questions revolved around Aldo Rossi, who, by that time, had reached international fame. Young emerging intellectuals such as Peter Brew (who is now a colleague at RMIT), Kim Halik, Leo Edelstein, and Yanni Florence asked me a lot of questions about Rossi, whilst no-one was interested in Gabetti. I guess they didn't know about him. Obviously, there was a strong interest internationally about La Tendenza, as well as about the relationships between Aldo Rossi, La Tendenza, and the philosophical, social, and political positions of the Frankfurt School.

SM And do you think that Rossi and Braghieri's entry to the Melbourne Landmark Ideas Competition in 1979 had some role in the rising interest in Italian postmodern architecture?

MB I think this competition entry may have had a bit of a role, but not in a relevant way. At the time of my interviews, ten years after the Melbourne Landmark Ideas Competition entry, Rossi was well recognised worldwide. His books were all very popular. His *A Scientific Autobiography* was even translated in English before being published in Italian. So, I'd say that everyone was well aware of Rossi, either for the positive or the negative.

JM I would guess that the people in Melbourne had a different understanding of Rossi than you would have had being in the office, and I am interested as much in what they misunderstood as what they understood. Could you maybe give us an example of what they grasped clearly and maybe what they misunderstood or projected onto Rossi?

MB The interview for *Transition* was conducted by a younger group of emerging talented minds, all very ambitious with their own ideological agendas. I thought they were highly ideological, much more ideological than Rossi actually was. Sure, Rossi was ideological: *The Architecture of the City* (Italian edition, 1966) is a testament to this as well as his early writings, which I have read and which were later published in the book *Scritti Scelti sull'Architettura e la Città*, edited by Rosaldo Bonicalzi (1975). However, and also in light of our earlier topic regarding the lack of intellectual discussion within his office, my impression is that the questions posed to me at the end of the 1980s were slightly misaligned, time-wise, with the day-to-day concerns of Rossi's practice in the second half of the 1980s and early 1990s, when I was part of it.

JM One of the first things I really liked about Rossi was an interview in which he talked about housing and his Gallaratese housing in Milan. He said he would only design terrace housing because villas were bourgeois and tower blocks were inappropriate in historic environments. This statement is strong. You know, this is Marxism! The attraction of Italian architecture for Australian progressives was the idea that Italian architecture was political. In Australia, everyone was aware of the dominance of the Communist Party and progressive politics in Italy, looking towards people like Gramsci. So, part of the interest of Australian architects in Italian architecture is the idea that it was an architecture that was politically progressive. Is that what you mean when you say the people who interviewed you from *Transition* were ideological? In that political sense?

MB Yes, I could feel that. I think that, at another level, Peter Corrigan was fond of Rossi for different reasons. Sure, Peter was certainly aware of the strong political character informing Rossi's theoretical writings and early architecture, but I believe Peter also liked Rossi's aesthetic, his formalism. He really liked his drawings and his compositions, both in graphic resolution and formal execution.

JM   Since you have been permanently in Melbourne, you've developed this great interest in Robin Boyd, who is a hero for many Melburnian architects. Do you think you come to Boyd differently because of your education in Italy?

MB   Possibly, yes. I know that Ian McDougall is also very fond of Boyd, but I think he looks at his work from a different angle. Many of the Italian architects I feel empathy for—not by coincidence, many of these are from the neoliberty generation—are able to operate at 360 degrees, applying their approach at many different scales, from furniture and product design to architectural and urban projects, as well as integrating practice and academic activities. Boyd, as we know, was not an academic. However, he was regularly involved in the delivery of public lectures at architecture schools and other places in Australia and overseas. He was extremely generous in devoting time and efforts to the cause of good design, and he wrote and spoke profusely, nationally and internationally through books, journals, and daily newspapers, even directing a program in collaboration with the Melbourne newspaper *The Age* for providing people with well-designed houses.

Beside his generosity and advocacy for good design, I like his design approach very much, in particular his ability to shift spatial proportions a little, as well as his inclination to integrate built and open spaces. Very often, he treats open spaces, hallways, balconies, and other 'servicing' spaces as additional rooms for spill-out or cross-program activities. To me, Boyd is somehow a 'localist', particularly when he directs attention towards the Australian landscape, and yet his work is certainly not vernacular. He is also somehow a postmodernist, someone capable of shifting from Modernism. It's not by chance that his work shares common ground with the Smithsons and Kazuo Shinohara, among others. He also wrote about these architects and shared an idea of architecture with them that was inclined to revisit the local but never through literal translations in the form of symbolic or metaphoric features.

From this point of view, Boyd is not that different from Gabetti; all these sorts of analogies came to me later, retrospectively thinking about the Turinese architect's work and drawing relationships with Boyd according to my personal interpretation of both these architects. Gabetti advocates for a localism that mainly focuses on paying attention to local sensibilities, local cultures, local landscapes, and local traditions, yet he is not interested in formalistically or metaphorically representing these. His architecture is about embracing the local and creating conditions—mainly spatial conditions—to integrate it with the new built outcomes.

SM   Mauro, when you arrived in Australia, did you recognise the contemporary architecture of that time as postmodern? Did you find a local postmodern culture and discourse?

MB I remember visiting many postmodern works in and around Melbourne. This was also thanks to the generosity of the *Transition* editorial group, who used to hire a car and take me around, showing me works by Edmond and Corrigan, ARM, Greg Burgess, Biltmoderne, Wood Marsh, and others. I have to admit these works were a bit like punches in the face—at that time I was still working on Rossi and Braghieri's projects and was therefore constantly engaged with a rather different idea of architecture. However, these works in Melbourne were also extremely fascinating to me. I always thought they were the expression of a type of postmodernism that was much quirkier, a bit crazy, definitely clumsier, and 'not-quite-right'—all terms that I'm using here with positive connotations—in comparison to the canonical type of postmodernism produced by the Americans. I remember I found analogies between the 'craziness' of this Australian postmodernism and the sense of 'beyond the world' that was well expressed, at least to me, in the film *Mad Max*. Rossi himself thought Australians were crazy; one day he asked me, "… but Australians, they're all mad, aren't they?"

SM Was that really Rossi's understanding of Australia?

MB Well, judging from that remark, this was indeed Rossi's projected image of Australia! Mind you, he never visited Australia.

JM The general understanding is that Melbourne architecture was very influenced by La Tendenza, of which Rossi was the undiscussed frontrunner. But then, when one talks to people like you and McDougall, one wonders if it was more about Neoliberty. Not that people at the time understood that, but in the longer term it's that relationship that becomes more important. What would you say to that?

SM Just complementing this question, let's acknowledge the role of *Domus* in the circulation of architectural ideas at an international level. *Domus* was a great vehicle for promoting Neoliberty architecture in and outside Italy. You know, there was awareness of their work worldwide.

MB Yes. Conrad Hamann tells me that prominent architects from Melbourne travelled to Italy as they really wanted to visit Neoliberty buildings and establish a direct influence with these works. Also, it's interesting to see that Boyd was interviewed by *Casabella* at a certain stage. So, he knew about Neoliberty too. Let's not forget that Neoliberty was just a name, a label; it was Portoghesi, I believe, who came up with such a name. And there were conflicting positions under Neoliberty. It depends what type of Neoliberty one wants to refer to.

SM   Mauro, just a clarification. We know that *Domus* paid attention to Australian architecture, especially when directed by Gio Ponti until 1979. That was not the case of *Casabella*. I've always wondered how Boyd managed to be interviewed by *Casabella*, being the only Australian architect to be involved with this journal.

MB   My hunch is that at a certain point they decided that an Australian architect should be involved in the discussion in *Casabella*. The magazine's editor Ernesto Nathan Rogers might have asked Vittorio Gregotti, member of the editorial board, for advice about inviting foreign architects into the discussion. And, again it's my speculation, Gregotti would have observed that there was an Australian guy writing for his same publisher George Braziller.

SM   Oh yes, *New Directions in Italian Architecture*, released in 1969.

MB   In 1962 Boyd had published a book on *Kenzo Tange*, and in 1968 a book called *New Directions in Japanese Architecture*, both for the same publisher. So, Braziller and its series on new architectural directions in the world is the connection.

JM   Mauro, I am curious about your practice and your design, particularly Baracco+Wright's Garden House (2014) in Westernport, Coastal Victoria that's been so prominently publicised recently. That house seems to reflect back on the architecture of the period of your training, but it's also a very Australian house. How do you reflect on your practice now?

MB   Yes, you are right; Louise and I share a strong affinity in our interest towards Neoliberty, Boyd, and ideas revolving around the notion of the local.

SM   The house looks somehow postmodern with its big gable roof!

JM   As a conclusion of our dialogue, could you talk a little bit about where Baracco+Wright are now and how you see this period of history that we're talking about, from the 1970s to the present?

MB   Louise and I are interested in designing 'architectural spaces' more than 'architectures within space': spaces informed by levels of integration between indoor and outdoor, between built and open environment, between building and land. We believe that to relate to the local, particularly the local landscape and open environment, it's also primarily an act of 'reconciliation' with the land and the people who were capable of sustainably inhabiting the land of this country for thousands and thousands of years. Our projects are also interested in simple forms. The gable roof of the Garden House doesn't intend to be a postmodern gesture; it is simply the outcome of a constructive technique normally implemented for the very local typology of the rural shed. The Garden House was built, in fact, by a company specialising in rural sheds; however, the conventional proportions and materials of typical sheds are slightly altered here and reconfigured to also integrate the new volume with the existing open vegetated space. Architects such as Boyd and Shinohara are very interesting to us, as their design approach is inclined to a revisited type of vernacularism, where spatial resolutions are definitely more relevant than metaphorical or symbolic forms, which, in fact, are never really present in the works of these two architects and others for whom we feel empathy.

Encountering Italian Architectural Culture via USA and Australia

Conrad Hamann

in conversation with

Silvia Micheli

Conrad Hamann is an Associate Professor in Architectural History at RMIT in Melbourne. He taught contemporary architecture in the Arts faculty at Monash University from 1980, which was fed to a marked degree by a travelling scholarship in 1978–80. His current writing and interests are still affected by the take that was possible on contemporary architecture then and by the vistas presented by inclusive, pluralist, multivalent, postmodern architecture in the 1970s and early 1980s, the 'earlier' incarnation of architectural postmodernism.

Conrad Hamann
I was asked to outline teaching contemporary architecture in the Arts faculty in Melbourne's Monash University from 1981 and how that reflected a growing Australian interest in Italian architecture. That teaching was fed to a marked degree by a travelling scholarship in 1978–80, and the experience keeps giving. My current writing and interests are still affected by the take that was possible on contemporary architecture then and by the vistas presented by inclusive, pluralist, multivalent, postmodern architecture in the 1970s and early 1980s, the 'earlier' incarnation of architectural postmodernism. This architecture and the critical positions associated with it were formed pre–Hal Foster, critical regionalism, the early 1980s backlash, pre-deconstruction and its formal elisions, and before postmodernism was conspicuously claimed for Europe.

Silvia Micheli
What was the presence of Italian architectural culture in the US?

CM At the start of the 1980s, European architectural circles, in publications generally and certainly in the United States, distanced themselves from the emerging plurality and visual complexity of American architectural culture in public, and with some ferocity. And in the United States itself, Western hemisphere affiliates, especially those broadly aligned with Neo-Rationalism and the Italian *Tendenza*—from Peter Eisenman and John Hejduk to Mario Gandelsonas and Diana Agrest—largely rejected early architectural postmodernism as outside a Marxist orbit culturally, as populist and too accommodating of an existing social and class order. But Italian architectural experience profoundly informed both neo-rationalist and American pluralist or 'inclusive' architecture in these years. The leading figures of architectural change in 1960s and 1970s America all drew widely on Italian experiences, and neo-rationalism, which was at its core, and Italian movement. It appears, too, that Italian mediation had a primary role in bringing neo-rationalist and American pluralist architecture together and became a major factor in making their collective ideas 'travel'. For me, US architectural culture, Yale University, and New York's Institute of Architecture and Urban Studies (IAUS) were both a constant mediation for Italian architecture and a means of viewing it at closer range. It also meant I came back to Australia alerted to Italian affinities and parallels in a spectrum of local architecture, of the 1950s and 1960s especially.

SM After post-doctoral study in the US, in 1980 you came back to Australia and started teaching at Monash University, with emphasis on postmodern architecture. How did you structure the course and what role did the Italian architectural discourse have in it?

CM   The Monash course in Postmodern Architecture, Visual Arts 223–323, commenced on the night Roy Grounds died, 7 March 1981. The course began discussing mainstream modern architecture's problems and assumptions, followed by, per week: Robert Venturi and Denise Scott Brown; Charles Moore; Robert Stern and newer inclusives, Ricardo Bofill and Hans Hollein; Frank Gehry's suburban-based architecture in Los Angeles and the East Coast; Stanley Tigerman's Chicago-based designs; the inheritances of German expressionism in Hans Scharoun, Sergius Ruegenberg, Bernhard Pfau, and Gottfried Boehm; Neoclassicism and its legacy in Michael Graves; mannerist inheritances from Giulio Romano and Michele Sanmicheli via Lutyens and Le Corbusier; 1900s art nouveau, free styles, and their legacy; Scandinavia through its own distinctive classicism, Swedish grace and empiricism informing Alvar Aalto's and Ralph Erskine's pluralist and multi-valent designs; the New York Five, especially Michael Graves' 'turn' towards a recast classicism; James Stirling's engagement with traditional forms and in particular 1840s German romanticism; Louis Kahn's directions and legacy; Italian Neo-Rationalism; Carlo Aymonimo and Aldo Rossi and their parallels with both the Krier brothers and Latin Americans such as Diana Agrest; and finishing with a survey of Romaldo Giurgola's architecture from the early 1960s up to his Australian Parliament design. Paolo Portoghesi's projects and a specific discussion of Italian Neoliberty's inheritance were included from 1983. I visited and photographed numbers of Enrico Taglietti's Canberra buildings in early 1982, but incorporated his architecture, primarily, in a course on Australian architecture that I began later that year.

Though I travelled in Italy in 1978 and 1980, the Monash course largely reflected the architectural movements and tension I encountered in the US, and for me the East Coast US *was* the mediation, primarily in New York City—Columbia, the Institute of Architecture and Urban Studies (IAUS)—in Philadelphia, guided especially by the historian Edward Teitelman, and two subsequent years at Yale in postdoctoral research supervised by Vincent Scully and George Hersey. I don't believe the US acted as a conduit for Italian architecture to Australia generally at this time, though in Melbourne the architect Peter Corrigan had begun subscribing to the IAUS journal *Oppositions*. By 1981, RMIT University library had a run of *Oppositions* going back to 1973. I knew nothing of the IAUS in Australia previously, though that may have just been me; Rem Koolhaas put me onto it when I sought him out in London in 1978.

SM   What was the take on Italian architecture by the Americans?

CM   In the US, Italian elements were refracted through American debates and the direct Italian experience of various Americans—Vincent Scully, Louis Kahn, Robert Venturi, Peter Eisenman, Michael Graves—and by expatriates working in the United States; Alan Greenberg from South Africa, Kenneth Frampton from England, Mario Gandelsonas and Diana Agrest from Argentina, Massimo Scolari and Romaldo Giurgola from Italy itself. These circles saw Aldo Rossi and Neo-Rationalism as pivotal in future directions. Most of the expatriates had clear links with Marxist and related critiques of contemporary architecture, especially by Manfredo Tafuri, where the principal text was his *Architecture and Utopia*, available in translation through MIT (1976), and his collaboration with Francesco Dal Co on *Modern Architecture* (Electa-Abrams, 1975). Kenneth Frampton's *Modern Architecture: A Critical History*, 1980) was under their influence. In 1978–80, the standard retrospective used in IAUS referencing was Leonardo Benevolo's *History of Modern Architecture* (1960), published in English by MIT Press in 1977, despite his strange blind spots on theatre as a social condenser. During this period, I attended Frampton's lectures and seminars, both at the IAUS and at Yale. Arguably, Frampton's account and its positions could not have been possible without the Italian work that went before.

SM   What were the critical substrata directing your History of Architecture course at Monash University?

CM   The Monash course emphasised differing perspectives on contemporary architecture; it was not about a single viewpoint, whether Charles Jencks, Robert Venturi, Manfredo Tafuri, or Vincent Scully. Prompted by Scully's arguments that contemporary Italians held much common ground with Americans such as Venturi, I argued reconciliation of what were often seen as diametric opposites by contemporaries; Venturi 'versus' the expressionism of Giovanni Michelucci and his older German counterparts or the context-based generation of architectural form then encouraged in Italy. Nordic empiricism and Italian Neoliberty—Paolo Portoghesi, primarily—led me to examine work by 'Modernists', as Charles Jencks and other critics saw them, whom I saw as directly participating in multivalent and inclusive architecture. The Monash course was primarily about what linked a spectrum of movements in contemporary architecture. By that time, Portoghesi's newly translated critiques of the prohibitive (and predominantly British) modernist critical orthodoxy in 'The Presence of the Past' (1980) and *After Modern Architecture* (1981) seemed equally defining as an 'arena'; I stressed that heavily in arguments after 1982. Portoghesi's argument was prompted by Reyner Banham's 1959 *Architectural Review* encyclical on Italian Neoliberty and, for me, was emphasised by continuing eruptions of what Portoghesi called "prohibitionism" and "the functionalist statute" abroad and locally in 1981 and 1982: Aldo van Eyck, Berthold Lubetkin, James Marston Fitch, and, certainly, Harry Seidler locally. At the same time, I became more wary of the conspicuous systematisation in what Charles Jencks was terming postmodern classicism, especially as he argued it reflected a "convergence of strategies" (wills?) into a new and curiously Banham–Richards–Pevsner mainstream. And classicism was, indeed, how the general pluralist development in the post-war period was ultimately caricatured from the 1990s.

The course also reflected the beginnings of a historiography of postmodern tendencies, mooted variously by Vincent Scully at Yale, Alan Greenberg in New Haven, Stuart Wrede at Columbia, and Demetri Porphyrios in London.

My own perspective was shaped widely in the US by a study I was making, also between 1978 and 1980, of American free style, arts and crafts, and art nouveau architecture from the 1890s though to 1930. At the same time, Neo-Rationalism, as it was known, was unfolding its main texts in new English translations: Tafuri and Francesco Dal Co's *Modern Architecture* (1979); Tafuri's *Architecture and Utopia* (1976); Tafuri's *Theories and History of Architecture* (1979); Aldo Rossi's *Architecture of the City* (1982) and *A Scientific Autobiography* (1981). I incorporated all these texts into the unit's reading between 1981 and 1984. I also emphasised reading from articles and to that end secured Monash subscriptions to the Australian journal *Transition*, which promoted Italian architecture, and the Italian journals *Casabella and Domus*, among other periodicals.

Now, even in this framework you can see the Italian crossovers and gain a sense of their potential variety. Vincent Scully, Louis Kahn, Robert Venturi, Romaldo Giurgola, Charles Moore, Michael Graves, Peter Eisenman, and Colin Rowe all had substantial links with Italy and with recent architectural developments there. Giurgola was Italian-born and trained, while the others all toured there. Apart from Graves, they had all studied there between 1949 and 1952, and Kahn had toured and sketched and painted there earlier still, in the late 1920s. Graves was there from 1960 to 1962. Kahn, Venturi, Scully, and, much later, Graves, all had substantial contact with Frank Brown at the American Academy in Rome, and Rome in those years was, significantly, a focus for the realist and pluralist tendency we now term 'Neoliberty'. Among their outcomes were Louis Kahn's *Travel Sketches* and paintings, especially of Siena and of the EUR; Robert Venturi's 1953 *AR* article on the Campidoglio; and Vincent Scully's eloquent commitment to monumental and typological urbanism, seen especially in his writings after 1960. In the more rationalist territory of Milan and the North, you can also see Colin Rowe and Peter Eisenman revisiting the Italian territory that so interested Scully and Kahn, especially when Rowe explored links between Palladio and Le Corbusier (1946–47) or Eisenman studied Giuseppe Terragni and the implications of formal transformation (1965–68).

The Institute for Architecture and Urban Studies in New York (IAUS), dubbed *istituto nero* by one New York wag, was crucial in collating much of this experience; Venturi, Denise Scott-Brown, and Charles Moore excepted.

The IAUS was funded by Philip Johnson and led by Peter Eisenman. By 1978, it had gained direct influence in John Hejduk's Cooper Union, in Princeton, Cranbrook, Harvard, Cornell University, and SUNY Syracuse University. Yale soon took up a series of IAUS affiliates in its theory and history seminars, then chaired by the dean, Cesar Pelli, who was broadly sympathetic to the inclusive direction embodied in Venturi and Scott Brown. IAUS personnel were clearly on the star circuit of American colleges, as Portoghesi later termed it: Massimo Scolari, Eisenman, Rem Koolhaas, Michael Graves, Charles Gwathmey, Kenneth Frampton, Stanford Anderson, and "the Argentinians" could variously be caught on energetic campuses around the US at any given time of the year. The IAUS was the engine room, literally, for *Oppositions*, the journal and the books printed by MIT. The IAUS owed its impetus above all to a modern tradition in Italian design that encompassed the currents of rationalism, context, typology, the School of Venice, and, to me, an extraordinarily open and flexible interest in historical phenomena and history as a subject. This was apparent when I joined Mario Gandelsonas's seminars and his emphasis on something that at least was unfamiliar to me; *urbanism* and, to a large degree, typology and built context were considered central to the history of modern architecture rather than an option to be included by some thoughtful architects. The IAUS's Italianate criticism was also exciting in its abandonment of architectural evaluation by checklist or by ticking formal and thematic boxes, except when a box called American Populism was detected. Even in that moment of resistance, the IAUS approach was primarily a reflection of Italian thinking and a broader concern, almost a signature in rationalist architectural circles, for quarantining European culture from American popular influences. So, too, despite the usual architectural inconsistencies, was the conspicuously Italian connection between architecture and political *paths* sharpened by the Marxism of Tafuri and Rossi. And the Italians studied their *political* position, in contrast to American architects, who seldom showed strong political positions beyond a widely shared, fairly tacit aversion to America's Republican Party. But stepped-up politics was just one facet of the IAUS and its wider program: it was bringing primarily European values to receptive American architects.

SM Before visiting the US, what kind of architectural references did you have?

CM My pre-US perspective around 1975–78 was in a predominantly British tradition; James Stirling, brutalism, Archigram and Cedric Price, Ralph Erskine as participation, rough finishes and genuineness, pipes and primary colours, visual toughness. It was like British music's beat boom of 1963–66 applied to architectural perspectives. The general historiography primarily focused on the Bauhaus and Le Corbusier as convergence points in a Nikolaus Pevsner line from the arts and crafts in what might now be called "'art historians' modern architectural history". Largely framed by doctrinal purism, it guarded eternally against backsliders and fought to preserve Team Modernism's formal revolution; Corbusier's five points and the abolition of ornament. By the 1970s, this was being re-textured in an assortment of counter-cultural and rock music responses; as cop-outs, sell-outs, *pig architecture*. The primary target was large commercial architects working with similarly large corporations. Developed leftist engagements that resembled Italian political alignments were rare; John Macarthur cites his circle at the University of Queensland among early participants, but elsewhere there seemed little of that level of political thought.

In the mid-1970s, Australian architects showed very limited tolerance of inclusive or pluralist readings in contemporary architecture that would mark the postmodern phenomenon, especially of Venturi and Scott Brown, who were then widely categorised as 'Pop' or 'Camp'. I only encountered 'postmodern' as a term around 1976, when reading an old article of Joseph Hudnut's in *Progressive Architecture* (ca. 1953). In Australia, Venturi and Scott Brown's use of roadtown and advertising imagery was seen as allowing *The Australian Ugliness* back in by stealth. Charles Moore was accepted, interestingly enough, by Robin Boyd and other Australians such as Peter Corrigan, and the Melbourne architect and teacher Jeffrey Turnbull had studied and worked with Moore for several years.

The Australian affinity was primarily for Moore's Sea Ranch Condominium (1963–65), which in retrospect looks among the most Italian of his designs, replete with piazzas, campaniles, and masses of internal subdivisions that repeated medieval Tuscan proportions. Robin Boyd and Kevin Borland clearly admired Moore. Moore was clearly excited by the highly compressed and perspectively forced centres of Italian hill towns, much as Kahn had been. And Bernard Rudolfsky's images of Italian hill towns, published in his *Architecture without Architects* (1963), found parallels in contemporary Australian projects. These included Hely, Bell & Horne's Housing (1963) at Glebe; Hassell's Elderly People's Housing (1971) in Adelaide; Earle, Tompkins and Shaw's Lygon Street Housing (1970–73) in Melbourne; and Daryl Jackson and Evan Walker's City Edge Housing (1972–74) in South Melbourne. The detailed grain in these projects, however, was largely from outside Italy. Rather, the sources were in the new brutalist British terraces of Neave Brown and Patrick Hodgkinson; James Stirling's Greenhouse Chamfering; partial acceptances of Nordic Empiricism via Erskine. In Australia during the 1970s, Italy's architectural culture and its influences were viewed uneasily from within what was still a recognised modernist mainstream.

SM   What was the general understanding of Italian architecture?

CM   Among Australian architects, Italy was good for *industrial* design and *flair*, for worthy historical examples, and for its perceived conduit to European urbanity. All those crimson and mustard-coloured Alfas and Fiats that architects and designers drove here were a testament, there among the green MGs. But building design? Actually, it was a Fiat-driving American academic, Memory Holloway, who alerted me to Paolo Soleri and his Arcosanti in her architectural teaching at Monash. His community was conspicuously counter-cultural, and I found it hard to incorporate his studio's work in my own Monash teaching, though I duly visited the Arcosanti in 1979. It is only very recently that I have reviewed Soleri in my own RMIT teaching. Carlo Mollino seemed unknown in Australia at that time, and I only learnt about him, basically, when his monograph lobbed in to Peter Corrigan's bookshelves in 1987.

SM   What about the Italian architects operating in Australia?

CM   The prominent Italian expatriates in Australia were the Milanese Enrico Taglietti, of course, and, with more dramatically popular forays, the Triestino architect Ermin Smrekar (1931–2016), mostly active in Melbourne. In their differing ways, both were, in my mind, related to the highly sculptural reinforced concrete architecture in Italy. Aldo *Loris* Rossi's work in the Naples area was at one end of that spectrum; Carlo Scarpa was at the other, in the Veneto. Both had considerable coverage in contemporary publications, *Domus* and *Abitare* especially. But I found it hard to lecture or teach on Carlo Scarpa; as Gevork Hartoonian notes, the fragmentary and episodic character of his work made it hard to translate, in my case, into lectures and seminars. Margaret Plant was able to develop teaching around Scarpa later, as part of the Museum Studies courses she developed at Monash (1984–85.). Neither Taglietti from Milan nor Smrekar from Trieste were admitted to a wider Australian fellowship in architecture at that time, despite Norman Day's early championing of Smrekar among Melbourne Young Turks around 1975–82 or Taglietti's rather sporadic coverage in *Architecture Australia*. Both were way outside Australian architecture's prevailing ruralist convergence and its celebrations of platonic pavilions in a benign landscape. And, in Australia, neither *seemed* sufficiently persecuted to be ranked (in compensation) as visionaries or heroes. Smrekar sat in on my postmodernism lectures and we worked together on an RAIA housing jury in mid-1981, which became known quickly as 'the Postmodern Jury'.

SM   How was Banham's analysis of Italian architecture perceived in Australia?

CM Reyner Banham was feted here, and, though he was interested in Italian architecture, most of his efforts were aimed at bringing Italian architecture 'to heel'. But in this, interestingly, he was isolated from Robin Boyd and other local friends, who might normally have adopted a similarly proscriptive line. In 1970, Boyd personally championed and invited Giancarlo di Carlo, certainly a transgressive Italian figure, to initiate a series of annual lectures on architecture for the Victorian chapter of the Institute of Architects. Banham's pop-psych pejoratives on Italian architecture—neuroses, infantile regressions, etc.—did not get a real reprise till Harry Seidler re-used them on postmodernism as a more general phenomenon in the early 1980s. After that, the more established end of the local culture, especially in Sydney, began seeing neuroses everywhere.

SM The Venice Biennale of Architecture was a big component for the dissemination of postmodern architecture. Did you visit its first exhibitions?

CM Nothing in my Australian background prepared me for Vittorio Gregotti's 1978 exhibition in Venice (Venice Biennale of Architecture No. 0), held in the salt warehouse and coupled to the Art Biennale being held around it. My first response on visiting it was *reaction*; I was startled by the pronounced neoclassicism of many of the exhibited designs and the reiteration of Giuseppe Terragni and the rationalist architecture of the 1920s and 1930s. Neoliberty was more subdued as a presence: Gregotti had moved against it.

SM It is interesting that you mention Neoliberty, as it is quite a controversial page of Italian twentieth century architectural history.

CM In Venice, I still sought out Ignazio Gardella's nearby Zattere House (1953), being keen to see it after reading a hostile commentary by Banham. My next real contact with Neoliberty as a tradition was when travelling in Denver, Colorado, in 1979, where a local family (fundamentalist Baptists) introduced me to Gio Ponti's North Wing of the Art Museum (1971). Literally a castle, it reads as strongly scenographic; thin-skinned, yet with castle thickness in its imagery, glittering with glazed tiling, layered and brittle in its shaping and incisions. It has affinities with work both by Taglietti and Smrekar, without the sculptural weight you see in Taglietti designs. The verticality, re-entrant angles, and texture in Ponti's design also seemed much closer to Paolo Portoghesi, who eventually visited and lectured in Australia during the 1990s. Portoghesi's writing on baroque was on university reading set by Monash colleagues from at least 1980. Portoghesi's *own* projects and designs, the chronology and influence of his building designs, and his reception in Australian architectural circles still needs to be charted in detail.

After US-based study, I went back to Italy in 1980, seeking out Neoliberty and neo-rationalist buildings more deliberately. BPPR's Torre Velasca (1950-58) and Ponti's Pirelli Tower in Milan were obvious destinations, but I was also struck by the abundant Neoliberty and contextualist residential design in Verona, especially in areas where I had gone to explore Michele Sanmicheli's fortress gateways, encouraged in this interest by Vincent Scully's admiration of Sanmicheli. Subsequently, I lectured on Sanmicheli in Monash's Renaissance art courses (from 1982 or 1983, as I recall) and moved to tease out some of the connections that Scully had observed between Sanmicheli and Edwin Lutyens. This raises questions of how postmodern architecture drew from another, more formally direct Italian connection, sixteenth-century mannerism. But clearly the linkage of mannerism and what people now see as postmodern architecture is much broader, and their future affinities were prefigured in a remarkable essay of Bruno Zevi—never ultimately a friend of postmodernism—on Palladio in the Italian *Encyclopedia of Art* (1957).

SM   How did Neoliberty impact on Australian architecture?

CM   Teaching postmodern architecture in an Australian setting alerted me to 'precursor' Neoliberty affinities in local architecture by Australians, though the boundary between that and a parallel affinity with Scandinavian empiricism was not always clear-cut. Empress Towers (1965–67) at Battery Square in Hobart, which I looked at in 1983 and later, was a case in point. On the one hand, it recalled the Point Housing in Orebro, Sweden (1946), by Sven Backstrom and Leif Reinus. But it also evoked, for me, the angled walls and skillion roofed Tiburtino Housing (1944–54) in Rome by Ludovico Quaroni and Mario Ridolfi. Italian Neoliberty and Scandinavian Empiricism clearly worked in conjunction for Australia's architects in the 1950s and 1960s. Dennis Rourke's North Sydney House (1964) struck me this way: its framing and asymmetrical window placement and brick infill bays recalled Neoliberty work for me, as with Mario Ridolfi's Viale Etopia Housing (1950–54) in Rome. In 1985, Ken Woolley observed in an interview published in the Australian journal *Transition* that he had sought out Grounds, Romberg, and Boyd in Melbourne for interviewing before his first major overseas travels in 1959. His main reason was their perceived affinity with Italian Neoliberty architecture, then associated particularly with Grounds' personal friend, Ernesto N. Rogers. Woolley soon got me thinking about Grounds, Frederick Romberg, and Robin Boyd and the sense they gave of an acute response to context and typology, unusual in Australian Modernism generally at that time. All three were, in partnership and as separate practitioners, broadening their historical resonance to a degree that was seen by 1960 as transgressive, especially with Grounds. Their Ormond College Buildings were the immediate evidence—Grounds' use of finials and gazebo form with his Vice Master's House alterations (1958) and the evocation of summer-house forms in his Master's Lodge (1959). Romberg's Picken Court (1961–63) reworked the canted bays on Joseph Reed's original building (1887) nearby but through a markedly Neoliberty system: pronounced but lightly scaled cornices, an exposed concrete frame, infilled bays with raw brick and offset windows, repeated polygons, evocation of the Gothic in tapering and acute angled edges, and chamfered concrete supports that gave an echo of BBPR's Piazza Meda Offices (1958–69) in Milan.

SM   Robin Boyd followed Italian architecture very closely, directly interacting with Italian architects.

CM   Robin Boyd was affected as well. He had previously written for the Italian journals *Casabella, L'Architettura. Cronache e Storia,* and his refurbishment of Jimmy Watson's Tavern (1959–62) in Carlton, combining three terrace houses behind a single new façade with arched openings and decoratively roughcast texture and string cornice, shows the scales and textures of contemporary Italian work. His revision of Romberg's 1965 design for Ormond College's new McCaughey Court dormitory (1965–68), completed after Romberg moved to Newcastle, was closer to Scandinavian empiricism in its historical and out-of-mainstream resonances and its lack of a *directly* contextual scaling and mass. The structuration here, and his later use of diagonal concrete struts in Menzies College (1969–71), has distant echoes of BPPR's Velasca Tower but is more likely prompted by the off-form concrete Boyd was then admiring in Japan and Britain and the conspicuous use of struts by earlier Australian architects such as Harold Desbrowe-Annear. Though he retained the original chamfered square plan, Boyd effectively discarded Romberg's design of 1965, removing, in particular, its Neoliberty grain; the light scale and its precast, interlocking concrete aprons that also recalled the accentuated, rusticated stonework of Reed's 1880s College Buildings again right alongside.

In larger buildings such as these, Romberg and Boyd were paralleled by Grounds' Victorian Arts Centre design (1958–59) and his John Medley Tower (1965–70) at the University of Melbourne. Philip Goad and I wrote separate essays on the early years of the Arts Centre project, Philip emphasising how Grounds toured Milan's Castello Sforzesco with Ernesto Rogers in 1958. He argues how this contact informed the Gallery's final form and ideas, and it is certainly evident in the courtyard divisions and the separate triangular barbican, reworked by Grounds to form the Building on St Kilda Road (1968) for the National Gallery of Victoria School of Art. Until Philip's essay, though, I personally missed the Castello Sforzesco connection entirely, though it makes perfect sense when you see the Gallery building.

In 1977 interviews, Grounds spoke to me more of echoing the great banking families' palazzo tradition, of Florence's Medici-Ricardi palace by Michelozzo in particular, but his response seemed undeniably Neoliberty in its grain. My "Backlogue" essay argued links to Neoliberty architecture by Luigi Caccia Dominioni, Ignazio Gardella, and Mario Ridolfi, largely citing examples illustrated in Gregotti's *New Directions in Italian Architecture* (1968). I was also interested in the design's fusion with elements of Scandinavian modern Classicism and New Empiricism, a crossover that Alan Colquhoun has observed in Italian Neoliberty designs. Their affinities here were not wholly Italian, though, by any means. Grounds had other interests: there was his traditional Japanese usage in line, scale, and proportions, carried through from Grounds' Embassy Buildings (1960–62) in Canberra; there was a persistent Scandinavian Classicism in the grain of the original fountain courtyard (now gone); an unashamedly scenographic Errol Flynn–Hollywood mead hall with minstrel balconies reshaped as the Gallery's Great Hall; and an unsuccessful grappling with homestead verandahs applied in the drama court (now gone).

Grounds' John Medley Building (1969–71) for the Arts Faculty at the University of Melbourne makes thorough sense in this Italian context. Its central Bridge of Sighs, accommodating a shared staffroom so staff might mingle, its rectangular concrete hood-aedicules, the proportions and breadth of the tapering cornices with their crimped and panelled soffits, all speak of Italy's palazzo tradition, especially as Neoliberty architects might have made the linkage. Ignazio Gardella's housing springs to mind. Grounds' Robert Blackwood Hall (1965–71) at Monash University, with curiously smudged imagery, suggested a medieval cathedral. But it also completed another primarily Italian reference in a little-remembered but remarkable episode in urbanism.

SM   Was Italian Neoliberty well received across all Australia?

CM   This interest was by no means restricted to Melbourne. Ken Woolley's earlier interest in Neoliberty resurfaced in details of his collaboration with Ross King in work for Edward Herbert Farmer on the State Government Offices (1961–64) in Sydney. Indeed, what struck me when shown the design in 1997, was the way the building breathed Neoliberty. This shows in the glittering stalactite-box light diffusers enveloping the lift foyer ceiling; the flattened arches over the main foyer doorways; the flattened arches lining the short podium along Philip Street; the polished stone and other materials when one was away from the external frame and its expression; and the almost medieval slot windows shielding the public service drafting annexe from the western sun. There were other recurring Italian affinities, rationalist and Neoliberty, in Sydney work: think of the legacy of Giuseppe

Terragni's Casa del Fascio in Como so evident, ironically enough, in Bunning and Madden's now-demolished Returned Services League Offices (1949–57) in College Street or their International House (1967) at the University of Sydney. The pervasiveness of these themes was again mediated by Scandinavian empiricism.

SM   Romaldo Giurgola was a postmodern architect, who bridged his Italian architectural sensibility to Australia via the US. Could you please give your interpretation of his work?

CM   Giurgola had a unique take on the broader American inclusive tendency I had tracked in the Monash Postmodern course. I grew interested in Giurgola through American magazines before travelling over there and from Robert Stern's coverage of his earlier designs in *New Directions in American Architecture* (1968, 1976). Stern emphasised the inclusive and pluralist concerns in a body of Giurgola's American work and brought home to me, early on, that American pluralism could range outside Pop and responses predicated on roadtown. I sat in on Giurgola lectures in Renaissance Architecture (Columbia, 1978) and his IAUS lecture on his own current work (also 1978), studied his reworking of Columbia's Mathematics building (1976–78), watched his involvement in Australia's Parliament House competition (1979), and read his essay on the Partial Vision in *Perspecta* (1965, read 1979–80).

In *Perspecta* and his later *New Directions in American Architecture* (1968), Robert Stern presented Giurgola as one of a pluralist, inclusive trio: the other two were Venturi and Moore. In 1974, Vincent Scully scooped Giurgola into his own inclusive, historically resonant pantheon in *The Shingle Style Today or The Historian's Revenge*. I was, again, personally interested through seeing an affinity between several of his houses (the Dorothy Shipley White house, Chestnut Hill, Philadelphia, 1963; the Mount Desert Visitors' Center project, Maine, 1962) and the free style persistence of American Edwardian forms that I was then exploring in postdoctoral work. So, I included Giurgola in my Postmodern course at the beginning, and his commission to design the Australian Parliament (1979–88) was further reason. The Parliament was much more classicising than his earlier work and stands stock still compared with the flash-by imagery in the Mount Desert pavilion, with its 'glimpse' of a New England quadrant window or the pivoting masses in the Dorothy White house. The New Parliament also makes an interesting reference to Michelangelo's trapezoidal Capitoline Piazza in its inscribed desert lake and the converging berms of its forecourt. I confess, in retrospect, to preferring Giurgola's St Thomas Aquinas Parish Church (1989) in Charnwood and his additions to Parramatta Cathedral (1996–2003). The new Parliament seemed too immediately British Empire/Red Fort/Lutyens and Baker, a general interest among American inclusives at the time. But the Parliament is certainly the closest that a major Canberra building has come to embodying the constituent spaces, progressions, and encounters that mark a city. Here, Giurgola tackled Canberra's lack of an urban sense as much as imaging a national capitol. In that sense, again, you are reminded that Italian architecture, in its urbanism, its drawing on typology, and at so many points its sheer boldness in combination, is central to the development we now view as postmodern, pluralist, inclusive; it's another reminder of the close link between the postmodern phenomenon and currents in Italy's modern architectural culture.

We All Loved Tafuri!

A conversation between

Gevork Hartoonian, John Macarthur and Paul Walker

Gevork Hartoonian, John Macarthur and Paul Walker were inspired by the work of Italian historian Manfredo Tafuri at the start of their academic careers. Each of them approached Tafuri from different socio-political and cultural environments: the University of Pennsylvania (USA), the University of Queensland (Australia), and the University of Auckland (New Zealand), respectively. Beyond their common interest in Tafuri, these academics were equally intrigued by Italian architects, intellectuals, and architectural historians' engagement in the political praxis of post-war Italy. When Gevork, John, and Paul came together at the Italy/Australia Postmodern in Translation symposium in Canberra, they recalled their initial encounters with the work of Tafuri and reflected on where their views of the Italian historian intersect and diverge.

Gevork Hartoonian

To have a conversation about Manfredo Tafuri is like opening Pandora's Box, especially in the present situation marked by the advent of globalisation and digital reproducibility. More challenging is to reconsider Tafuri's work in the context of the Australian academic environment today. Tafuri's reception in Anglophone countries took place at a time when structuralist and post-structuralist discourses were seasonal. For reasons that are beyond the scope of this conversation, 'theory' as such is now *passé*. To me, therefore, any discussion on Tafuri needs to be assessed in a different matrix.

Still, the historical and political differences between the USA, Italy, and Australia make this game of juggling a little bit more complex. Especially so because of the recent writings of Pier Vittorio Aureli, who has tried in a very complex way to connect Aldo Rossi, Massimo Cacciari, and Tafuri with the political movements of Italy, and we know that, for some time at least, both Rossi and Tafuri were members of the Communist Party in Italy, the strongest Marxist group in Europe.

For myself, I should say that my thinking has developed from Marxism; I was even a little bit Maoist at one point in America, and I got the chance to teach Tafuri for a PhD Colloquium at Columbia University in Fall 1999.

Let me mention a couple of doubtless familiar background issues. It's good to remember that the end of the 1970s and the beginning of the 1980s was marked by the appearance of relevant publications, including Jean-François Lyotard's *The Postmodern Condition: A Report on Knowledge* (1979), followed by a host of scholarly publications on the subject; Fredric Jameson's *Postmodernism or The Cultural Logic of Late Capitalism* (1983) and Jürgen Habermas's 1981 speech, entitled "Modernity: An Incomplete Project". In reference to the Venice Biennale of Architecture of 1980, Habermas, in a very interesting way, plotted three architectural tendencies. First was a Venturiesque historicism or eclecticism; the second was the deconstructive debate vigorously pursued by the New York Five; and third was a critical continuation of the notion of the incompleteness of modernity through Frampton's discourse on critical regionalism. This last direction, I believe, drew from Vittorio Gregotti's editorials in the Italian architecture magazine *Casabella*.

The situation of architecture in the 1980s also witnessed Manfredo Tafuri's *Theories and History of Architecture* (1968), the English edition of which appeared for the first time in 1979; then, of course, *Architecture and Utopia* (1973), translated in 1976—the so-to-speak bible—followed by *The Sphere and the Labyrinth* (1980), translated into English in 1987.

Now, relevant to Australia, I should say that one can't forget the fact that Tafuri disseminated a Marxist reading of history shared by most members of the Italian Movimento Operaio [labour movement]. I am reminded of the letter Tafuri wrote to Joan Ockman after the exposure of the United States east coast intelligentsia to his work. He wrote: "Over there [the USA east coast academies] you guys have no clue about the political situation in Italy, or what is my stand, because of east coast architects and intellectuals have no political dimension in their work."

Now, I'm also very much aware that John Macarthur reviewed Tafuri's book *The Sphere and Labyrinth* for issue 32 of the architectural journal *Transition* in 1990, commissioned by editors Karen Burns and Harriet Edquist. Is that correct?

John Macarthur
I was having difficulty getting published at the time and they were kind.

GH   It is a very long review presenting a comprehensive analysis of the text, which I read from A to Z! In the background of John's review, my first question concerns the issue of the task of the historian that Tafuri articulated in the historical project. I just want to read a very short quote from the book. Tafuri claims the historian's role is "to construct a history that, after having upset and shattered the apparent compactness of the real, after having shifted the ideological barriers that hide the complexity of the strategies of domination, arrives at the heart of those strategies—arrives, that is, at their modes of production."

John, would you mind reflecting on this notion of the task of the historian; how does it work in the context of Australian socio-political and architectural culture?

JM   I had thought that we were going to approach such serious questions through life stories. But I suppose a relevant story of how I came to read Tafuri may come back to your question. I read Tafuri, like a lot of people, as theory not as history. In the politics of the academy at the time, in the architectural school at the University of Queensland, this was very much about factional conflicts between architectural science and architectural design. What Tafuri stood for was a possibility of a coherent design theory that would give thinking about design, particularly the cultural aspects of design, a kind of intellectual credibility that would allow it to stand up against climatic determinism and a lot of architectural design methods based on positivistic science.

I read *Architecture and Utopia* on my own account around 1980, and my Master's thesis of 1984 was entitled *Foucault/Tafuri/Utopia*. The first time I taught Tafuri was in 1990. I took over a course from Peter O'Gorman, who was an architect, design teacher, and builder who had run a small seminar on Tafuri the semester before. Peter wasn't really equipped by his education to read Tafuri, I think, but he enjoyed it and had a great deal of insight. He saw that kind of weighty thinking as a defence of the complexity of design thinking, a manner of seriousness that would give creative work some intellectual credibility to stand up against the kind of scientific discourse that was going on at the school at the time. Although I knew some Marxism and historiography, my excitement about Tafuri was not so different from Peter's and focused on the persona and position of the theorist, as much as any theory. Much later Andrew Leach and I wrote an essay about the persona of Tafuri as a theorist; "Tafuri as Theorist" in *ARQ: Architectural Research Quarterly* 10, 3–4 (2006).

Although I was enrolled in Architecture, significant parts of my intellectual education were from the Arts Faculty at the University of Queensland. My sister studied in the French department, and she would teach me semiotics informally before I enrolled to study semiotics under Anne Freadman and moved on to read post-structuralist historiography such as Roland Barthes on the narrative form of history. I didn't believe in history. I didn't think the task of the historian was at all as serious as Tafuri takes it, so I was much more pluralist and relativist at that time than I am now. What interested me were conceptual constructions that used the data of the past.

In some ways, when I first taught and thought about Tafuri, I was trying to rip out some kind of theory of architecture from the historiographic aims of the books, but also out of Tafuri's Marxism. Like you, Gevork, I think it mistaken not to account for the Marxist enterprise in Tafuri's thought. But, again, this is perhaps because of my own education. In the 1980s, I was in the Marxist Literary Theory Group of the English department at the University of Queensland, led by Dan O'Neil, an inspirational teacher who had been a student leader at the University of Queensland in the anti-war and civil rights movement of the late 1960s. While the group's original enemy was the high mandarin view of culture of F.R. Leavis, by the 1980s there was a factional split between a hard left, who, to exaggerate a little, wanted to practise small arms assembly during the seminar, and those of us who were already, kind of, post-Marxist. We were reading semiotics, the Annales School, Louis Althusser, Michel Foucault, and Jacques Derrida, so we considered ourselves post-Marxist, and we tried, I guess, to rescue a nimble leftist project out of what we saw as the teleological determinism of Marxism.

So, when I read Tafuri, I was trying to strain out Marxist historiography, the big Hegelian themes, and I was uninterested in the wider questions of a proper historiography. I was interested instead in trying to recuperate some genuine theory of architecture that would be applicable in the studio, in design, for architecture of that time. I think that's just something of my eccentric Australian take on Tafuri of that time.

GH Yes. But, in your review, the issue of technique comes often, even in the subtitle. Technique turns to be the initial question in approaching Tafuri: how do you reconcile that, or why the emphasis on technique?

JM Well, again I'm channelling the debates that were had between Marxist historiography and the historiography of Michel Foucault or the French Annales School. Having been schooled in that kind of theory of historical formations and their rupture, I was very much opposed to a narrative teleological history and indeed the kind of metanarratives that you were announcing before in your paper and which Tafuri indulges in. Your claim that there could be some sort of relationship between an architect's understanding of present historical circumstances and those of an architecture of the fourteenth century seems to me to be wild, basically. Why would you assume that there was an essence or concept of architecture stable or even comparable across such a time frame, when you could look much more concretely at the way in which institutions and techniques were directly transferred?

So, following Foucault and his books on power/knowledge, I was looking for aspects of architectural culture that could reasonably be supposed to transfer across the historical ruptures of what architecture was and had been. The one that interested me most was planning; how planning (a definite technique, a definite teachable knowledge) was neutral in itself, neither good nor bad, neither capitalist nor communist, neither oppressive nor a matter of freedom, and how you could understand that kind of neutral technique. It seemed to me that plotting the history of such techniques was possible. By then, I was doing historiography.

GH We can discuss Tafuri's interpretation of architectural history, but we can also examine how his thinking is relevant in other countries. Andrew Leach, for one, has taken up Tafuri's historiography, but I haven't yet read any historiography of Australian or New Zealand architecture from a Tafurian point of view. Should we distinguish between historiographical principles and an actual historiography of the architecture of a given time and nation?

Andrew Leach's PhD dissertation became a book entitled *Manfredo Tafuri: Choosing History* (2007), the first interpretation of the Italian historian written in the region. It is quite interesting, and I reviewed it for *Architectural Theory Review*. Leach presented a comprehensive 'textual' reading of Tafuri: a structuralist tendency sealed by the Barthian notions of the 'death of author' and autonomy popular among major circles of the Italian left of the 1960s. More recently, Marco Biraghi has published a book entitled *Project of Crisis: Manfredo Tafuri and Contemporary Architecture* (2013), which Paul reviewed in 2014. Paul, how should we bring these two books together; because they have two different takes on Tafuri?

PW Andrew Leach was my student in Victoria University, Wellington, so, I suppose, I'm responsible for introducing him to Tafuri. The work he did for his research Masters degree in Wellington was based on a local case study and used some American cultural studies theory in relationship to it.

I recall talking to him about Tafuri when he was thinking about potential PhD topics, but this did not seem like an obvious path to follow at the time.

I think you're absolutely right to raise the question of the relationship of Tafuri's work to geographically specific architectural history. This would be a very good question to direct at Andrew because he has made major contributions to New Zealand architectural history through his study of Frederick Newman (originally Neumann), a very significant migrant figure, a Viennese modernist with experience in the Soviet Union who came to New Zealand and worked in government circles.

I'm not going to answer your question directly, but I think that the Biraghi book at least helped me understand some things that I didn't understand about *Theories and History of Architecture* when I read it in the 1980s. I probably read *Architecture and Utopia* first, but I didn't find that a very persuasive book because Tafuri's argument in *Architecture and Utopia* is that the protocols of planning invented by architecture were appropriated by capitalism. But the book does not explain the mechanisms by which this appropriation occurs. It's too small a book to delineate the process through which this transfer might happen. At least, I couldn't imagine how this had occurred.

Theories and History of Architecture seemed to me to be a much more profound book because it treated architecture as a significant discipline in its own right and took architecture's historiography seriously. Tafuri certainly wanted to rescue architectural history from its having been instrumentalised by the modern historians, and, though *Theories and History of Architecture* had a reputation for being difficult to read, that aspect of its argument was understandable to me.

The thing that I took out of the book was that Tafuri treated architecture as a serious matter. In the period of the 'theoretical turn' of architecture in the 1980s, it seemed that a lot of what we were reading was written by architects appropriating various species of cultural theory that turned architecture into an exemplification of that theory. They did this to demonstrate their understanding of the theory rather than their understanding of architecture.

One of the things I admired deeply about Tafuri was that he could refer to Foucault, he could refer to Derrida, quite lightly or allusively and make points with their work, which were pertinent to architecture. I thought that was a really impressive achievement. He introduced me to some writers who I didn't know previously. Walter Benjamin, for instance. He wasn't a figure talked about in the Auckland architecture school, though I am sure there were circles elsewhere in the University of Auckland where he might have been. "The Work of Art in the Age of Mechanical Reproduction", I thought—and still think—is one of the most profound reflections on twentieth century culture. It was memorable for me in any case.

GH   So, you read Tafuri through Walter Benjamin?

PW   Yes, "The Work of Art in the Age of Mechanical Reproduction" is very helpful in coming to an understanding of Tafuri's view. The comparison that Benjamin makes between architecture and cinema as two popular art forms, which are consumed collectively in a distracted mode, is key to understanding *Theories and History of Architecture*.

What I couldn't follow in *Theories and History of Architecture* is Tafuri's discussion of the work of many Italian architects. I did not know their work, so often the explication through these examples was not accessible to me at the time. Architectural history was not a strong point at the Auckland School of Architecture when I was an undergraduate. When I was recently reading the Biraghi book, his discussion of Tafuri's treatment of the architects of the international canon—Mies, Kahn, and so on—helped me to follow the development of Tafuri's work. My review of Biraghi's book is a little negative in the end because, although I think it helps one understand why Tafuri was so infuriated by Kahn, for example, I do not find the use of the idea of 'crisis' in relation to this very compelling, though Biraghi's insistence that Tafuri sees history itself as a project may be.

But perhaps this distaste for 'crisis' is another reflection of my own history. One of the first things I was asked to read when I started architecture school in Auckland in 1977 was an article by Malcolm MacEwan entitled "The Crisis in Architecture", and, by the time I'd finished my PhD, I felt that I had been continuously told architecture was in crisis, and yet it continued—more or less—to do things. No doubt architecture is a very compromised discipline, which has lost its great ambitions of the 1920s or the 1950s. To be sure there is crisis in terms of its broader socio-political role. But it is not the case that architecture as a discipline is entirely defunct or reduced to the mere styling of real estate.

GH   One of the interesting things about Biraghi's book is its title, *The Project of Crisis,* and the way he explores the subject. What are the potentialities in crisis? Instead of being totally negative, he looks into the positive outcomes of the crisis. If you take a dialectical understanding of the term, there is something to discuss in Tafuri's treatment of Louis Kahn in *The Sphere and the Labyrinth*. I was a bit shocked, if not surprised, to see that Biraghi wrote one chapter on Kahn. We typically talk about Tafuri through his take on Piranesi or Mies. Why then is Kahn highlighted in Biraghi's book? I think Kahn's work is a formalistic game, which in a very radical way was later articulated by Peter Eisenman.

But let me go back to these two books on Tafuri; Leach's and Biraghi's. The title of Andrew Leach's book, *Choosing History,* suggests a psychological factor in Tafuri's career; trained as an architect, he later chose to pursue history. Leach told me that he has seen Tafuri's beautiful drawings, which are still unavailable to the public due to difficulties with Tafuri's estate. So, Leach chose to write of the historian's choice of history. But what should we make of the notion of crisis emphasised by Biraghi? John, in his review of *The Sphere and the Labyrinth*, wrote that "Tafuri's supposition that Modernism maintains itself by creating a perpetual state of crisis has not been proved false by the collapse of that sense of crisis, on the contrary. But, the collapse of the crisis and the rise of an orthodoxy on the same foundation has had the unfortunate effect of casting Tafuri's analysis in a light less critical and more historical that is susceptible to appropriation." What do you mean here?

JM Wow, did I write that? It sounds as portentous as Tafuri! I was talking about the historical success of postmodernism. I think Andrew's title *Choosing History* has two meanings. The first is the biographical point made by Gevork and the relation of practice and history that unfolds. The other point is choosing history over theory. Tafuri's base concept is that history can provide the resources to critique theory, and by theory he means ideology. I think Andrew also means that history gives us the material to critique present ideologies. I guess in the statement that I made there I was saying that, to read Tafuri in the 1990s about events in the late 1970s, we're caught in a strange paradox. Tafuri is presenting all these historical bullets to fire at the 'Whites' and the 'Greys', but that moment's already passed. His analysis then becomes bound into the historical progression of postmodernism over late Modernism.

PW I would also observe that getting to know Tafuri as a historian was very enlightening. I think that a really profound essay that he wrote is the "Disenchanted Mountain" about the skyscraper. It's included in the book *The American City* (1973), translated into English in 1979. It's not a highly theorised essay; he just goes through so much dense material, thus making it available. It may not be Tafuri's most significant work, but reading a historian taking this material very seriously, trying to write a narrative with it without losing its complexity, for me it was terribly important as an exemplar of historical work. Perhaps this is where we can see some pertinence in Tafuri's work for more local or specific histories.

GH We talked of postmodernism as something of the past, a subject for historians. Have we taken enough account of the architect's use of history? Tafuri was good in highlighting buildings that used history to mark historical ruptures that were 'epoch making'. There is a difference between an antique fragment in Piranesi's reconstruction of Rome and Venturi's quotations. Tafuri picks up Piranesi in order to lash out at the postmodern quotations. For me, this is interesting because it says something about Tafuri's love affair with the New York Five architects. I guess he was saying something like:

"See how smart these kids are, playing and learning that you will hit the wall that capitalism has set up every time, no matter what you do." In that sense, I think there are lessons to learn from his historiography, if put in terms of architectural work and the role of the historian.

But what about postmodernism? Tafuri never used the word 'postmodernism'; he used 'hypermodernity' instead. In his resistance to the term postmodernism, you can read his emphasis on modernity as a historical project over a long period of time—*longue durée*—within which little changes such as postmodernism are almost irrelevant!

JM I want to mention the American literary critic and Marxist political theorist Fredric Jameson's essay on Tafuri, "Architecture and the Critique of Ideology" (1985). One little justification that I can see, other than them both being Italian: Jameson stirs some Gramsci into his version of Tafuri. A Gramscian notion of a counter-hegemony within the institutions of capitalism seemed to offer a way for a left architecture to operate without waiting for a complete revolution in the means and relations of production. I think I was far from alone in reading Jameson's essay as a way of recuperating Tafuri into issues of postmodernity, if not postmodernism. If there is a Tafuri in Australia, it's probably a Jameson Tafuri.

PW As I said earlier, one of the things that I found profound in *Theories and History of Architecture* was the lesson that Tafuri drew in that book from Benjamin, particularly that the distracted state of attention is a political state. That helps us understand why he sees architects like Mies as important; those whose architecture is not singular objects but series. His indulgence of the New York Five is also because he sees them as looking at the systems of architecture rather than focusing on exemplary objects. I don't know why he chose not to use the word 'postmodern', but there is no doubt that he was disdainful of turning buildings into spectacles to be contemplated along with architects who deployed history to justify the spectacularisation of the objects that they designed. I think that's why Louis Kahn was such a thorn in his side. Perhaps he thought that Kahn, when he set out on his career, could have been more like Mies in terms of dealing with conditions of production and reception, but instead he turns into a producer of spectacular buildings.

Again, I think it would be very useful to go back to "The Work of Art in the Age of Mechanical Reproduction" and think about what those arguments might mean now with the mediatisation of architecture.

JM I'm not so sure Paul. It seems to me that a lot of Tafuri's postures and his descriptions of the circumstances of architecture follow Theodor Adorno's work, which is to say the next iteration of his friend Benjamin's argument, made after the war and into the 1960s. For Adorno, Tafuri's description of the retreat of European high culture into a self-referential game or system would be a good thing in that it's an honest recognition of the only possibility of art bearing on the world, through negation. Adorno thought that history had shown Benjamin to be utopian, to engage directly with reality. The problem of art later in the Twentieth Century is how to negotiate its difference from empirical reality. The great patrimony of Western culture is in a crucible and almost implodes upon itself, and, for Adorno, this is a necessary fact of history. But it's exactly what Tafuri seems to decry in similar language.

GH It seems "we all loved Tafuri"!

Canberra: The Invisible City

Enrico Taglietti

The Milanese architect Enrico Taglietti came to Sydney in 1955 to set up the exhibition "Italy at David Jones" about Italian design, architecture and lifestyle. After visiting Canberra, he decided to move to Australia permanently. He made a significant contribution to Canberra's postmodern public and domestic architecture, merging his Italian design method with the uniqueness of the local culture and landscape. He was the 2007 RAIA Gold Medallist.

Fig. 47—50

Being in search
of a "philosopher's stone"
that could transform
edifices into Architecture
and chaotic unliveable cities
into dream cities,
I left Milan.

I left with a companion,
Francesca, my Virgil
and a Matilda
containing two amulets.

Amulets that every committed architect
in search of his philosopher's stone
should have in his sack.
A poem and a book.

My amulets were:
Leopardi's poem "The Infinite",
to remind me of the dead seasons,
6000 years of past classical architecture;
and to confront me with the present one alive,
the book, *Utopia*, by Thomas More.

Our journey took us to
Istanbul,
Lalibela,
Moscow,
Granada,
New York,
Marseille,
Tokyo,
Sydney
and, finally,
to Canberra.

Canberra
the city without history,
an INVISIBLE city.
Audible
as silence
and silencing

as only music
can be.
The dream of a city
yet to be born.

—

A city of 30,000 inhabitants
with the same dream.
The dream
of spaces different
from any other.
A cohesive and welcoming city.

Canberra
the city of elsewhere,
when the elsewhere
was not to be found anywhere.

A city so culturally and spatially
alien to the world,
it must be the only city
where it was possible
to dream the impossible dream.

What made us stay
was love at first sight.

Canberra was a city of emptiness
with a golf course waiting to become a lake.
Nobel laureates, atomic scientists,
Chinese scholars, Etruscan masters
and a prime minister,
all in love
with Canberra's future
as capital of Australia.

—

Canberra was then, and still today
I believe,
the city described by Italo Calvino
in his book *Invisible Cities*

Enrico Taglietti

Zobeide, the city of fulfilled desires.

"... After six days and seven nights
(the time it took us to fly from Milan to Canberra)
you arrive at this white city,
well exposed to the moon,
with streets wound about themselves as in a skein."

They tell this tale about its foundation:
men of various nations
had an identical dream.
They saw a beautiful woman
running at night through an unknown city.

She was seen from behind,
with long hair, and she was naked.
They dreamed of pursuing her.

As they twisted and turned,
each of them lost her...
They decided to build a city
like the one in the dream.
In the laying of the streets
each followed the course of his pursuit.

—

At the spot where they had lost the apparition
they arranged spaces and walls
differently from the dream,
so she would not be able to escape again...

This was the city where they settled,
waiting for the apparition to happen again.
The streets are the streets where they go to work every day,
and the houses are the places where they dream every night.

Other men are arriving now,
men who do not understand
what drew people
to this trap of a city,
so incredibly different from other cities.
Zobeide, the city of fulfilled desires.

Let me then dwell
on Architecture
as I see it.
The one that has no presence,
only existence.
My approach to the design
of architectural work
is to silence reason,
and create a theatre
where questions asked
are more important
than answers.

Architecture to me
is the shaping of the voids within.
You create the voids
then you cover their surface
with appropriate materials.

Architecture is, for me,
an open work,
it is the inhabitant's e-motion
that reveals it.

The INVISIBLE
within the voids
should be speaking to the inhabitants,
listening and responding to their e-motions.
This is the aloofness of Architecture
and its essence.

Ultimately, architecture is a balancing act,
to see buildings giving the sun its shadow.

Remember Socrates?
People and planners
are chained inside a cave
in such a way that they can see but mirages.
Few of them escape to reality,
at first they are blinded by the light,
but they recover and Socrates says to them:

Enrico Taglietti

at last you were able to see the invisible.
"The prison house is the world of sight,
the light of the fire is the INVISIBLE
and you will not misapprehend me
if you interpret the journey upward
to be the ascent of the soul
into the intellectual world."
Unfortunately, the people in the cave
think that the few escapees are mad.

Remember Louis Kahn?
"Architecture has existence but NO PRESENCE.
Only the architect's works have presence.
Those works are made as an offering
to Architecture in the urging of industry,
and when the dust settles
the work gives the sun its shadow."

Remember Lao-Tze?
"To make a building,
you cut out doors and windows
in order to have light.
You adapt the Nothing
therein to the purpose in hand,
and you have the enjoyment of the building.
Thus, what you gain is something.
Yet it is by virtue of the Nothing
that the building can be put to use."
Canberra is a unique city,
it is Utopia ready to be realised,
it is the city of no-where,
when 'no-where' exists any more.

Politicians and planners have yet to see the INVISIBLE,
they still live in the cave of the conservative.

The rationalist architect's doctrine
asserted that form
should follow function.
The resulting equation is
that given a function,
if it is resolved perfectly,
a single form will be produced.

This is what Socrates referred
to when he said the world of sight
is the prison house,
you will not see the INVISIBLE, the ascent of the soul.

Functional requirements change,
the essence of the soul does not.
Therefore, let function follow form.
Functions will change in time,
the urban architectural envelope,
if properly designed,
should not.

The precinct will always rotate around the sun
with the same yearly pattern,
the protected views will always be there
embedded with the emotion of living there.

There is not enough time
to express all my dreams
and concerns
for my INVISIBLE city
Canberra.
It is Utopia ready to be realised,
it is time to step out of the cave.

So, we must tell the politicians:
it is not the violin
that makes the music.
It is not the building
that makes Architecture.
It is not the planner
that makes the cities.
It is not development
that makes richness.

It is us,
pursuing the impossible dream
of a unique city.
A unique city,
invisible as the infinite,
and as silent as music.

Dream the impossible dream
to reach the unreachable star
fight the invincible foe.

—

A Vision for Canberra: In 1904, the Australian capital was conceived, more, it seems, by artificial insemination than through passionate love. It took nine years to see the light and another fifty years to grow to puberty, when the golf course became the lake.

The city is now self-sufficient and will continue to grow, but it still lacks the passion of love. Canberra is and has been for some time at a historical moment of choice, a choice between a healthy growth and a malignant one. Our first duty is to ensure that its future development be as visionary as the site our forefathers expected.

I believe the current planning and designing philosophy of Canberra is forcing the city in the wrong direction and should be stopped. We need to make an effort to tell the politicians that Canberra is the Australian capital, not Sydney or Melbourne.

City design should not be in terms of isolated buildings to satisfy current temporary functions and political expediency but should bend in terms of aesthetically integrated precincts.

The concept of precinct design is not new; it is only to be rediscovered and not copied.

Please, no trams or boulevards. No motorboats on the lake, no more lakeshore private developments.

One of Canberra's singularities is its physical confinement within the bounds of the Griffin Plan, protected by green corridors and hills creating well-defined limits of growth.

These well-defined limits, if we don't succumb to the greed of infill, would allow an accurate determination of optimum sustainable development and a well-defined division of precincts within central Canberra.

Index

A+U, Architecture and Urbanism, journal
   93, 103
Aalto, Aino
   166
Aalto, Alvar
   70, 78, 168, 196
AASA (Australasian Architecture Student Association)
   39, 77, 89, 173
Abitare, journal
   7, 201
Abraham, Raimund
   24
Ackerman, James
   112, 117
ACT (Australian Capital Territory), Australia
   160, 163
AD, Architectural Design, journal
   14, 15
Addison, Rex
   37, 38, 45, 77, 78, 85, 152–155, 172
   Burrundulla Garden Housing, Kambah, Canberra, Australia
      155, 178
   Post Office, Nerang, Queensland, Australia
      154, 178
   Villa Carbone, New Farm, Brisbane, Australia
      174
Addison, Susan
   175, 177
Adjmi, Morris
   185
Age, The, journal
   34, 66, 73, 189
Agrest, Diana
   50, 51, 59, 195–197

Albini, Franco
   39, 176
Alighieri, Dante
   26
Almaas, Ingerid Helsing
   16, 17, 21
Also Architects, office
   86
Alsop, Will
   24
Althusser, Louis
   211
Ambasz, Emilio
   50
American Academy, Rome, Italy
   8, 14, 108, 198
Amsterdam, The Netherlands
   184
Anderson, Stanford
   199
Andresen, Brit
   78, 83–85, 87–89
   Burrell Museum, Glasgow, UK
      78
Andrew Metcalf Architects
   43
   House, Rose Bay, Sydney, Australia
      43
Annales School
   211, 212
Archigram
   24, 77, 199
Architectural Association, London, UK
   20, 81, 83, 89
Architectural Research Quarterly, journal
   211
Architectural Review, journal
   78, 88, 103, 197

Architectural Theory Review, journal
   212
Architecture Australia, journal
   35, 45, 46, 57, 61, 65, 73, 89, 201
Architecture d'Aujourd'hui, La, journal
   37, 93
Architettura. Cronache e Storia, La, journal
   204
Arcosanti, Arizona, U.S.A.
   201
Arkitektnytt, journal
   17, 21
Arkitektur N, journal
   16, 21
Arkkitehti, journal
   37
ARM Architecture (Ashton Raggatt McDougall), office
   32, 148, 149, 150, 151, 165, 169, 170, 190
   Competition entry for Federation Square, Melbourne, Australia
      32
   Library and Heritage Centre, Geelong, Victoria, Australia
      148, 166
   Scheme for the National Museum of Australia (NMA), Canberra, Australia
      32
   Shrine of Remembrance, Melbourne, Australia
      32
ARQ: Architectural Research Quarterly, journal
   211
Art + Text, journal
   54, 60

Artforum, journal
24

Arup, office
79

ASM (Architecture Student Magazine), journal
46

Asplund, Gunnar
111

Aureli, Pier Vittorio
51, 59, 61, 209

Avant garde
26, 59, 60, 64, 69–71, 74, 114–115

Aymonino, Carlo
35, 63

Backstrom, Sven
203

    Point Housing, Orebro, Sweden
    203

Baghdad, Iraq
175

Baird, George
50, 53, 55, 61

Bandini, Micha
28, 34, 56–58, 61, 131

Banham, Reyner
168, 183, 197, 201, 202

Baracco, Mauro
158, 180

Baracco+Wright Architects, office
158, 191

    Garden House, Western Port Bay, Victoria, Australia
    158, 191, 192

Barak, William
32

Barbieri, Umberto
185

Baroque
17, 110, 112, 166, 202

Barthes, Roland
211

Bass, Brian
80

Bates, Smart & McCutcheon, office
24, 33

Baudrillard, Jean
54

BBPR (Banfi Belgiojoso Peressutti Rogers), office
32, 176, 204

    Piazza Meda Offices, Milan
    204

    Velasca Tower, Milan
    204

Beck, Haig
14, 61

Bee Gees, musical group
42

Behrens, Peter
70

Bellini, Mario
32

Bendigo, Victoria, Australia
166

Benevolo, Leonardo
8, 197

Benjamin, Walter
55, 106, 116, 213, 214, 216

    "The Work of Art in the Age of Mechanical Reproduction"
    213–214, 216

Besley, Jo
80

Besley, Peter
80

Biltmoderne, office
31, 190

Biraghi, Marco
212–215

    Project of Crisis: Manfredo Tafuri and Contemporary Architecture
    212, 214

Birrell, James
37, 45, 173, 174

    Project for a Multistorey Hotel, Port Moresby, Papua New Guinea
    174

    Union College, St Lucia, Brisbane, Australia
    173

Blainey, Geoffrey
37, 45

Bligh, Graham
79

Bligh, Rod
79, 88

Bligh Voller Architects, office
79

Boehm, Gottfried
196

Bofill, Ricardo
196

Bonicalzi, Rosaldo
20, 188

    Scritti Scelti sull'Architettura e la Cittá
    188

Bonnemaison, Sarah
81

Borgelt, Julie
86

Borland, Kevin
34, 168, 200

Borromini, Francesco
30, 110

Bosch, Theo
184

Boullée, Étienne Louis
117, 186

Boyd, Robin
32, 34, 44, 46, 54, 168, 180, 182, 184, 189, 190–192, 200, 202–204

    Australia's Home: Its Origins, Builders and Occupiers
    44

    New Directions in Japanese Architecture
    191

    The Australian Ugliness
    44, 200

Braghieri, Gianni
25–28, 120–123, 180, 184–187, 190

Bramante, Donato
112

Brawne, Michael
78, 79, 88

    The New Museum: Architecture and Display
    78, 79, 88

Braziller, George
191

Brisbane, Queensland, Australia
9, 24, 37, 39, 54, 77, 79–81, 83–89, 172, 173, 175, 176, 187

Brookes Crescent, North Fitzroy
65

Brown, Neave
200

Brutalism
63, 199

Building, journal
33, 35,

Bull, Henrik
17

Bunning and Madden, office
205, 206

    Returned Services League Offices, Sydney, Australia
    206

    International House, University of Sydney
    206

Buonarroti, Michelangelo
106

Burgess, Greg
70, 190

Burns, Karen
35, 46, 61, 72, 73, 210

Butcher, Mardi
68, 70

    Kew Children's Cottages School of Nursing Extension, Melbourne, Australia
    68

Caccia Dominioni, Luigi
205

Cacciari, Massimo
50, 60, 209

California, U.S.A.
41, 54, 113

Calvino, Italo
183, 220

    Invisible Cities
    220

Canberra, ACT, Australia
8–10, 19, 20, 32–34, 43, 44, 46, 60, 107, 112, 147, 150, 155, 172, 178, 196, 205, 207, 208, 218–225

Capitalism
13, 16, 18, 19, 59, 65, 73, 105, 106, 113–117, 176, 209, 213, 216

Capp, Julia
80, 101

Carr, Bill
78

Carter, Louisa
80

Casabella, journal
7, 32, 37, 45, 46, 49, 59, 70, 77, 190, 191, 198, 204, 209

Castelvecchio Museum, Verona
77–81, 83–85, 88, 136

Castiglioni, Achille
32

Caulfield, Victoria, Australia
166

Chalk, Warren
24

Chossegros, Pascal
81

CIAM (Congres International d'Architecture Moderne)
14

CIRCUS
77, 79–81, 84, 86–88, 135

Ciucci, Giorgio
34, 50, 53, 60

    The American City: From the Civil War to the New Deal
    34, 53, 60

Clarke, Alison
25, 34

Clark, Tony
167

Classicism
7, 70, 71, 167, 196–198, 202, 205

Collins Place, Melbourne, Australia
24

Collins Street Defence Movement
29, 34

Colquhoun, Alan
50, 51, 205

Columbia University, New York
59, 107, 209

Communist Party
117, 188, 209

Contextualism
13, 58, 87

Conway, Hudson
30

Cook, Peter
15, 61

Coop Himmelb(l)au, office
24

Cooper Union, New York
199

Cornell University
199

Corrigan, Peter
30, 31, 35, 43, 44, 53, 61, 66, 68–70, 73, 127, 156, 157, 168, 182, 183, 186, 188, 190, 196, 200, 201

Cox and Partners, office
43

    The Market Three Campus, NSW Institute of Technology, Sydney, Australia
    43

Cranbrook, Michigan, U.S.A.
199

Crone, Peter
66

Crown Casino, South Bank, Melbourne, Australia
30

Dal Co, Francesco
50, 52, 53, 58, 60, 79, 88, 167, 197, 198

    Carlo Scarpa: The Complete Works
    79, 88

    Modern architecture
    60, 167, 197, 198

    The American City: From the Civil War to the New Deal
    53, 60

Dance, Su
55, 61

David Jones, store
7, 39, 46, 218

Day, Norman
29, 43, 126, 201
   Public Housing, Northcote, Melbourne, Australia
   43, 126

DCM (Denton Corker Marshall), office
24, 28, 34
   South Bank Grand Arbour, Brisbane, Australia
   24

De Carlo, Giancarlo
32, 35, 176

De Felice, Ezio
32

De Gruchy, Graham
34, 54

Deen Brothers
81

Deleuze, Gilles
54

Denver, Colorado, U.S.A.
202

Derrida, Jacques
8, 72, 211, 213

Desbrowe Annear, Harold
204

Desney, Paul
91, 93–103, 139–142
   Ana Kindergarten, Auburn, Sydney, Australia
   91–94, 101–103

Devenish, John
35, 66

Dezzi Bardeschi, Marco
41

Diamond, Jack
24

Digerud, Jan
17, 21
   Sheraton Oslo Fjord Hotel, Sandvika, Norway
   17
   Radhusgata 23B, Oslo, Norway
   17

Dods, Robin
175, 178
   St Brigid's Catholic Church, Red Hill, Brisbane, Australia
   175

Dogliani, Italy
183

Doherty, Rachel
80

Domus, journal
7, 24, 28, 32, 34, 37–42, 44–46, 73, 74, 77, 79, 80, 117, 126–128, 172–174, 177, 181, 184–187, 190, 191, 198, 201

Donovan, Brian
84

Donovan Hill, office
84–86, 137, 138
   The HH House, Highgate Hill, Brisbane, Australia
   84–85

Dovey, Kim
29, 35

Downton, Peter
29

Drexler, Arthur
27, 34

Drew, Philip
54

Dunster, David
30, 35

Durham, Kate
45

Earle, Tompkins and Shaw, office
200
   Lygon Street Housing, Melbourne, Australia
   200

Eco, Umberto
183

Edelstein, Leo
187

Edinburgh University
79

Edmiston, Leona
45

Edmond, Maggie
43

Edmond and Corrigan, office
35, 53, 70, 156, 157, 182, 190
   Kay Street Infill Houses, Melbourne, Australia
   43, 127

Edquist, Harriet
210

Ehn, Karl
27

Eisenman, Peter
14, 49, 50–53, 57–61, 71, 72, 77, 167, 195, 196, 198, 199, 214

Elliott, Peter
32

Empiricism
114, 196, 197, 200, 203–206

England, UK
14, 165, 175, 197

Erskine, Ralph
196, 199, 200

Espie Dods Architect
43
   Ashton House, Sydney, Australia
   43

ETH Zurich (Eidgenössische Technische Hochschule Zürich)
30

Farmer, Edward Herbert
205
   State Government Offices, Sydney, Australia
   205

Fausch, Deborah
114, 117

Field, Erastus Salisbury
31

Fine Art Gallery of Ballarat, Victoria, Australia
42

Fitch, James Marston
197

Fitzgerald Inquiry
80

Fitzroy, Melbourne, Australia
167

Florence, Italy
34, 176

Florence, Yanni
187, 205

Forster, Kurt
51

Foster, Hal
63, 72, 116, 195

Foucault, Michel
56, 67, 73, 210–213

Frampton, Kenneth
50, 51, 61, 103, 112, 113, 117, 197, 199, 209

Frankfurt School
187

Freadman, Anne
211

Freeland, John Maxwell
54, 60

   Architecture in Australia: A history
   54, 60

Freeman, Yuncken
65

   BHP Corporate Tower, Melbourne, Australia
   65

Freud, Sigmund
30

Functionalism
8, 16, 49

Futagawa, Yukio
31, 32, 35, 88

GA, Global Architecture, journal
31, 35, 79, 88

Gabetti, Roberto
181–184, 187, 189

Gabetti e Isola, office
183

   Bottega d'Erasmo, Turin
   183

Galvagni, Mario
24

Gandelsonas, Mario
50–52, 59, 195, 197, 199

Gardella, Ignazio
202, 205

   Zattere House, Venice
   202

Gardens of Bomarzo, Italy
166

Gasson, Barry
78

   Burrell Museum, Glasgow
   78

Geddes, Robert
106

Gehry, Frank Owen
61, 176, 196

Getzel, Stefano
25, 26, 120–123

Ghirardo, Diane
49, 58, 59, 61

Gilbert, Cass
28

   Woolworth Building, New York
   28

Ginzburg, Moisei
51

   Style and Epoch
   51

Giriodi, Sisto
182, 183

Giurgola, Romaldo
10, 19, 20, 43, 46, 105–117, 144, 147, 196–198, 206, 207

   St Patrick's Cathedral, Parramatta, New South Wales
   110, 144

   St Thomas Aquinas Parish Church, Charnwood, Canberra, Australia
   206

   Newman Residence, Bedford, New York
   111

Glasgow, UK
78, 91, 134

Globalization
21

Goad, Philip
34, 35, 45, 60, 61, 73, 204

Goldberger, Paul
109, 117

Goodman, David
49, 59

Goodsir Baker Wilde Architects, office
174

Goodwin, Bill
68, 132

   24 Hour Police Station, Campbellfield, Victoria, Australia
   68, 132

Gramsci, Antonio
56, 188, 216

Granada, Spain
219

Grassi, Giorgio
50, 63, 69–71, 74, 167, 168

Graves, Michael
14, 50, 53, 55, 60, 61, 182, 186, 196, 198, 199

Greene, Charles
54

Greene, Henry
54

Greenhatch, Betty
32, 125

Greenhatch, Kevin
32, 125

Gregotti, Vittorio
191, 202, 205, 209

   New Directions in Italian Architecture
   191, 205

Griffin, Walter Burley
44, 54

Grounds, Roy Burman
32, 35, 159, 196, 203–205

   Building on St Kilda Road, National Gallery of Victoria School of Art, Melbourne, Australia
   204

   Embassy Buildings, Canberra, Australia
   205

   John Medley Building, University of Melbourne
   205

   John Medley Tower (1965–70) at the University of Melbourne
   159, 204

   Ormond College Buildings, Melbourne, Australia
   203

Robert Blackwood Hall, Monash University, Melbourne, Australia
205

Victorian Arts Centre, Melbourne, Australia
204

Guattari, Félix
54

Gwathmey, Charles
199

Gzowska, Alicja
18, 21

Postmodernizm polski — Architektural Urbanistyka
18, 21

Habermas, Jürgen
209

Haddad, Elie
15, 20

Hadid, Zaha
71, 176

Half—Time Club
29, 32, 34, 35, 67, 70, 71

Halik, Kim
32, 187

Hall, Russell
85

Hamann, Conrad
35, 61, 72, 159, 168, 182, 190, 194

Hamer, Rupert
23, 30, 35

Hampson, Alice
80, 86, 88, 89, 138

Hampson Brans, Catharina
85

Hartoonian, Gevork
8, 117, 201, 208

Harvard, Cambridge, Massachusetts, U.S.A.
81, 116, 199

Hassell, office
28, 200

Elderly People's Housing, Adelaide
200

Hatzisavas, George
32

Hays, K. Michael
49, 59, 60, 74

Heidegger, Martin
17, 113

Hejduk, John
195, 199

Hely, Bell & Horne, office
200

Housing, Glebe, Sydney, Australia
200

Henriksen, Arne
17, 21

High Tech
168

Hill, Timothy
84, 86, 89

Hodgkinson, Patrick
200

Hogben, Paul
35, 46, 53, 59, 60, 72, 73

Holl, Steven
24, 34

Anchoring: Selected Project 1975-1988
24

Pamphlet Architecture 7: Bridge of Houses
24, 34

Hollein, Hans
20, 61, 196

Holmes, Andrew
81

Horner, Max
84

Hudnut, Joseph
200

Hughes, Robert
63

Hutson, Andrew
68, 70, 132

Gisborne 24 Hour Police Station, Victoria, Australia
68, 70, 132

IAUS (Institute of Architecture Urban Studies), New York
49–55, 57–60, 195–199, 206

Industrial Design Council of Australia, Melbourne
39

International Architect, journal
35, 93, 103

International Design Centre, Berlin, Germany
42

International Style
13, 18, 39, 108

INXS, musical group
42

Irace, Fulvio
42, 44, 46

Irwin Johnson and Partners, office
65

BHP Corporate Tower, Melbourne, Australia
65

Istanbul, Turkey
219

IUAV (Istituto Universitario di Architettura di Venezia), Venice
50, 53

Jackson, Daryl
28, 29, 200

City Edge housing, South Melbourne, Australia
29, 200

Jameson, Fredric
8, 9, 18, 73, 105, 116, 209, 216

Postmodernism or The Cultural Logic of Late Capitalism
73, 209

Jan & Jon (Jan Digerud and Jon Lundberg), office
17, 21

Villa Normann, Jessheim, Norway
17

Japan
57, 204

Jencks, Charles
14–16, 19, 20, 29, 63, 65, 72, 73, 170, 197

The Language of Post—Modern Architecture
13, 19, 20, 63

What is Post Modernism?
13, 20

Jiřičná, Eva
24

John Price Architect, office
86, 87

Johnson, Phillip
43, 199

Jones, Charles Lloyd
39

Jones Evans, Dale
31

Journal of Architecture, The, journal
15, 20

Jung, Carl
30

Kahn, Louis
19, 21, 51, 54, 91–100, 102, 103, 106–115, 117, 196, 198, 200, 214, 216, 223

    Congress Hall, Venice
92

    Jewish Bath House, New Jersey, U.S.A.
111

    Goldenberg House, Pennsylvania, U.S.A.
111

    Phillips Exeter Academy Library, Exeter, New Hampshire, U.S.A.
99

Keniger, Michael
80, 88

Kennedy, Ken
56, 61, 130

Kierkegaard, Soren
113

King, Ross
205

Kirk, Richard
80

Klein, Lidia
18, 21

    Postmodernizm polski — Architektura I Urbanistyka
18, 21

Koetter, Fred
63, 72

    Collage City
63

Koolhaas, Rem
50, 53, 55, 61, 71, 196

Delirious New York
55

Korzeniewski, Swetik
54, 91–103, 139–142

    Ana Kindergarten, Auburn, Sydney, Australia
91–103, 139–142

    Whale Beach, Sydney, Australia
92

Krier, Léon
16, 24, 50, 72, 196

Krier, Rob
196

Lae, Papua New Guinea
174

Lalibela, Ethiopia
219

Lambert and Smith Architects, office
86, 89

    CSIRO's Queensland Centre for Advanced Technologies, Pinjarra Hills, Queensland
86

LaoTze
223

Lapidus, Morris
41, 46

Lasdun, Denys
91

Le Corbusier, pseudonym of Charles Édouard Jeanneret
51, 52, 178, 181, 184, 196, 198, 199

Le Grew, Daryl
29

Leach, Andrew
211, 212, 214, 215

    Manfredo Tafuri: Choosing History
212

Leavis, Frank Raymond
211

Lebanon
176

Lewerentz, Sigurd
78

Lewis, Miles
29

Lyons Architecture, office
53

Lyotard, Jean François
18, 54, 209

    The Postmodern Condition: A Report on Knowledge
209

Lo Cascio, Giorgio
24

London, UK
65, 77, 79, 81, 83, 91, 166, 196, 198

Loos, Adolf
27, 28, 31, 43, 50, 70, 110

    Project for the Chicago Tribune
28

    Spoken into the Void: Collected Essays 1897–1900
31, 50

Lowe, Jenny
24, 124

Lubetkin, Berthold
197

Lundberg, Jon
17, 21

Lutyens, Edwin
196, 203, 206

Macdonald, Chris,
81, 83, 84, 89

    Oriental Museum competition entry, Durham, UK
84

MacEwan, Malcolm
63, 65, 72, 73, 214

    Crisis in Architecture
63, 65, 72, 73, 214

Machado, Rodolfo
50

Mackintosh, Charles Rennie
178

Macy, Christine
81

Mad Max, film
42, 190

Magagnato, Licisco
79

Mallgrave, Harry Francis
49, 59, 106, 116

Mamino, Lorenzo
182, 183

Mangiarotti, Angelo
176

Manieri Elia, Mario
53, 60

    The American City: From the Civil War to the New Deal
    53, 60

Mannerism
54, 203

Marciniak, Piotr
18, 19, 21

Marseille, France
219

Marsh, Randall
31

Marx, Karl
27, 116, 117

Marxism
8, 57, 188, 195, 197, 199, 209, 211, 212, 216

Mazzariol, Giuseppe
79, 88

    Carlo Scarpa: The Complete Works
    79, 88

Mazzocchi, Gianni
38

McCaughey, Patrick
23, 33, 204

McDougall, Ian
28, 32, 35, 43, 53, 60, 61, 70, 89, 125, 164, 182, 183, 189

    Kensington Community Health Centre, Victoria, Australia
    70

    McDougall's House, Melbourne, Australia
    43

MCG (Melbourne Cricket Ground)
187

McKinnon, Kathy
45

McLeod, Mary
49, 59, 69, 74

Meanjin Quarterly, journal
66, 73

Meier, Richard
43

Melbourne, Victoria, Australia
14, 23–35, 43, 53, 54, 55, 60, 63, 65–67, 69, 70, 71, 72, 73, 80, 120, 121–127, 159, 164, 165–169, 180–182, 186, 187–190, 194, 196, 200, 201, 203, 204, 205, 225

Melbourne Landmark Ideas Competition
23, 30, 34, 35, 120–125, 187, 188

Men at Work, musical group
42

Mendini, Alessandro
40–42, 44–46, 181

Metro Arts Gallery, Brisbane, Australia
80

Meyer, Hannes
70

Michelucci, Giovanni
197

Milan, Italy
7, 24, 25, 27, 31, 32, 35, 37–40, 50, 77, 174, 176, 181, 183–185, 188, 198, 201, 203, 204, 218, 219, 221

Milan Polytechnic
39

Milan Triennale
14, 20, 39

Missingham, Greg
31, 61

Mitchell, William
81

Mitchell/Giurgola Architects, office
109, 117

    Acadia National Park Headquarters, Maine, U.S.A.
    111

    Administration Building at the Academy of the New Church, Pennsylvania, U.S.A.
    111

    Kasperson Residence Conestoga, Pennsylvania, U.S.A.
    109

    Penn Mutual Tower, Philadelphia
    109, 147

    United Fund Building, Philadelphia
    115

    Walnut Street Garage, Philadelphia
    115

Mitchell/Giurgola & Thorp Architects, office
43

    New Parliament House, Canberra, Australia
    43, 54, 107, 206

Modena, Italy
27, 28, 49, 52, 56, 60, 72

Modernism
8, 20, 29, 34, 37–40, 42, 45, 59, 63, 64, 66, 70, 71, 78, 88, 105, 108, 109, 114, 116, 168, 172, 178, 181, 182, 184, 189, 200, 203, 215

Mollino, Carlo
201

MoMA (Museum of Modern Art), New York
14, 20, 27

Monash University, Melbourne, Australia
32, 72, 194, 195, 197, 205

Moneo, Rafael
50, 52, 60, 64, 67, 72, 73

Moore, Charles
31, 54, 61, 77, 196, 198, 200

    Sea Ranch Condominium, California
    200

More, Thomas
219

Moroney, Paul
77

Morrissey, Peter
45

Moscow, Russia
219

Munday, Richard
29, 35, 53, 55, 60, 61, 70, 103, 167

Murphy, Richard
77, 79, 81, 88, 163

Murray, Shane
67, 68, 73
   McKinnon High School Music Complex, Melbourne, Australia
   67, 73, 74

Natalini, Adolfo
25, 26, 28, 34, 124

Neo-avant-garde
70, 71

Neo-Functionalism
52, 59

Neo-Rationalism
71, 195–198

Neo-Rats (Neo-Rationalist)
63, 69, 71, 72

Neoclassicism
196, 202

Neoliberty
9, 168, 183, 189–191, 196–198, 202–205

Nervi, Pier Luigi
39

Neue Sachlichkeit
105, 106

New Empiricism
114, 205

New Haven, Connecticut, U.S.A.
43, 198

New South Wales, Australia
43, 91, 110, 144

New York, U.S.A.
20, 31, 34, 43, 49, 53, 54, 59, 60, 69, 73, 117, 185, 195, 196, 198, 219

New York Five
51, 52, 55, 196, 209, 216

New Zealand
34, 59, 72, 73, 208, 212, 213

Newman, Frederick
213

Newson, Marc
38

NGV (National Gallery of Victoria), Melbourne, Australia
31, 32, 35, 42, 187, 204

Nietzsche, Friedrich
56

NMA (National Museum of Australia), Canberra, Australia
32, 150

Norberg-Schulz, Christian
16, 17
   Genius Loci: Towards a Phenomenology of Architecture
   17

Norman Day Architects, office
43, 126
   Public Housing, Northcote, Melbourne, Australia
   43, 126

Norway
16–19, 21

Nouvel, Jean
169

O'Gorman, Peter
78, 84, 89, 210

O'Neil, Dan
211

Ockman, Joan
49, 58–61, 74, 209

Oppositions: Journal for ideas and criticism in architecture, journal
32, 50, 51, 52, 54, 58–60, 64, 71, 72, 196, 199

Opposition Books
31, 49, 50, 51, 52, 59, 60, 74

Ostoja-Kotkowski, Stanislaus
24

Oxlade, Brian
175

Palladio, Andrea
173, 198, 203

Papadakis, Andreas
14, 15, 20

Papua New Guinea
172, 174, 178

Pataphysics, journal
187

Patel, Nimish
81

Paris, France
15, 20, 42, 46, 81, 160

Pelli, Cesar
27, 43, 199
   Pacific Design Center, Los Angeles, California
   27

Perret, Auguste
70

Perspecta, journal
111, 117, 206

Pfau, Bernhard
196

Phenomenology
17, 87, 107, 116

Philadelphia, Pennsylvania, U.S.A.
91, 106, 107, 115, 147, 196, 206

Philadelphia School
19, 106, 116

Pie, Geoffrey
173

Piranesi, Giovanni Battista
166, 214, 215

Pisa, Italy
176

Poland
16, 18, 19, 21

Pompidou Centre, Paris
42

Ponti, Gio
37–40, 42, 46, 77, 173–175, 177, 191, 202, 203
   Office Building, Baghdad, Iraq
   175
   Pirelli Tower, Milan
   203
   North Wing of the Art Museum, Denver, Colorado, U.S.A.
   202

Pordenone, Italy
176, 177

Porphyrios, Demetri
72, 83, 198

Portoghesi, Paolo
7, 16, 17, 181, 191, 196, 197, 199, 202

Postmodernism
10, 13–21, 38, 40, 41, 45, 63, 64, 71–73, 87, 105, 106, 108, 113, 114, 116, 169, 170, 178, 180–182, 184–186, 190, 194, 195, 202, 203, 209, 215, 216

Price, Cedric
24, 199

Princeton, New Jersey, U.S.A.
51, 199

Progressive Architecture, journal
106, 116, 200

Proust, Marcel
183

PROV (Public Records Office of Victoria), Melbourne
23, 33, 34

PWD (Public Works Department of Victoria)
63, 66, 70, 71

Qualls, George
106

Quaroni, Ludovico
203

Tiburtino Housing, Rome
203

Queensland, Australia
37, 43, 77–81, 85–89, 174, 175

Queensland Architectural Students Association
77

Querini Stampalia Library, Venice
92

QUT (Queensland University of Technology)
77

Radice, Barbara
40, 46

Raggatt, Howard,
169

RAIA (Royal Australian Institute of Architects), Melbourne
29, 50, 53, 57, 58, 89, 93, 166, 201, 218

Ranciere, Jacques
105

Rationalism
41, 98, 103, 199

Redpath, Norma
24

Reed, Joseph
204

Reinus, Leif
203

Point Housing, Orebro, Sweden
203

Renaissance
7, 112, 203, 206

RIBA (Royal Institute of British Architects), London
65

Ridolfi, Mario
168, 203, 205

Tiburtino Housing, Rome
203

Viale Etopia Housing, Rome
203

Rijavec, Ivan
67, 69, 73

Victorian Coronial Services Centre
67, 73

Whittlesea College of TAFE
67

RMIT (Royal Melbourne Institute of Technology)
182, 183, 186, 187, 194,196, 201

Roche, Kevin
43

Romano, Giulio
196

Romberg, Frederick
203, 204

Picken Court, Ormond College, Melbourne, Australia
204

Rome, Italy
55, 77, 78, 86, 107,108, 110, 113,115,167,176, 198, 203, 215

Rogers, Ernesto Nathan
39, 46, 77, 191, 203, 204

Rossi, Aldo
7–9, 17, 20, 25, 26–28, 30–35, 40,43, 49–53, 56–61, 63, 67,70, 72, 73, 87, 108, 117, 120–123, 131, 166–169, 180, 184–188, 190, 196–199, 201, 209

"Analogous City", The
27, 30, 31, 56

Architecture of the City, The
7, 31, 32, 49, 50, 52, 53, 57–59, 61, 129, 166, 167, 186, 188, 198

Architecture School in the Miami University Campus
185

Cemetery of San Cataldo, Modena
27,48,52,56

Competition entry for the Civic centre tower, Pesaro, Italy
27

Gallaratese housing, Milan
27, 31, 52, 188

Hotel on the Grand Canal in Cannaregio West, Venice
27

Hotel Il Palazzo, Fukuoka, Japan
185

Il Teatro del Mondo, Venice
27, 31

"Architecture assassinée, La"
52

Molteni Family Tomb, Giussano, Italy
185

Monument to the Resistance, Segrate, Italy
52

Scientific Autobiography, A
31, 49, 50, 53, 59, 186, 188, 198

Elementary School, Fagnano Olona, Italy
27, 52, 56

Student Housing, Chieti, Italy
27, 52, 70

Villa, Borgo Ticino, Italy
27

Rossi, Aldo Loris
201

Rourke, Dennis
203

North Sydney House
203

Rowe, Colin
50, 63, 72, 198

Collage City
63

Rudolfsky, Bernard
200

Rudolph, Paul
43, 108

Ruegenberg, Sergius
196
S.H. Ervin Museum and Art Gallery, Sydney, Australia
35, 42
Salter, Peter
24, 83, 84, 89
   Oriental Museum competition entry, Durham, UK
   84
Salway, William
33
Samona, Giuseppe
8
San Francisco, California, U.S.A.
15, 16
Sandell, John
186
Sanmicheli, Michele
196, 203
Sartre, Jean-Paul
113
Saunt, Deborah
166
Scarpa, Carlo
9, 32, 35, 77–88, 91–94, 96–98, 100–103, 201
   Brion Vega Cemetery, San Vito d'Altivole, Italy
   92, 96, 101
   Castelvecchio museum, Verona
   77–81, 83–85, 88,136
   Fondazione Querini Stampalia, Venice
   79
Scharoun, Hans
70, 196
Schellino, Giovanni Battista
183
Schinkel, Karl Friedrich
30, 70, 186
Scolari, Massimo
20, 24, 60, 197, 199
Scott Brown, Denise
108, 196, 198–200
Scully, Vincent
16, 196–198, 203, 206
Seidler, Harry
37, 40, 42, 45, 46, 197, 202

Selenitsch, Alex
31, 68, 133
   Scheme for Regional Prison, Castlemaine, Victoria, Australia
   68, 133
Shaw, Earle
29, 200
   Housing Co-operative scheme, Carlton, Melbourne, Australia
   29
Shinohara, Kazuo
61, 189, 192
Siena, Italy
176, 198
Sillett, Jeanne
81
Silvetti, Jorge
51
Sinnamon, Ian
78, 88, 175
Sky, Alison
31, 35
   Unbuilt America
   31, 35
Smith, James
33
Smithson, Alison
77
Smithson, Peter
24
Smrekar, Ermin
201, 202
Sola-Morales, Ignasi de
50
Soleri, Paolo
201
Solidarnosz, movement
18
Sottsass, Ettore
31, 35, 42, 46
Spring, Martin
14
St John Wilson, Colin
83
Stern, Robert
14, 182, 186, 196, 206
Stirling, James
43, 51, 77, 196, 199, 200

Stone, Michelle
31, 35
   Unbuilt America
   31, 35
Strada Novissima, La, exhibition
181
Stradbroke Island, Queensland, Australia
84, 86
Studio Nizzoli, office
24
   Domus Editorial Headquarters, Rozzano, Milan
   24
Superstudio
25, 26, 34, 124
   Monumento Continuo
   26
Switzerland
185
Sydney, New South Wales, Australia
7, 9, 35, 38, 39, 42, 43, 45, 46, 54, 56, 65, 66, 91, 92, 101, 103, 139–142, 176, 202, 203, 205, 206, 218, 219, 225
Sydney College of the Arts
38
Syracuse University, New York
199
Tafuri, Manfredo
7–9, 25, 26, 28, 32–35, 50 53, 55–61, 64, 71, 72, 74, 87–89, 106–108, 113–117, 130, 167, 181, 197–199, 208–217
   Architecture and Utopia: Design and Capitalist Development
   32, 51, 52, 55, 60, 167, 197, 198, 209, 210, 213
   History of Italian Architecture, 1944–85
   34, 35, 51, 72, 74, 89, 116, 117
   Modern Architecture
   197, 198
   Sphere and the Labyrinth, The
   51, 116, 209, 214, 215
   Theories and History of Architecture
   32, 51, 55, 58, 60, 115, 117, 198, 209, 213, 214, 216

The American City: From the Civil War to the New Deal
34, 53, 60

Taglietti, Enrico
7, 9, 39, 46, 149, 162, 196, 201, 202, 218

Tange, Kenzo
191

Tartaglia, Filippo
24

Taylor, Jennifer
53, 54, 60, 74

Tendenza, La
9, 20, 63, 64, 67, 69, 71, 72, 112, 167, 187, 190, 195

Terragni, Giuseppe
60, 72, 198, 202, 205

   Casa del Fascio, Como, Italy
   205

Tessenow, Heinrich
70

Thompson, Martyn
45

Thomson, Sheona
80, 86

Tibbits, George
29

Tigerman, Stanley
61, 196

Timpano, Francesco
68, 133

   Scheme for Regional Prison, Castlemaine, Victoria, Australia
   68, 133

Tokyo, Japan
185, 219

Transition, journal
28, 29, 32, 34, 53–58, 60, 61, 63, 66–71, 73, 80, 93, 95, 103, 130–133, 164, 167, 187, 188, 190, 198, 203, 210

Trieste, Italy
52, 77, 176, 201

Tschumi, Bernard
71

Turin, Italy
181–183, 187, 189

Turin Polytechnic
181, 182, 187

Turnbull, Jeff
54, 200

Turner, John
63, 72

   Freedom to Build
   63, 72

Udine, Italy
38, 45, 77, 174, 176

UIA (International Union of Architects)
19

UK (United Kingdom)
9, 16, 24, 46, 61

University of Adelaide
164

University of Melbourne
29, 32, 35, 45, 53, 159, 204, 205

University of Pennsylvania
91, 102, 106, 107, 116, 208

University of Sydney
45, 56, 91, 92, 101, 103, 206

UQ (The University of Queensland)
37, 77, 79, 84, 85, 175

Urbino, Italy
176

Uren, Tom
100

U.S.A. (United States of America)
9, 18, 21, 24, 50, 108, 111, 208–210

Ussher, Beverley
166

Valle, Gino
37, 77, 172, 174–178

   Manzano House, Udine
   174

   Zanussi Headquarters, Porcia, Pordenone
   177, 178

Van der Rohe, Ludwig Mies
18, 21, 108, 168, 181, 184

Van Eyck, Aldo
184, 197

Vattimo, Gianni
183

Venice, Italy
16, 27, 31, 50, 59, 60, 73, 77, 78, 83, 88, 92, 103, 199, 202

Venice Biennale of Architecture
14, 17, 41, 181, 182, 202, 209

Venturi, Robert
14, 17, 21, 31, 43, 49, 52–54, 59, 77, 91, 103, 106, 107, 111, 113, 114, 115, 117, 177, 178, 196–200, 206, 209, 215

   Civic Center, Thousand Oaks, California
   113

   Complexity and Contradiction in Architecture
   49, 91, 103, 114, 117, 177

   Vanna Venturi House, Chestnut Hill, Pennsylvania
   17, 114

Verona, Italy
77, 79, 88, 136, 203

Vicenza, Italy
91, 92, 102

Victoria, Australia
23, 33–35, 63–66, 69, 71, 73, 120–126, 162, 187, 191, 202

Victoria and Albert Museum, London
14

Victorian Ministry of Housing, Melbourne
29, 35, 43

Victoria University, Wellington, New Zealand
212

Vidler, Anthony
51, 52

Viollet-le-Duc, Eugene Emmanuel
98

Viterbo, Italy
166

Voysey, Charles
178

Walker, Evan
29, 34, 200

   City Edge Housing, South Melbourne, Australia
   29, 200

Walker, Ronald
30, 35

Warhol, Andy
115

Watson, David
29

Watson, Donald (Don)
    175
Watson, Jimmy
    204
    Tavern, Carlton, Melbourne, Australia
        204
Weese, Harry
    24
Weiner, Joseph
    15
Weir, Peter
    42
Westover, Virginia
    15
White, Deborah
    66, 73
Whitlam, Gough
    93
Williams, Lloyd
    30
Wilson, Peter
    24, 124
Wittkower, Rudolf
    107
    Architectural Principles in the Age of Humanism
        107, 116
Wood Marsh, office
    31, 190
Wood, Roger
    31
Woolley, Ken
    203, 205
    State Government Offices, Sydney, Australia
        205
Woolloomooloo, Sydney, Australia
    65
Wrede, Stuart
    198
Wright, Frank Lloyd
    110
Wronska, Anna
    18
Wurundjeri willam, clan
    32
Yale University, New Haven
    21, 195

Zanuso, Marco
    39
Zaveri, Parul
    81
Zevi, Bruno
    203
Zuber, Claude
    186

www.ingramcontent.com/pod-product-compliance
Lightning Source LLC
Chambersburg PA
CBHW041507010526
44118CB00006B/181